POLISH
CIVILIZATION

Essays and Studies

THE POLISH INSTITUTE OF ARTS AND SCIENCES
OF AMERICA

The Polish Institute of Arts and Sciences of America is an American non-profit organization for cultural, educational and scholarly activities founded in 1942 by six members of the Polish Academy of Arts and Sciences of Cracow.

Membership in the Polish Institute is without regard to race, religion, national origin, sex or any other criteria beyond scientific, artistic, and scholarly achievement and interest. The Institute publishes The Quarterly Journal, *Polish Review*.

POLISH CIVILIZATION

Essays and Studies

Edited by
Mieczysław Giergielewicz

in cooperation with

Ludwik Krzyżanowski

A Polish Institute of Arts and Sciences of America Book

Published by New York University Press • New York

JW

Copyright © 1979 by New York University
Library of Congress Catalog Card Number: 78-52747
ISBN: 0-8147-2972-X

Library of Congress Cataloging in Publication Data

Main entry under title:

History of Polish civilization.

    1. Poland—Civilization—Addresses, essays,
lectures. I. Giergielewicz, Mieczysław.
DK4110.H57   943.8   78-52747
ISBN 0-8147-2972-X

Manufactured in the United States of America
10 9 8 7 6 5 4 3 2

Contents

v

Acknowledgments

The Polish Institute expresses its gratitude to the Jurzykowski Foundation, especially to Mr. Alexis D. Coudert, President, and Mr. Morris Cohen, Trustee, for the generous grant, and to the Kościuszko Foundation for the financial assistance which made translation, editing and publishing of this volume possible.

Acknowledgment is made to the following publishers who have granted permission to reprint selections included in this anthology:

Orbis Books, Ltd., for chapter by Cezaria Baudouin de Courtenay Jędrzejewicz, "Polish Rituals and Seasonal Customs," originally published in *Polska i jej dorobek dziejowy,* London: Orbis, 1956.

Authors' Agency Ltd. (Warsaw), for two excerpts by Henryk Barycz, "Seventeenth Century Padua in the Intellectual Life of Poland," based on *Spojrzenie w przeszłość polsko-włoską,* Wrocław: Ossolineum, 1965, and Stanisław Pigoń's "Recollections of the Camp at Sachsenhausen," originally published in *Z przędziwa pamięci,* Warsaw: Państwowy Instytut Wydawniczy, 1968.

Martinus Nijhoff's Boekhandel en Uitgeversmaatschappil B.V., for Wacław Lednicki's "Mickiewicz at the Collège de France," originally published in *Bits of Table Talks,* The Hague: Martinus Nijhoff, 1956.

Arts, Inc., for Adam Żółtowski's "Catholicism and Christian Democracy in Poland," originally published in *Church and Society,* New York, Arts, Inc., 1953.

Roy Publishers, for Feliks Gross' "The Working Class in Poland," based on *The Polish Worker,* New York: Roy Publishers, 1945.

Introduction

The task the present work sets itself is by no means easy. By definition any anthology cannot help but be selective and for this very reason will not satisfy every reader alike. The task is even more difficult when the subject matter does not lie in a domain that evokes an immediate response of familiarity, which is the case in this instance. Aware of the shortcomings inherent in the situation the method adopted by the editor was to choose from the abundance of possible source materials that seemed most characteristic, significant and comprehensive.

Although not presenting a running story the respective studies and essays are arranged chronologically and are meant to speak for themselves offering a sort of continuance.

Considering the fact that until recently Poland was primarily an agricultural society it is fitting that the peasant customs and rituals find an extensive treatment at the hands of an outstanding ethnologist.

In turn attention is focussed on the medieval Polish towns and their burghers in a specialized historical essay.

Though comparative latecomers on the European historical stage, the Poles quickly overcame this handicap. They participated in all the great religious, intellectual and cultural movements of the West: Humanism, Reformation, Counter-Reformation, Enlightenment, Classicism, Romanticism. To each of these trends they made signal contributions. If on the whole they were not leaders in cultural development, they certainly were partners and adapters of Western cultural values. One achievement, however, excels above all others personified in the figure of the father of modern astronomy, Nicholas Copernicus, shown here by a specialist within the framework of Renaissance European culture.

This scientist received the rudiments of his education at the University of Cracow, an institution founded in 1364 modelled originally on Bologna and after its reorganization on Paris. Polish scholars not only were at home in Western Europe, but played a distinguished role in its learned bodies, not infrequently advocating ideas advanced for the age. Thus a rector of Cracow University, Paulus Vladimiri, at the Council of Constance (1414–1418) postulated the thesis that the Christian religion may not be forced upon non-Christian peoples.

Rightfully considerable space has been dedicated to an aspect of Polish culture comparatively little known or even ignored, viz., Poland's significant participation in the Reformation in all its ramifications and in particular Poland's role in the development of "Arianism," "Anti-Trinitarianism" or "Unitarianism" as it was finally called.

From the XVIth century on pre-partition Poland was a so-called "gentry democracy." A primary description of life in the tumultuous XVIIth century is supplied by a typical member of that middle gentry. Discovered only in the XIXth century the Memoirs have become a classic taking its place in the history of Polish letters.

Owing to Poland's civilizational juniority, literature in the modern sense of the word did not blossom forth until the sixteenth century considerably indebted to the influence of the Reformation and the impact of its religious controversies, in fact the role of "father of Polish literature" is usually ascribed to the vigorous and racy Protestant Nicholas Rey. The company of the brilliant writers of the Golden Age is headed by the greatest poet of Renaissance Poland, Jan Kochanowski (1530–1584), an unsurpassed master of language, which under his pen shines with unexcelled richness and purity. The development of Polish language and style owes much to the classic translation of the Bible accomplished, following several Protestant versions, by the Jesuit Jacob Wujek in 1599. Its role in Polish literature is comparable to that of the Authorized Version in the English-speaking world.

Also within the framework of the Reformation is the advanced political and social thought of Andrzej Frycz Modrzewski, while the leading figure of the Counter-Reformation is Poland's foremost ecclesiastical orator, the Jesuit Peter Skarga, who imbued his prose with majestic dignity and ardent religious and patriotic feeling.

The life span of our memoirist marks the period of epic poetry represented by Samuel Twardowski and Wacław Potocki who celebrated the Polish Christian knight and defender of the faith long after his counterpart in Western Europe had become an extinct species.

A chapter that must not pass unmentioned is that of Poland's treatment of the Jews. Jewish immigration into Poland began in the early middle ages, and probably at first came from the East. However, Polish Jewry was derived mainly from the West— Germany, Bohemia and Moravia and the influx of these "Ashkenazim" resulted from the outbreak of persecutions in such cities as Prague (1389), Vienna (1420), Speyer (1420), Cologne (1435), Austria (1496), Nuremberg (1503), Brandenburg and Regensburg (1519), and Frankfurt (1612). In Poland the Jews were welcomed and granted privileges (the first major one in Kalisz (1264) and protective legislation was extended over their communities and religious practices. The matter is extensively and expertly treated by a recognized scholar.

Poland's close cultural ties with Europe are exemplified by the role the University of Padua played in the education of the Polish intellectual élite.

After an existence of eight hundred years with periods of growth and greatness, weakening and decline, Poland ceased to exist as an independent state. That the nation should have built up a large federal state in the debatable borderlands between Central and Eastern Europe may appear as an interesting phenomenon; that this federal State should have fallen prey to the aggression greed of three strong military monarchies around it, was, if not unique, unprecedented as an international occurrence.

Not only did the Polish people survive the partitions, but they made constant heroic efforts to regain their freedom and in the very period of political eclipse produced their highest creative achievements in many fields of human endeavor.

The essay by the great novelist specializing in re-creating the great figures of the past is devoted to Julian Ursyn Niemcewicz, who is also connected with the United States where he spent the first years of the XIXth century. His activity spanning several decades is exemplified in the present excerpt by his role in the so-called Kingdom of Poland created by the Congress of Vienna. Niemcewicz may be considered a bridge between the independent Poland and the era in which the Poles had to act, deprived of their own statehood.

Any mention of XIXth century Polish cultural, literary and political life would be inconceivable without referring to the towering figure of the poet Adam Mickiewicz. He is shown here in his role of propagating the Polish spirit before an international audience at the Collège de France. Written by the foremost Polish expert on Russo-Polish relations, Wacław Lednicki, it presents this one aspect of Mickiewicz's role.

Considering the fact that from the Xth century on Poland was a member of the Catholic Church, it is proper to include a chapter on the development of the role of the Church in social and political thinking.

In the post-partition century the Polish people were prevented from enjoying even the most common political and social privileges. However, generation after generation was intent on preserving the national cultural identity and eventually to regain independence for their country. Under these circumstances an underground system developed which enabled the Poles not to lose touch from each other and obtain books and papers and to maintain their morale. Therefore, it seems natural that a segment of the Memoirs of an outstanding political figure should be included to stress life as it existed under the partitions.

The image of Polish society would not be complete without drawing attention to the origin and development of the working class. This task is fulfilled here by an outstanding sociologist and labor leader.

After the Nazi invasion and occupation of Poland the new masters aimed at the complete annihilation of the Polish people that would be achieved by the destruction of the intellectual leadership. This sad chapter in the history of Polish culture is described by a great scholar who with hundreds of his colleagues was deported to a German concentration camp. This chapter offers an insight into the tenacity of the Polish spirit which even under the most atrocious conditions tried to maintain their national and human dignity.

In presenting this work to the American scholarly community as well as to the general reader interested in the affairs of Eastern Europe we hope that it will contribute to a better knowledge of Poland, her role and participation in Western civilization.

Ludwik Krzyżanowski

Polish Peasant Rituals and Seasonal Customs

Cezaria Baudouin de Courtenay Jędrzejewicz

The rituals and customs of the Polish people, like those of other peoples, constitute the strongest traditional link that binds individuals into groups.

This is hardly surprising, since ritual of any kind is designed to stress the cohesion of a given group of people. Therefore, people who more or less consciously recognize their solidarity (with a people, nation or religious group) preserve greater loyalty to tradition and pass it on to the following generations even when in other fields of life (e.g., art, literature, politics) they are not among the so-called conservatives.

This explains the fact that although we find some practices in rituals that come from very recent times, they also contain ancient elements. Nevertheless, these ancient elements are very much alive, since living people incorporate them into the realm of their existence.

Some of these Polish rituals reach back to prehistoric times, as do the beginnings of the Polish language. Others belong to the Christian era, and were formed under the influence of the Church and other factors.

For centuries, Poland was an agricultural country, a rural land; that is why agricultural traditions, woven into the liturgical Church year, have determined the style and character of Polish customs.

THE CYCLE OF RITUALS DURING CHRISTMASTIDE

We call the cycle of rituals and customs beginning on Christmas Eve and ending with the Epiphany feast days. They are related to the ancient rites associated with the solstice, although their main emphasis now is placed on one of the two most important holidays of the Christian Church. We are dealing here with a number of much older "new year" rituals and customs connected with the winter solstice. The sun wins. Days begin to get longer. A new season of growth begins. Therefore, on the threshold of a new solar year, one must most solemnly petition for a good harvest in the fields and orchards, blessings for the family, fruitfulness in the barn, poultry roost and beehive. . . .

The day before Christmas, despite the work that is still in full swing on the farm and in the cottage, tears the people away from everyday reality right from the morning, and draws them into the realm of another existence. Everything takes on special meaning. One must concentrate and be vigilant, since every step, every action can bring down calamity if some procedure is not respected. But if things are done according to custom, danger can be averted for good fortune.

The farm and the cottage must be cleaned, made ready, and properly decorated before the star of Bethlehem appears. But in some hidden corner a little dirt must be left because if it is all thrown out, some happiness may be thrown away as well. Lending anything to anyone must be avoided, to guard against indigence. Even in places where the old mortar and pestles have long since gone out of daily use, they are now brought out for the performance of a ritual role. Grain is milled in them for the preparation of Christmas Eve dishes.

As evening approaches, the peasants' cottages grow still, as though transformed into rural shrines. Depending on the region, the farmer brings a sheaf of grain into the house, stting it in the corner next to the holy pictures or in the eastern corner of the room. In other regions, sheaves of various grains, some-times beautifully decorated, are placed in the corners of the room. They are called "old man" or "farmer," which is charac-teristic of agricultural customs, closely connected with the cult of ancestors who continue to watch over their land and farm even after death.

In the Wilno region, in Podlasie, under the Christmas Eve "consecrating" table, the farmer and his wife place grain for the poultry; farmers of Poznan and Kujawy spread sheaves of hay or bundles of straw which are later used for shielding fruit trees. In the Sandomierz region, grain is scattered under the plates at the table, and two pieces of bread with a blessed wafer between them are placed on the hay. The farmers will share this bread and wafer with their cattle and they will share the hay from the table with the horses. The grain will be reserved for threshing. In the towns, hay alone is usually spread under the tablecloth.

All kinds of decorations (varying according to the region) are hung from the ceiling at the center of the room or over the table, to stress the meaning of the solstice and relate it to the mystery of the Birth of the Savior. Stars and chandeliers are made of straw and decorated with multicolored tissue and tin-sel. Pinewood tips are hung upside down. These evergreen "little trees of life" symbolize constantly regenerating nature and are related to the "new spring." The Christmas tree also symbolized the return of spring and the renewal of nature. The Christmas tree made its first appearance in Poland at the end of the eighteenth century. It became very popular at the begin-ning of the nineteenth century; it became an essential part of Christmas tradition, first in the cities and later in the manor houses, in the last decade of that century. The popularity of the Christmas tree in Poland, as throughout the rest of Europe, is not surprising. Behind it is the familiar concept of the ever-green as a symbol of the regeneration of nature, and the joy it brings to children. Even in Orthodox Jewish homes, during the feast of Hanukkah, the tree has found its place.

The place of honor in a peasant's room is occupied by the "table-altar" where all members of the household and other close friends gather for the festive supper. In the middle of the table, sometimes among other ritualistic baked goods, lies the most expressive symbol of temporal life, bread, in various forms depending on the region and the wealth of the house: long loaves of decorated plaited white breads, oval flat cakes, country cakes also called (in the Lublin region, *Podlasie*) *korowaj* (wedding cake) and strudels, prodigal breads (*szczodraki*—tiny cakes of white flour), "nuts" made of rye flour or carrots (*Pomerania*).

The traditional pastry, regardless of its variety, has a twofold meaning. It was an agricultural as well as a Christian symbol. Proof of this finds reflection in the shape sometimes given to the plaited white bread, separated at one end in the form of an infant's feet. The opposite end is rounded to resemble an infant's covered head (in accordance with the tradition of a landed Polish family from the Ukraine: "In our part of the world, in the manor house and in the village, a flat cake like that was always prepared, because Jesus Christ is born on this night"). Holy wafers were placed on this flat cake. They were also put on the plate before the person occupying the place of honor who broke the wafer to begin the meal, but symbolically to "gather strength from this holy bread" as the old Rocho said in Reymont's epic *The Peasants.* In the patriarchal peasant culture, the man of the house fulfills this function.

The Christmas Eve supper (called *wilia,* from Latin *vigilia*) is an example of a Church practice that arose from an ancient, pre-Christian tradition. It is a fasting meal that excludes even dairy products of any kind. Even the decorated traditional pastry may be eaten only after the Midnight Mass. Thus, all dishes consumed during the day are cooked only in vegetable oils. The great quantities and varieties of fish dishes, including fish soup, which are put on the Christmas Eve tables by others, do not belong to the *wilia* menu of peasant culture, save for herring. But even the herring is not offered everywhere. By contrast, in the fishing villages of Pomerania not only the traditional salted eel is served at *wilia,* but also other fish dishes.

As a rule, the dishes clearly bring out the agricultural character of this solemn, ritual feast. They are prepared from the harvest of the fields (rye, wheat, and buckwheat flour, cereals of all kinds), the harvest of the orchards, vegetable gardens (with the inevitable peas, cabbage, beets, poppy seeds), the harvest of the forest (mushrooms especially), and honey. None of these gifts of God and fruits of the work of man can be left out, lest there be a shortage of them in the coming year. Therefore, regardless of regional differences in the dishes and their names, or the differences that run through the divisions of social groups among the Polish people, everywhere we encounter the same basic ingredients.

During the preparation of the supper and the baking of pastry, the women scatter crumbs in the corner for the house spirits. Food is also left on the *wilia* table all through the night for the dead ancestors in many parts of Poland. The people do this during this special ceremony to unite their ancestors with their clan, to assure protection for their descendants. Food for them is also scattered about the house, especially near the threshold. The more grains of cereal disappear from the Christmas Eve bowl, the better the crops will be! Also, throughout the evening various magical incantations are made to obtain prosperity and protection of people and their property against evil. Thus, in some regions they "toss handfuls," throwing cereal so high that it sticks to the ceiling. The more that stays up there, the better the harvest will be. In the Sandomierz region and other sections of southwestern and central Poland, farmers spread straw on the floor after the Christmas Eve supper. Then they pick out straws and throw them into the crevices of the log walls, behind the holy pictures or overhead on the ceiling beams. The more straws that remain there, the better the crop will be.

The holiday fare is often shared with the domestic animals either on Christmas Eve (before or after the Midnight Mass), on Christmas Day, or on the day after Christmas (called the second day of Christmas). In the Lowicz region, after their Christmas Eve supper the farmers' wives, in the company of other members of their family, offer the wafer to the cows and the sheep. In many Mazovian villages this takes place early the following morning. In the vicinity of Lancut and elsewhere in Little Poland the cattle are offered their gifts on St. Stephen's day (the second day of Christmas). The cows are given straw, pieces of bread, and the wafer from under the Christmas Eve tablecloth, the horses—hay from under the table, the poultry—crumbs of all kinds. The farmers make the rounds of beehives to announce to the bees "the news of the birth of the Holy Infant." It is a widespread belief (for instance, in the Lublin region) that the bees then awake for a moment and answer with joyous buzzing.

On their way to the Midnight Mass, the farmers from the Sandomierz region take with them sticks of wood and poppyheads. They hold them out during the asperges (blessing the congregation with holy water). On their return to their farms, they scatter the poppyseed in the orchard, so that there should be as much fruit in the fall as there are seeds in the poppyheads. They strike the trees with the sticks "to force a good harvest out of them." In many parts of Poland on Christmas Eve the trees are wrapped with straw binding (made from the straw that covered the floor during the supper) and their trunks are whitewashed. In Little Poland, the "forcing of a good harvest" is brought about through a dialogue between the farmer and his wife. The farmer goes to the orchard with an axe and straw bindings in his hand, and stands before the apple tree:

"Will you bear fruit?" he asks.

And the farmer's wife, standing in the doorway of the cottage, answers: "I won't, I won't."

"Then I'll cut you down!" shouts the farmer, raising the axe.

Then the farmer's wife calls out: "I will, I will bear fruit."

The tree is spared the axe, and a good harvest is assured. The farmer binds it with straw, and then binds the rest of the fruit trees, with the help of his farmhands and sons.

And, of course, on the eve of the great holiday, the fields are not forgotten. Before nightfall, a little fertilizer is spread around so the fields can refresh themselves at the start of the new year.

If the village is far from the church or other reasons prevent people from attending the Midnight Mass, they pray at home. At midnight all kneel before the crucifix in common prayer. Then the farmer reads from the Gospel according to St. John and the singing of carols begins.

Immediately after the Midnight Mass, the young people of

Poznan, Kalisz and Pomerania go from door to door singing carols. Boys and girls in the vicinity of Wilno and among the Byelorussians near Wolkowysk, "walk around like sheep" and bleat as they make the rounds of the neighboring farms. They stop bleating only when the farmers invite them to the table for treats. This is to ensure the "thriving of the flock," or its fertility. In Pomerania the carolers, dressed up as animals and soldiers, begin their rounds right after supper, led by "Gwizdz" (the Whistler), the companion of "Little Star." The carolers offer sweets to the children and in turn are given treats by the people they visit. Around Sulmierzyce the carolers set out as soon as it begins to get dark, dressed up as "old Josephs" with long, false beards. After supper, the "star carriers" carry a long pole with the star of Bethlehem, skillfully made of gold and multicolored paper.

In Mazovia, Little Poland, and other parts of the Commonwealth, the families are drawn together not only on the evening and night of Christmas Eve at the hearth, but also on Christmas Day. The day is spent in prayer. The sound of carols fills the air. Only the young men go out to visit other homes with greetings. In some areas the "goat" visits the farms on Christmas Day. A boy dresses up in a sheepskin coat with the wooly side out, sometimes wearing a mask of bark with horns attached, or simply blackened with soot and wrapped in pea stalks and girdled with a straw binding. The goat is the most popular. There exists a belief passed down from very ancient times to various peoples, that the goat is the personification of the strength that brings fertility and a good harvest:

> "Where the goat goes,
> the rye grows! . . ."

sing the boys, beginning the songs in a serious vein. In later stanzas the song becomes more and more ribald. The "bear" may appear here and there, wearing an old fur coat to play all sorts of pranks.

The dread of man and beast—the wolf—was also one of the dramatic figures visiting the neighbors, both near and far. Among others, Rej of Nagłowice (1505–1569), a brilliant expert on customs, mentions "running around caroling, with a wolfskin." In the vicinity of Garwolin, I was told by an old farmer in 1929, that on St. Stephen's day he donned a wolfskin, attached a "huge red tongue" and "ran around caroling."

Long-beaked storks, cranes, sometimes cocks, wander around in the crowd of other creations. They all bleat, neigh, howl, clack and crow to make as much noise as they can.

The animals are accompanied by old men and women, kings and queens, orphans, a Hungarian, a Slovak, or some other itinerant vendor, a Jew, a Gypsy couple and many other characters wearing home-made bark masks, horned and decorated with crowns of moss and forest pine cones, in sheepskins and pea stalks, flecked with colored bits of material, shining with tinsel. In the Lancut vicinity, "ruffians" go around in caps made out of straw binding, in cloth masks and with straw belting around their waists.

The animals are imitated because the people are celebrating customs based on the very old cultures that flourished before an agrarian life was evolved, in the forests, when men herded sheep and goats, and hunted for their livelihood. Also, this is the reason why little round buns are baked for the *wilia* table; they imitate nuts and preserve the old ties with the forest and its bounty.

After the mass on St. Stephen's, oats, lupine, chickling, broad beans, peas, and rye are blessed in the churches (in many localities in Poland). People pelt each other (and especially the farmers) with oats, as they do in some regions on the feast of the Blessed Virgin of Sowing.

There is an old saying: "Everyone is his own master on St. Stephen's." And indeed there is a loosening of the restraints that hold people back from excessively boisterous gaiety on the first day of Christmastide. The carolers, already wearing masks of all kinds, visit the neighboring farms in greater numbers and fill the villages, town, and the suburbs of larger cities with their clatter, singing, and music. Boys sing courting songs to the girls, accompanying themselves on various instruments. Little boys recite greetings in verse which they have learned from the older youths. (Some of these poems were created in the distant past, the times of the Cracovian schoolboys and others studying in

Polish convent schools before the first partition.) The children also have the task of "awakening the earth from its winter sleep." From the first days of the Christmas to the New Year, little boys run through the fields with bells, as harbingers of Spring (the "new summer"). Since hens begin to lay in January, the young people make the rounds on St. Stephen's Day of the neighborhoods in the Zywiec region, with a stuffed rooster (*kur*). In other parts of Poland this tradition belongs to the repertoire of spring rituals.

Farmhands are hired on St. Stephen's, the threshold of the New Year. Most often, the farmers invite the candidates to the tavern. They discuss the deal as they treat the prospective farmhands to vodka and holiday fare. In the lands of the former Grand Duchy of Lithuania, the farmers ride "with the bell" attached to the harness of the horse's head in sleighs covered with a beautiful homespun blanket to the home of the future farmhand. As is the custom when the deal is agreed to, the contract is sealed with a drink.

The holidays begin with the fasting *wilia*, and then blossom into frolic and gaiety on the second day of Christmas. The activities really gain in intensity before the New Year. (These activities are kept in check only by certain prohibitions that regulate the course of work and play.)

On New Year's Eve, the farm women bake a new batch of "cookies" for the New Year guests. In the Sandomierz region, the "ruffians" come in their linen masks and moustaches made out of yarn to sing under the window:

> Good luck, good health on this New Year,
> Let your wheat and peas grow well.
> And rye and millet and everything,
> That you may not go barefoot.

How could one turn them away and not shower them with cookies?

In Pomerania (in the Gniew district), they baked a "new summer" of dough on New Year's Eve, i.e., human figures, little trees, animals, and placed them in glass cabinets. In the Lubawa district, the arrival of the New Year's day is greeted in the orchard by binding the trees with straw and inserting pastry crosses on them with the following words:

> Here, my tree, you have the new summer (Spring).
> Give me a good summer,
> You will get me abundance for it.

In the Kielce region there was another custom—still surviving in some villages—of taking fir branches to high mass on New Year's Day; these were stuck in the belt, and later the rafters at home. At the same time, the girls pin branches of flowering cherry blossoms to their kerchiefs. They had placed these branches in water on the feast of St. Lucia, December 13. The girl whose branches blossom the soonest will be the first to marry.

In the period between New Year's and the feast of the Purification of Our Lady, parish priests and vicars, accompanied by their organists, visited their parishioners, blessing their families, hearing their children's catechism, collecting offerings.

Before the First World War, older gentlemen in larger Polish cities, especially in Warsaw, dressed in frock coats and high hats, made New Year's calls from morning till night. New Year's wishes were also sent on calling cards.

Doormen and mailmen made their appearance with their greetings and to collect the traditional cash tip. In Cracow, on this occasion the mailmen distributed a printed poem or a whole collection of poems they themselves had composed.

Besides the carolers going around with a star, small bands of amateur actors also made the rounds of city homes as well as farms. Most often, these were craftsmen who had prepared for their roles during Advent. Some of them belonged to the "Herod" troupe. Entering the room, they sang carols. Then Herod, clad in a robe, with a scepter in hand and a crown on his head, would sit in a chair. Attendants in armor of paper, wearing helmets and wooden swords at their sides, stood on either side of him. They were accompanied by a Jew, a devil, death and musicians. The performance ended, naturally, with the death of Herod and his abduction by the devil. During Christmastide there was also caroling "with paradise." Paradise is represented by a spruce, the tree of life, hung with apples and ribbons and carried by one of the boys. In southwestern Little Poland, toys are made "with Dorothy" (from an ancient play, whose heroine is St. Dorothy), and the "Three Kings," accompanied by a smaller or larger group of companions.

During this time, "From Christmas to the New Year, the spinners work till dusk. But from New Year's to Epiphany right until supper." Disobedience of this interdiction, as well as interdictions against plucking feathers, chopping wood, and threshing from Christmas Eve to Epiphany will affect people's happiness and their property, the state of the chicken coop and the barn. For example, if spinning is done at any forbidden times, chicks may hatch with twisted necks, and if wood is cleared, a two-headed calf may be born.

Until a hundred years ago, spinning was carried out in the homes during the winter months; now, of course, most of the spinning is done all year in mills. In the past, the flax was sowed in May, and the fiber harvested in the fall and the spinning was begun during the second half of November. The thread was readied by Shrovetide and then the women began to weave the thread, to have their fabric finished before the onset of work in the fields and gardens in the spring.

The spinning evenings were an important setting for the expression of the Polish culture, and the Poles have sung about them for centuries. During such evenings, the old people would tell tales and pose riddles. And dances were born from the spinning, like the *"oberek"* with an extremely fast tempo and the dance for the "high flax" or *"lenek."* These evenings were interrupted only from the day before to the second day of Christmas.

From St. Stephen's to Epiphany, and sometimes even longer, the Old Marketplace in Cracow was filled with creches and puppet shows famous for their beauty. The puppeteers were invited into homes, if they did not come of their own accord, with their theater of marionettes or dolls skillfully manipulated on the stage by directors and actors hidden from public view, who spoke and sang for them. Up to 1939, in the suburbs of Warsaw, in the Old Town and Praga, as well as in the area of Nowogrodek and elsewhere, these holiday spectacles were continued. Besides scenes whose content related to Christmas, the puppet shows featured humorous scenes, characteristic of regional Polish types, along with dashing dances and songs.

The eve of Epiphany is called the Generous Evening in Poland. In the region of the Grand Duchy of Lithuania, the population calls the Generous Evening the "Great Christmas Supper," to distinguish it from the "Little Christmas Supper" of Christmas Eve. Even in some provincial houses of the gentry the supper consists of the same dishes served at *wilia*, but there is no breaking of the wafer, and the mood is less solemn.

On the day of Epiphany, the people write three letters, separated by crosses with chalk blessed that day with incense, over the entrance door to the house and over the doors of the farm buildings: K + M + B (Kasper, Melchior, Baltazar, the names of the three Kings or Magi who came to the Child with gifts). In granaries in northwestern Poland, the grain is sprinkled with holy water.

SHROVETIDE

The feast of the Purification of Our Lady on February 2 (Candlemas Day) is the last day for priests to make their annual visits to parishioners and generally marks the end of the period related to Christmas. Folk tradition associates it with protection from the storm and lightning, as demonstrated by the name for the candles *"gromnice"* (*grom*=thunder) consecrated in church that day. These play a role in family life, since they are given in the hands of the gravely ill or placed near the bed of the dying. The *gromnice* are lighted during a fire; rounds are made with these lighted candles near the herds starting out for the first grazing of spring; a sign of the cross is burned out with this candle on the main beam of the ceiling. But, above all, these candles are lighted during a storm to gain protection from lightning.

Shrovetide! The last rich meat days before Lent. Joy increases. Now Shrovetide mummers proliferate in the villages and cities. But where people hold fast to the old traditions, it is unseemly for country girls to dress in disguise and go around

with the carolers. That is why the Cracow girl appearing together with a Cracow boy is really a boy in disguise.

At Shrovetide (in Great Poland) they whittle a figure of a goat
or boy, called "under the goat," and put it near the musicians.
Stopping before it as they dance, the boys sing a courting song.
The girls put money for the musicians "under the goat."

Midnight of the Tuesday before Ash Wednesday approaches.
The "Shrove-Horse" in Mazovia and Kurpie charges in wildly.
They sing to him:

> Prance, prance, little horse
> On the red reins

In Pomerania, the "Shrovetide horse" is led around. But the
Shrove is relentless. The violins and violas are silenced. In
Great Poland the people drive a musician out to the fields; a cat
is released there, and is allowed to escape as "the sound escap-
ing from the body of the slain musician." Or, the people place a
bundle of straw on the shoulders of the violinist and then light
it. Thus the musician is symbolically burned, or sometimes
hanged. In Sokolniki the musician rips off the strings of his
violin. The boys cover his head with their caps and at that
moment the oldest person present scatters ashes over the heads
of everyone attending the party.

On Mardi Gras in the Poznań region, the people dance at the
tavern. The celebration is called "under the goat." The girls
also dance "the abundant flax." In the Poznań region, the boys
drive the "kur" (or cock) around in a cart, for good fortune in
the chicken coop. In Pomerania the spinners, carrying their
spindles, dance around the spinning wheel. The fishermen
dance around a draped net, jumping as high as they can for
good salmon catches.

Finally, a boy wearing a beard and dressed as a prince, surrounded by equally well costumed servants, arrives at the
tavern to put an end to the revelry.

On Ash Wednesday the priest sprinkles the heads of the
faithful with ashes. The boys hang pots of ashes to branches of
roadside trees or over doorways, so that the ashes fall on those
who pass by. Or else lurking farmhands throw ashes at the girls.

And they stealthily pin small pieces of wood or paper to the backs of anyone who did not marry during the winter season. (As late as the nineteenth century, unmarried young people were made to plough the field with a log on that day. Sometimes they were harnessed to the plow.) The older farm women grab the young brides and carry them in wheelbarrows to the tavern, where they are made to stand a round of drinks for the older women to buy their way into their group. Then, once again, all the women dance together or with their husbands at the tavern for the flax, for the hemp, for the oats, jumping as high as they can.

LENT AND EARLY SPRING

At this time the young animals are born in the sheep house, the barn, the pigsty. The farm women ready the warps for the loom, covering the fences and walls with flaxen or dyed thread, and then sit down to the weaving.

During Lent the cranes and storks come home for the season. On the feast of St. Joseph, the patron of family life, a girl and boy climb on to a selected thatched roof to prepare a nest for this protector of the homestead. In honor of the return of the larks and other birds, the companions of sowers and plowmen, little cookies in the shape of swallows and cuckoos are baked and distributed to the children.

In the countryside, the Sepulcher of the Lord is visited on Good Friday at the parish church. In towns, "rounds of the Sepulcher" are made at various churches. The Sepulchers were prepared with great care. In front of the Sepulcher in the larger parochial churches a decorative little garden was made of oats, cress, and boxwood grown in flower pots. Empty spaces were filled with sand. The Sepulcher was surrounded with lemon and orange trees and decorated with flowers and lamps with colored shades. On Good Friday, small crosses were blessed in the churches and then buried in the fields to ensure a good harvest. Also, little "crowns of thorns" made out of blackthorn and holly were blessed and then placed over the entrance to the barns and sheep pens and under the eaves of the roof for protection against all evil.

The houses had to be thoroughly cleaned for Holy Saturday and the "old fires" doused with water. During the first Mass, bonfires were lit in the church courtyard. A great tub of water also was placed there. After the Mass the priest blessed the bonfire and the water whereupon people snatched up twigs to light a new, holy fire in their homes and poured the water into flasks. In addition, people took Easter baskets to the church on Holy Saturday filled with colorful hard-boiled eggs tucked into the coils of sausages and resting on a bed of salt. On top of it all they put a loaf of bread.

RESURRECTION AND EASTER

The pealing of bells announces the Resurrection and the beginning of the Resurrection Mass, as solemn as the Midnight Mass of Christmas. But even during this greatest Mass of the liturgical year, the men and women from the farms do not forget to ask a blessing for their worldly goods and the fruits of their labors. After the Mass, the people return home and the Easter table decorated with the Easter lamb and especially the colorful eggs. Eggs have had a great significance to many races since prehistoric times, symbolizing the power of life and its continuity—in the life of nature and the immortality of the spirit. And the painting of eggs amongst the Polish people with traditional ornaments continues to have a magical and ritual meaning. Just as they share the wafer at Christmas, so do all of those gathered at the Easter table share the blessed eggs before the festive meal.

The Polish people begin the Easter breakfast with eggs and then eat an abundance of fresh meat and game, especially the roasted suckling pig with the traditional red egg in its snout, along with a variety of smoked meats. They have, as well, cheese, and bread, and pastry, including cheese cake and the so-called "mazurkas," which the bourgeois consider indispensable, as well as pastries flavored with raisins and almonds, enjoyed by the more prosperous farmers.

The Feast of the Resurrection is a time of happiness, of the victory of life over temporal death. Although in many parts of the country the people remain at home on the first day of the feast, they begin to make the rounds with holiday greetings. Children beg for treats and dress up as bears, old men and women, or gypsies. They sing under the windows of the cottages the ancient "greetings to the young ladies," and a refrain "about wine, green wine, and about the golden chalice." Again, as at Christmas, they take the rooster around to the houses while they sing Easter songs. The girls also go about with a fir tree decorated with colored paper, spangles and ribbons to greet the "new summer."

A good harvest must be conjured up at this time. And one ancient way is to sprinkle water on the ground. (In the country the boys sprinkle water on the girls so that there would be no drought and the earth would bear well.)

In :Cracow, the people remembered the dead on the third day of Easter by planting trees on a mound commemorating Krakus in the Krzemionki Hills along with silver coins, called the coins of St. John. It was assumed that people who dug them up later would think of the dead as heroes who had played various games, especially fencing, on the funeral mound. And because of this, games are also played, the most characteristic now being one in which the youths must climb a greased pole to reach a prize placed on top.

Finally, on the fourth day of Easter, egg shells and crumbs from the holiday feast are buried in the fields to prevent storms from beating down the crops. And during this Low Week, all accounts of the winter are settled. Symbolically, the boys and girls drown an idol made of rags stuffed with straw (called a "*smiertenka*" or "*marzanka*").

Among the old Christian traditions that spread into Poland from the West are the customs associated with St. George. St. George was the patron of farmers and breeders in Palestine and he was readily accepted into the traditions of a Europe in the process of becoming Christian. Churches were named after him and county fairs held in his honor late in April. Farmers dance with their wives in Silesia, jumping up as high as they can, so that their hens should lay as well as possible. In the Lublin region, Podlasie, eastern Mazovia, the territory of the Grand Duchy of Lithuania and in eastern Poland in general, St.

George has remained a great saint in the calendar of annual work and ceremonies. On his feast day, masses are offered for the success of the harvest. In the left corner of a side altar in Wilno-Nowogrodek, a St. George offering is placed: eggs, cheese, a country cake, a bolt of linen. Sowing begins between "the Polish and the Ruthenian St. George." On that day a boy dressed in green, with a loaf of bread on his head, is led around the fields or a large loaf of bread is rolled through the fields. The farm men and women roll on the ground of their culti- vated fields.

* * *

St. Florian (Florentinus, or flowery) was made one of the first official patrons of Poland in the Middle Ages. He also became a guardian of St. George's so-called flower month, and some of the elements of the old spring customs have become associated with his name. His feast day was celebrated, depending on the changes in the calendar, either on the 4th or 7th of May.

In Poland the importance of St. Florian faded in the course of centuries and his role was narrowed to patronage over fire- fighting and other lesser functions that varied according to the locality or parish.

WHITSUNTIDE AND CUSTOMS ASSOCIATED WITH CORPUS CHRISTI

May, as the month of the most beautifully blossoming spring, is dedicated to the Blessed Virgin. Wayside figures and holy images attached to the trees are decorated with garlands by the girls, and during the evening all the residents of the village recite the litany before them, singing hymns to the Mother of God. May services are also held in the churches. Pentecost or Whitsuntide is connected with the cycle of Easter Holy Days, as is Corpus Christi. In folk tradition, Whitsuntide symbolizes the "new summer" in full bloom and therefore houses and streets are decorated with budding trees, branches, and flowers. The paths leading to the houses are sprinkled with sweet rush. In some localities a bird, symbolizing the Holy Ghost, is hung from the ceiling. Sometimes the bird is woven of straw.

Priests visit the fields in the company of the farmers, blessing the land as they go. For protection against hail, branches of hazel, alder, or Easter "palms" are stuck in among the grain that has already come into ear. For the same purpose, in Little Poland and Silesia boys run through the fields, carrying lighted bundles of straw stuck on poles ("to chase away evil"). These people also light fires in the fields on the eve of Whitsuntide. Youngsters jump over this fire (in some regions the girls as well) and drive the cattle over it.

Whitsuntide, a time of verdant and luxuriant pastures, is ceremoniously observed by shepherds. Some elements of these indigenous customs, especially the shepherds' races and other traditional games, point to their distant connection with the customs of central-Asian pastoral tribes. On that day the horns of the cattle are decorated with flowers and red ribbons or streamers. Led by "kings and queens," the shepherds collect eggs in their village or the farmers bring food and liquor out to the pastures.

Pentecost also marks a turning point in the life of the people. Many children receive their First Communion then. Often apprentices are raised to the rank of master. In the country, boys who had been examined for their ability to gather hay successfully were accepted as adults. They were crowned with garlands, and, of course, had to pay for their acceptance into the group by offering a round of vodka and food.

On the second day of Whitsuntide, people in Poland went on picnics. In Warsaw and Cracow, they went to "Bielany," where they romped and danced in the woods surrounding the monasteries. Kiosks, laden with food and drink, and their noisy vendors added color and character to these suburban holiday outings.

The feast of Corpus Christi is a holiday that most distinctly unites the Polish people with the Church. The most important event, stressing Poland's alliance with Christ, is the procession through the main streets of the town in the direction of four altars that have been erected in the church yard. The procession circles the church and stops at each altar, as one of the four gospels is read in turn. The focal point of the procession is the monstrance, carried under a canopy by the highest church dignitary. In Cracow, the guild craftsmen prance about the head of the procession with hobby horses, which are a fleeting reminder of the camel drivers of the rich merchant caravans. Before the first partition of Poland at the end of the eighteenth century, the king assisted the archbishop in the procession. During the period of independent Poland, between 1918 and 1939, the ceremonies were attended by the president of Poland or the premier. Of course, throughout Poland the processions included representatives of the many groups that were important locally, such as the monastic clergy, the army, representatives of state and municipal authorities, university presidents and professors, teachers and students of secondary and primary schools, guilds, merchants' associations, various religious fraternities, all carrying banners and flags. Children with garlands on their heads strewed flowers before the Blessed Sacrament. The streets were flooded with flowers adorning houses and balconies, from which hung colorful, patterned carpets.

In the course of the whole holiday week, women and girls bring small bouquets to the church and garlands, made of herbs especially chosen for the occasion (medicinal and those that are said to offer protection from all kinds of danger). The priests bless them during the last vespers. Later, these blessed garlands will be buried in the fields, placed under the foundations of a new house, under the first sheaf of grain brought from the fields to the barn, or they are hung near the pictures in the household or over the entranceway. They may be placed over the gate to the barn, sheep pen, or stable. They are burned as incense near the fields and kneading troughs.

ST. JOHN'S

The feast of St. John the Baptist is interrelated with pagan celebrations that marked the longest day of the year, or the summer solstice. The cult of St. John is probably one of the oldest in Poland, having been spread by the first missionaries who baptized the converted people "with water." The customs of St. John are centered around fire, as well as water. Bonfires are lit; the young people leap over them to gain purification and to secure protection against the spells of witches and sorcerers. The cows, as well, are driven through the fires to protect them against spells that might deprive them of their milk. The farmers also protect their cows from the witches by keeping them from the pasture until the sun rises after St. John's eve. The farmers also incense their cows with blessed herbs to protect them from evil. The whole night and morning of St. John's harbors a great many supernatural mysteries.

But in Cracow and many other cities the people float garlands with candles flickering in them into the rivers. They draw great crowds, as do the fairs held at the same time.

SUMMER AND THE HARVEST SEASON

Haymaking begins about St. John's Day in southwestern Poland and, a little later, on Sts. Peter and Paul's Day in the north. And on June 29 the people hold fairs, especially in the larger towns. The farmers offer prayers to St. Peter, asking for good weather, so that the hay could be dried easily in the fields. The harvest is ended with celebrations of the "harvest home." First, the farmers leave in the fields a tuft of grain uncut. The girls braid sheaves and decorate them, while they sing songs which are clearly very ancient. The sheaves, that have been woven into either open or closed wreaths, are carried by one or more people, led by the foreman to the manor house. When they enter the yard, boys pour water on the girls for good luck and a good harvest. The lord of the manor receives the wreath and gives a reward of money. Then follows a toast to the festivities and dancing. The party continues through the night.

Finally, ending this season, the feast of the Assumption of the Virgin Mary is held on August 15. It is also a celebration of Mother Earth, and the women carry bouquets of various grains, vegetables, fruits, herbs, and flowers to the church.

BEGINNING OF AUTUMN AND SOWING

September 8, the feast of Our Lady of Sowing (the Birth of Mary), is connected with the time that winter crops are sown. In the last century there was a custom (eastern Mazovia, Białystok region) of pouring grain into the riddle on that day. Small candles, blessed at the church, were attached to the rim. The grain was sprinkled with holy water and sown in a portion of the field.

October is the month for completing the last work in the fields. Potato fields are cleared, cabbage and beans brought in, then shelled by the young people in a happy mixture of work and play. This month also sees feverish work on getting fibers out of flax and hemp which had been drying on the fences during September, usually a dry month in Poland. The distaff must be prepared for the long evenings of spinning before the rains of the last month of the autumn—November. Then only inside work will be done, such as threshing and cleaning the chaff off the grain.

October 28 is a day devoted to Thaddeus Jude, the apostle to Armenia. During World War II, litanies to St. Thaddeus reached the hands of people imprisoned in the Łukiszki in Wilno by the Soviets, because St. Thaddeus Jude is considered the patron of things most difficult to achieve and solutions to problems that seem hopeless. Thus, he became the patron of Underground Poland during the German occupation. He is still considered to be the protector of Polish exiles in England and other countries of homeless wandering, standing at the side of the Virgin Mary.

ALL SAINTS' DAY AND ALL SOULS' DAY

All Saints' Day, which falls on November 1, and All Souls' Day, November 2, begin the time when families congregate by the hearth. At this time, the people place candles in the cemeteries, and at places of torment and execution. Cereal, made of newly threshed wheat, or special cookies are placed on the graves; the pastries are given to the old men who chant memorial hymns at the cemetery gates.

Legal and farming traditions have become associated with the name of St. Martin, who was a soldier in his youth. The man lived at the turn of the fourth century and was known for his compassion; in time he became archbishop of Tours (France). In religious art (iconography), he belongs to the group of saintly knights. Like St. George, he is depicted on a grey horse. In folk art we sometimes meet him at the side of St. George in the same picture (Rumania and Slovakia). Small wonder! In agricultural tradition, both saints became the guardians of legal contracts.

On St. George's Day, there was a custom (as during Christmastide) to make agreements between farmers and farmhands, and also to change and rent apartments. This tradition has survived to this day in the Near East and in Istanbul as a continuation of old Babylonian legal traditions regulating the agricultural calendar (Hammurabi).

St. Martin has also been drawn into the calendar of legal dates connected with accounts and reckonings of the work season coming to a close—beginning with the spring and ending in November. Haur, an economic writer of the seventeenth century, reports that on about St. Martin's Day the peasants' tributes had to be collected. According to the folk customs in certain localities, on St. Martin's, debts were paid off to the neighbors and justice was meted out to offenders as on St. Matthew's (September 21); for instance, for grazing on another's pasture, letting one's cattle damage another's property, stealing. St. Martin's Day was free of agricultural work. The mills were also silent, although they were very busy during November in many regions.

The custom of serving "St. Martin's goose" for dinner on that day is of German origin, as is foretelling the severity of the oncoming winter from its breastbone. Obviously, other very ancient prophecies based on the viscera of animals killed in the hunt or butchered at home have been preserved among the traditions of the Polish country folk.

ADVENT

The season of Advent begins on the threshold of winter, and the people look to St. Andrew to protect them as they cross a new milestone in the passing of time. They ask him to protect their herds from the wolves. They hold a great feast for him and follow the custom of telling fortunes about the forthcoming harvest and success in the barn and sheep pen. In the cities the people consider auguries connected with the marriage and the general future of the young people.

In past centuries, street entertainments were held on St. Andrew's day in Poland as well as in other Western countries. In Cracow high school and university students took part and played all kinds of pranks, running around the streets in costume. This is probably the origin of the term "andrus," to denote a naughty urchin. The expression "andrew boys," denoting jokesters and tomboys, comes from the same source as St. Andrew games that once took place in England.

Advent is a period of fasting and reflection, as well as a time of preparation for caroling and going around in disguise to various "new summer" parties. The country folk and some residents of towns attend church at four in the morning for a Mass to the Blessed Virgin, called "Rorates," from the first words of the hymn "Rorate coeli" (let the heavens release the dew). People, hurrying in the darkness through the forest to the often distant church, set afire straw torches to ward off wolves and all evil.

On December 4 the miners, raftsmen, and fishermen celebrate the feast of their patron, St. Barbara, the protectress against sudden death. It begins with a Mass in church. Then the merrymaking begins, lasting far into the night.

The feast of St. Nicholas also is celebrated during Advent, as a prelude to Christimas in southwestern Polish towns. Stalls were set up in the streets to sell toys and sweets to the children, especially gingerbread in the shape of St. Nicholas. In some urban homes, the children left their shoes near the stove or on the threshold, which their parents filled with gifts. St. Nicholas' Day is considered to be a day for children, but for some, it is still a time to ask St. Nicholas for protection from the wolves.

The feast of the Immaculate Conception (Our Lady of the Snows) is also connected in folk customs with the offering of Masses to protect homesteads against wolves. On that day, according to ancient beliefs, the virtuous farmer may see, deep in the woods, as on the feast of the Purification of Our Lady, St.

George seated at a table. There are lighted candles on it. St. George reads out of a book who of the farmers are neglecting their duties to the land or are bad neighbors, and then directs the wolves to mete out justice to the culprit. The wolves face the Saint, awaiting orders.

The victory of Good over Evil, Light over Darkness, the winter solstice and the Birth of Christ are approaching. The earth, resting during Advent, will soon awaken to new life.

Christmas trees, hung from the ceiling, standing on the floor or on white tablecloths, will soon light up. In their mind's eyes people will see the cradle rocked to the rhythm of carols sung by a whole nation, and over it the bowed head of the Mother.

2

Towns in Medieval Poland

Jan Ptaśnik

Virtually all towns in the Middle Ages were fortified. In Holland, every town was walled with the exception of the Hague, which always remained an open city. In Poland, besides major cities such as Cracow, Poznań, Warsaw, Lublin, Sandomierz and Lwów, even small towns, especially those near the border, as a rule were fortified very early. We know that Bolesław the Pious fortified Międzyrzecz by means of a moat and battlements in 1269 and that in 1295 Wacław II allowed the bishop of Cracow to fortify Sławków, Ilza, Tarszek and Kielce in the same way. Naturally, larger towns had much more elaborate fortifications. For instance, Poznań is said to have been surrounded by a moat and battlements right after it was granted the Magdenburg rights (German Laws), but already in 1277 it was also protected by a wall, with four big gates, running along its moat. Lwów increased its fortifications in 1410 by raising its ramparts, deepening its fosses, building another buttress wall and enforcing it with a palisade. Cracow and Poznań were also surrounded with a double wall. On the other hand, Wilno, even in the times of the first Jagellonians, was not walled and thus its inhabitants were required to stand guard duty around the castle; they were freed from this obligation only in 1522, i.e., when Wilno was already surrounded by a wall. Other towns were fortified later—by walls, moats, and palisades—such as Pilzno, Sambor,

Drohobycz, etc., and this is how Stanisław Orzechowski wrote about Tarnów in "The Life of Jan Tarnowski":

"Look at Tarnów, the seat of the Tarnowskis, what wealth among the burghers, how it is equipped with ramparts, walls and cannons for protection."

Many towers built into city walls served to strengthen the defenses; the highest rose over the gates, since these were the most exposed to danger. A drawbridge connected the gate with the far side of the moat. When this drawbridge was raised by means of special machinery, it closely blocked the entranceway, changing into a mighty barricade-gate with sharp iron fraises on its outer surface. The entrance to the town itself was closed with a heavy wrought iron oaken bolt (in the shape of a grate), which was raised when the gate was open, but in the event of danger the boltswere pulled out and the latch, usually weighted down, fell in place with the speed of lightning and terrific force, blocking the entrance. Sometimes a portion of the enemy contingent was purposely let in through the gate and then, through the sudden lowering of the bolt, was cut off from the main enemy force; it was either exterminated or taken prisoner. This is what happened in 1376 during the siege of Złotoria, which was then held by the adventurous Prince Władysław the White. Having discovered a conspiracy aimed at letting into the town the armies of the Great Poland Subprefect, Sędziwoj, he used his knowledge in the following way: he purposely left the gate open; when about 26 of the enemy had entered, the bolt fell suddenly, and the unwary knights were forced to surrender.

More important city gates were sometimes also guarded by a second gate, in the form of a bastion jutting out beyond the trenches. Such a gate, called *propugnaculum* in Latin, was an Arab invention that was referred to as a barbican. In the Middle Ages nearly all better castellated towns had mighty barbicans of this type, or smaller round bastions and outworks. Some of them have been preserved to this day, as for instance in Carcassonne in southern France, and in Lusatian Zgorzelec; there is also one in Cracow built as late as the end of the XV century.

In medieval towns, what concerned people most was safety, rather than convenience, so that the town gates were closed for the night and no one, not even the highest state dignitary, was allowed to open them without the permission of the mayor and the council. An ordinary councilor could not issue such an order on his own.

From sunset to sunrise all town gates and portals had to be locked and closely guarded, and only on a very special occasion could any of them be opened.

This led to incessant strife with the local subprefects who, if they were delayed on their way to town, often had to spend the night at an inn outside its gates. If it ever happened, especially in times of danger, that town gates were left open during the night, the town authorities were suspected of treason. In 1455, the Poznań council exposed itself to such accusations, and even to a lawsuit brought by the district authorities, when as a result of criminal neglect the town gates were said to have been left open for four nights running. The townspeople accused the council of attempting to hand the city over to the Teutonic Knights.

As is often the case, the dispositions of the kings and the town ordinances pulled in one direction, and the whims of the willful nobles in the other. How difficult it was for the administrations of smaller towns to resist the caprices of the magnates and what misfeasances they had to risk, since in Cracow, right under the king's nose, in the times of Stefan Batory the nobility ordered the gates to be opened at night, and if "the mayor did not act in accordance with their will right away, or did not wish to please them, they dared to break down his door, heap abuse on him and pry open the town gates or locks by force." In the XVII century, the towns even had to resort to the threat of using firearms against the brawling hotheads.

Not only were the town gates locked, but also the streets leading to them were closed off with heavy chains in several places to prevent possible flight from the town or, in times of disturbances, to keep people away from the square and town hall. Remnants of such chains have been preserved in Cracow to this day, namely near the Mariacki Square, at Sławkowska and Grodzka streets. The town gates and streets were usually closed at a signal from the town hall bell or, as was the custom in border towns, "drums were beaten from the tower, calling the town guard to close the town at the appointed hour."

The streets of the medieval town were narrow and cramped so that they could be defended more easily, and also so that the greatest number of houses could be built in the smallest space possible. Any concern for the comfort of the inhabitants developed rather slowly; it is small wonder, then, that the streets were paved fairly late in Germany, and in Poland even later. Only in Italian towns, where material was readily available, were the streets paved at a rather early date, in the XII century. Roman tradition played an important role here, since many towns still had old pavements from Roman times. Probably the same can be said of towns in the West, such as Cologne, Strassburg, Mainz, Trier, etc., which were also founded by the Romans.

In central Europe, we encounter the first reports of the paving of streets in Prague in 1331, then in Bern, and in Nuremberg only about 1368. But even in those times Nuremberg was drowning in mud, so that in bad weather it was difficult to get around even on horseback, if one is to believe the Chancellor of Charles IV, the bishop of Lutomia, John of Newmarkt, who provides us with a lengthy and humorous account of the trouble he had getting from his house to the castle where the emperor was staying.

In the XV century, larger towns in the West were already paved. The Viennese pavements were praised by Aeneas Silvius Piccolomini; Prague was compared to Paris by a certain Silesian knight and scholar, but in smaller towns one literally sank down in the mud during those times. It was for this reason that the town council of Tutlingen cautioned Emperor Frederick III against coming in the rainy season, and when he did not heed the warning, he sank into the mud up to his waist, together with his horse. An even worse thing happened to him in the town of Reutlingen, when he and his horse almost drowned in a street quagmire. During the drought, this quagmire changed into a hard crust above which rose clouds of dust. The streets were also littered with manure, since nearly all burghers kept herds of swine and cattle, which paraded freely on the streets or at least passed through them on their way to the municipal pasture lands. As we will see, conditions were not much better in the towns even in later times.

Things were not likely to have been better in Poland, but rather worse. It took a long time to make the streets—in towns

built on quaggy soil, such as Cracow, Poznań or Wrocław—
usable for vehicular traffic. They were probably no better than
today's country roads. In the rainy season, it was difficult to
cross from one side of the street to the other, so that in certain
places wooden planks were laid to form street bridges. In time
logs were thrown down all along the street, changing it into a
bridge, in German *brucke,* in other words paving it with wood.
We have a drawing of such a street from the beginning of the
XV century, Grodzka Street in Cracow led through quagmire,
and thus was paved with planks in such a way that it was elevated near the houses and formed a sort of channel or river
bed, deepest in the middle, to which the gutters emptied; in
case of rain it really changed into a rapid torrent. This was the
condition of Grodzka Street in 1412, with other streets probably not much better. So that people could walk from one street
to another during the rainy season, sidewalks were built
alongside the houses, first out of wood, and then stone. This
was done rather early, since we hear of paviors in Cracow not
long after the middle of the XIV century (1368), and of
sidewalks for which mighty boulders were hauled in at the end
of that century. Stone sidewalks were divided from the street
proper by means of stone poles. This is how it was in Cracow,
and possibly also Lwów, but in other towns wood was still used
instead of stone. Up to the present day, in north-eastern towns,
even in the old Lithuanian capital of Wilno, sidewalks are built
of wooden blocks.

The oldest cities in the West, whose past goes back to Roman
times, were built without a plan, especially if they were located
in hilly areas. This is the reason for their picturesque streets
and alleys that wind in a confusing labyrinth. On the other
hand, towns founded later, especially on the eastern plains,
were built in accordance with a certain set pattern. First the
square was marked out, and from its center four streets were
extended at right angles to the four ends of the earth. Thus the
streets formed a cross whose limbs met in the middle of the
square, dividing the town into four parts, or quarters (*quartale,
viertel*). Parallel to each limb of the cross ran other criss-crossing
streets, so that the newly-created medieval town had the form
of a chessboard with the largest square in the middle—a paral-

lelogram or quadrangle—the market place. In some towns this plan was altered to the extent that there were no streets crossing the middle of the square, but streets ran from its four corners in four directions. This was the pattern of all east German towns, as well as Polish cities such as Cracow, Wrocław, Poznań, Gniezno, Old Warsaw, Toruń, Lwów and others. Such a town chessboard, whatever its size, was surrounded by a wall to form a separate municipal entity. Buildings outside of its compass did not conform to this plan, but formed suburban communities (*suburbia*), under the jurisdiction of municipal authorities if they lay within the city limits. Otherwise they formed separate towns along the pattern outlined above, also surrounding themselves with walls or moats, as did Kazimierz and Kleparz near Cracow, New Warsaw, Toruń and other twin or even triple towns, as Rostock and Prague.

Since medieval towns were built in accordance with a certain plan, there had to be engineers at that time to lay out this plan. But we have no detailed information about them before the XV century. We only know that in the second half of the XV century the municipal builder in Nuremberg was the sculptor and stonecutter Jacob Grimm, and that Wit Stwosz held the same position in Cracow at the end of the XV century, before he moved to Nuremberg to take over direction of municipal construction after Grimm, besides continuing his own work. This was a very important task, since Nuremberg was a strong fortress as well as a city. To a certain extent, these were practical architects. During the same period in Italy there appeared theoreticians, who in their works on architecture also went into the problem of building towns in such a way that they should serve military needs as well as the greatest convenience of their inhabitants.

But this was already in the time of the Renaissance.

As for Poland, we know that in the second half of the XVI century, two brothers from Urbino named Genga, engineers by profession, spent time here. We know that the town of Zamość, as well as its powerful fortress, was built for Hetman Zamojski by Bernard Morandi, and that during the same period Domenico Ridolfini, a colonel in the armies of Stefan Batory, who was also a great architect of border fortresses in Poland

and Hungary, spent time in Poland, Lithuania and later in
Transylvania; that in the XVII century Francis Corazzini of
Avignon, a Lt. Colonel in the Foot Guards of the Palatine,
Andrzej Potocki, planned and built for him Stanisławów, con-
ceived as a fortress-town.

Having become familiar with the general outline of the town,
let us now look at its more important public buildings and institutions.

The center of the town was the main market place or square.
Near it, or right on it, were found the most important public
buildings, such as the town church, which was under the protection of the council, the town hall, the cloth hall, the town
scale and various other municipal or guild buildings.

The town and its patriciate cared for the magnificent appearance of the main parish church or cathedral; prosperous merchants and craftsmen built family chapels or at least altars in
these churches at their own expense, and never forgot to leave
a certain sum in their will for necessary church repairs.

While council families tended the main parish church, other
churches were cared for by the townspeople, especially those
who wished to be buried in them or in the cemeteries near
them. In the Middle Ages, every town, however small, had a
great many churches—lay churches, parish churches and
monastic churches. In private towns, especially in the east, in
time there rose up great sanctuaries in the Renaissance or
baroque style, built at the expense of the nobles who, although
they seldom concerned themselves with the Polish character of
the town population, did not stint funds for the erection of
Latin churches and the founding of monasteries for the salvation of their souls. As a matter of fact, Ruthenian churches were
also built and endowed through their efforts. To this day in
nearly all churches numerous monuments to the generosity of
the townspeople have been preserved—such as chapels and altars, paintings and church furnishings. We learn even more
about the devotion of the medieval burgher to their houses of
worship from their wills and bequests, as well as foundation
records.

Hospitals were surrounded with particular solicitude.
Whereas "love thy neighbor" was an idea alien to ancient civili-

zation, it blossomed as a result of the teachings of Christ in the Middle Ages, a time when hospitals and poorhouses were built, along with dormitories and hospitals for students; even grants for girls were provided who because of their poverty had no chance of marrying. The larger the town, the greater the number of such charity institutions, usually founded through the private generosity of the townspeople and clergy. All Polish towns built hospitals, large or small, devoting special care to the most wretched—separated from the rest of the population—the lepers. In mining towns there were asylums for miners who had suffered accidents and could no longer support themselves by working. In the wealthy West, things went even further; for instance, in 1360 Strasbourg built a free home for strangers who for some reason or other were not able to pay for their lodgings.

The hospitals, just as the churches, beside the main parish one, could be found in various regions of the town, and even sometimes outside its boundaries. Let us turn our attention to secular buildings serving the everyday needs of public and private life.

All the civic activity of the townspeople was concentrated in the market place. This is where their main seat, the town hall (*domus consulum, domus consilii publici, curia, praetorium*), could be found. Every town strove to have such a building from the moment it was founded. Larger towns already built them during the Middle Ages in the Gothic style popular at the time, but later, when the Renaissance and Baroque styles were predominant, they wished to alter them more or less in keeping with these later styles. This was the fate of the Cracow, Sandomierz and Tarnów town halls, and above all of the Poznań town hall, whose lower levels were already standing at the time that the Czech kings, Waclaw II and III, ruled Poland. The whole building, rebuilt in the second half of the XVI century by an Italian architect, has preserved a typically Renaissance character to this day. The nature of the Tarnów town hall is similar; in its main characteristics it is reminiscent of the town hall that is probably the most beautiful of the town halls preserved in Poland—that in Sandomierz. The Tarnów town hall was rebuilt by the most outstanding Italian sculptor and architect who spent time in

Poland, Gian Maria Padovano, since its Attica is reminiscent of the Attica of the Cracow Sukiennice. In some towns, especially those that were founded later or became important just at that time, the town hall was built from the ground in the then popular baroque, rococo or other style.

In little towns, the town halls, as all other houses, were built of wood. Thus until the end of the XVIII century Wadowice had a modest wooden meeting house, pompously called a town hall, composed of a court room, jail and little room. A 1767 account of Nowy Targ describes its town hall as "a newly built town hall out of sawed, planed wood with pillared arcades all round." It was the same in small towns of Great Poland. In Grabów, for instance, as late as 1773, in the middle of the market place could be found "a town hall out of pine wood, hewn into angles—a two-story building with porches, a small tower and in it a little campanile, and a shingled roof "—built in wood, located "on the road from the Sieradz province, and the Little Poland provinces to Śląsk." The Grabów town hall, although made of wood, was more showy than most, since it was a two-story building (or one-story in the modern European usage of the term) and boasted a tower.

In larger towns, not only did the council hold its meetings at the town hall and the town trials and meetings of citizens took place there, but also ceremonies, receptions in honor of princes and magnates, and sometimes even balls and wedding banquets of the sons or daughters of the councilmen were held there as well. The ground floor was usually occupied by a commercial hall and shops, often in the shape of niches in the outer wall; under the hall could often be found the council's cellar, where beer and wine were sold; the upper floor was devoted to municipal offices, the council chamber, court room, merchants' and guild halls and other rooms. On their walls hung paintings by the most distinguished artists, along with mottoes and maxims connected with justice.

Over the town hall hovered the tower with a clock and bell, and lower stories that housed prison cells, which bore various names in the different towns: In Cracow, for instance, they were called "the debtor" and "the coat" and in Międzyrzecz "the nightingale" and "hell." No town hall could be without a well-castellated chamber in which the most valuable furnishings were kept. This was the town treasury, *Aerarium civitatis*. Generally the plan of the rooms in the town hall in a smaller town was about as presented in the 1663 description of the town of Drohobycz:

"This brick town hall, in which on the ground floor there is a great hall with windows framed in lead, a good vault and locks. In this chamber the judge does his judging. Near this chamber a mighty vault, a good one, with fine iron doors and a stout lock—that is the treasury—where the wealth and other *necessaria acta* are kept; it is there that the sword of justice is kept as well, and there was a craftsman in town, who is no longer here; in the same treasury there are two suits of armor for the guards, and ten harquebuses. It is there that three bronze pipes lead from the tubes throughout which water flowed. On the third floor a brick room for the trumpeter, who is no longer here. Over this town hall a tower, with a plated roof, girded by balconies; on this tower a great sturdy clock and index, with towers on the side, but in need of repair; there is a watchmaker in the town. On the first floor a decent room for the scribe and chancellery, and under this writing room a bricked vault below ground, well castellated for the prisoners. Under the town hall, butchers' stalls made out of wood."

Along with the towns, the town halls suffered through difficult times. The brick, as well as wooden ones often succumbed to fire. The old town hall in Międzyrzecz, tiled in 1581, burned in 1666; only its lower part remained, to which in 1670 the empoverished town managed to add only one story out of wood and cover it with ordinary tiles. A new tower was also built at that time, reputed to have cost a great deal of money, to replace the one that had burned. After the white eagle was placed on it, the priests and students from the town schools sang to the accompaniment of music, and at the end of the ceremony a solemn *Te Deum laudamus* was intoned. In 1701 this town hall burned down too, so another was built, which met the same fate in 1827. The present town hall rose on its ruins. The Pilzno town hall, built in the XVI century, if not earlier, fell into ruin as a result of wars and the crossing of troops. Although it was partly restored in 1756, against the wishes of the subprefect of the time, Stanislaw Pininski, this restoration was not sufficient, since in 1765 observers commented on its lamentable state, adding that after the restoration "it should have been an ornament for the town, a convenience for the courts and a safe place to keep records." No one seemed in a hurry to repair it, and thus it crumbled from neglect. Nearly all of the old-time town halls suffered a similar fate. Sometimes they were torn down on purpose, as was the case with the Cracow town hall; all that remained of it was a lonely, stately medieval tower reigning over the Cracow market place and all of the city. Only a few Polish towns can boast of old town halls: Gdańsk, Toruń, Sandomierz, Tarnów and Poznań are the foremost among them.

Other municipal buildings were also located in the market place. Among them were merchants' houses, called "sukiennice" (cloth hall), housing the stalls of rich merchants, first of all clothiers, and the town cutting center; then there was the house of drygoods merchants, called "szmatruz" (*schmetter haus*), if it was not a part of the "sukiennice," and large and small scales, called "witnica" in Polish, which were sometimes located in the "sukiennice," although usually they formed a separate building.

The "sukiennice" (cloth hall) was the most splendid of public buildings. Quite a few of them have been preserved to this day, such as those in Strasbourg and Constance from the XIV century, and especially those in Flemish towns—Bruges, Ghent, Malines, etc. The Mainz cloth hall, built in 1313, was unfortunately torn down in 1812. It was especially interesting in that, before the Cracow cloth hall was restored, it bore the greatest similarity to them. The Cracow Sukiennice was built at the time of Casimir the Great, to replace earlier merchant booths of the XIII century. In its upper floors, it underwent extensive alterations at the time of the Renaissance, executed by the great sculptor and architect from Italy, Gian Maria Padovano. It owes its present form, quite different from the original one, to the reconstruction of the brilliant architect Pryliński.

In a few Polish towns, especially in the east, where there was an abundance of honey and what followed, enough wax for export, special town buildings were erected where workmen melted and kneaded the wax, weighed it and provided it with a town stamp. Only wax thus ensured against counterfeiting was shipped abroad, to Germany, Flanders and Italy. We read of such a wax processing plant as early as the beginning of the XV century in Lwów, and at the end of that century also in Wilno (1492), where the people called it a "zaboynicza"; Lublin also had one (1548), as did other eastern towns.

The market place was not in the least free of clutter, since places where there were no public buildings were crammed with stalls, benches and booths of vendors and artisans, appendages that clung particularly to the walls of the cloth halls and town halls, spoiling their appearance. For the swarm of people who descended on the market place, especially during the time of fairs, there was a need for public toilets. The towns built them (not all towns, as a matter of fact), in the most primitive manner possible, without much regard for their cleanliness. For example, Nuremberg issued an order for the cleaning of its seven public toilets near the river Regnitz only once a year, on St. Martin's day.

It was a real blessing for the town if it had a river near by, since this made it possible to keep the streets fairly clean. For purposes of communication, bridges, often reinforced with double towers, were built over the rivers. On the two sides of the river, two separate town communities arose, each surrounded by its own wall; in case of siege by an enemy, one community could support the other from across the river; after one was captured, the other had to be laid to siege. This is how it was in Regensburg, Basel, Prague, and also in Cracow. The bridges were wooden on the most part, but already in the Middle Ages there were quite a few stone ones. E.g., in 1325 a stone bridge was built in Erfurt; the famous bridge over the Moldau in Prague was built at the time of Charles IV, and in Coblenz over the Moselle in 1444; in Nuremberg, in the second half of the XV century, old bridges were reinforced and new ones built over the river Regnitz; in Wrocław, a vaulted stone bridge spanning the river Oława was built as late as 1507. But it was especially the times of the Renaissance and baroque that delighted in massive stone bridges, as generally in all other monumental secular buildings.

Polish towns, located mostly near rivers or even among lakes, needed bridges all the more. Thus Poznań had a larger bridge on the river Warta and a smaller one on the Cybina; Gniezno also had a bridge; in Cracow a bridge linking Kazimierz with Cracow bore the name of "royal," lending its name to the whole suburb: *Stradomia alias Pons regalis.* Beside this great bridge was another smaller one. They were built of wood, although we also hear of stone bridges during this period. So, at the end of the XIV century the bridge leading out of town over the Rudawa in the direction of St. Nicholas parish, was fashioned of tremendous boulders, and Casimir the Great built a stone bridge out of Cracow, near Czyzyny, on the way to Bochnia. Unfortunately, this interesting structure from the times of Casimir has not survived to the present day.

Polish towns tried to get their own aqueducts fairly early. We must mention that at least from the end of the XIV century Cracow used them, drawing water from the Rudawa by means of a special contraption and conducting it throughout the town, that separate pipelines even supplied water to the palace, and that we read of work in Lwów, right at the beginning of the XV century, connected with the installation of an aqueduct with clay pipes which finally, in the year 1407, at the time of the mayoralty of Piotr Stecher, for the first time supplied the town with fresh water. Smaller towns followed the example of the larger ones. Thus in 1461 Krosno gained the privilege of building underground aqueducts, Biecz three years later, and Pilzno in 1467. But before this last town had a chance to conclude this construction, it was destroyed by the Hungarians in 1474, so that it could resume work on it only in 1487, completing it the following year to the great joy of its inhabitants. Sanok got running water in 1510, while Lublin concluded an agreement with masterworker Jan already in 1514, but began to build the waterworks only in 1535. Drohobycz got them in 1544, whereas Sambor had them earlier, since in 1542 we hear of their renovation. Also fairly late, at the beginning of the XVI century, they appear in Wilno. A water system was first introduced by the local Dominicans, who drew water from a stream belonging to them, Wingra, and also supplied water to the palace, bishop's court and the Franciscans, and at a price also to the townspeople. In 1536 they sold their stream to the town, which agreed to lay a huge waterpipe leading to the monastery gates, while smaller pipelines were to be laid by those who wanted water. In the course of the economic decline of the towns, the aqueducts fell into disrepair and ruin. In Pilzno they were a thing of the past already at the beginning of the XVII century, and in Lublin they were destroyed in the same century by the Swedish wars; Drohobycz also lost its pipeline during these military defeats, since a comment of 1663 states:

"So that the wells according to need *ad necessitatem* for defense, God preserve us, when fire *incolae* of this town *publico sumptu* was built and this *rurmus,* which *nescitur* what way found its way to Sambor, was saved, and having been saved was placed in its former place *cum omni reparatione.*"

The pipelines conducted water to the town, to a main reservoir (*cista*) and from it smaller canals conveyed the water to various places. They facilitated the formation of wells and fountains, especially in the market place. It is interesting that Cracow, with its abundance of Renaissance and Baroque buildings from the time when magnificent decorative fountains were built everywhere, did not have any at all. But Poznań, Lwów, Old Warsaw and probably other towns did have fountains. The history of the fountain in Leszno, built by the council in 1755, is an interesting one. A rich Leszno brewer, one Gotfryd Szobel, was well known for his weakness for going to court; he was involved in litigation not only with the townspeople, but also with the town itself; having lost the case, he was made to pay such a sizeable sum of money that it was sufficient for the building of a fountain depicting Bacchus with the face of Szobel, sitting astride a barrel and holding a glass of beer in his hand. The insulted brewer again brought suit against the council, which finally removed the glass from the hand of Bacchus, replacing it with the cluster of grapes more appropriate for this god of drunkenness.

We do not know how hotels looked in Poland during the Middle Ages. At any rate, they could be found in border towns and in all larger towns; sometimes, as for instance in Będzin, they were the property of hereditary heads of villages. In Cracow, German artists, priests and scholars stopped at the hotel called "Under the White Lion," which existed on St. Anna Street at least from the end of the XV century and throughout the whole next century, in a house earlier called "Zarogowski"; in Toruń, a hotel called "Under the Cerulean Apron" has existed from 1489 to the present day. Most often, however, inns were located in the suburbs, as in Kleparz near Cracow, where the most famous was an inn located in one of the few brick buildings, thus called "Earthen Jar." For long years visitors to Poznań had to stop at five suburban inns, since there was no hotel in the town itself. Travelers managed by renting rooms in private homes, and then furnishing them with the bare necessities. There was such a need for lodgings for visitors, and such a demand for them, that speculators leased whole houses in order to rent out bare and dirty rooms to visitors. Only the Prussians, step by step, succeeded in introducing hotels and inns within the town. As for traveling journeymen and foreign craftsmen, they found lodgings in the guild houses, which had guest rooms alongside their taverns. Butchers, furriers, shoemakers, tailors, goldsmiths and probably others had such guild houses. Old guild houses of this type have been preserved in Toruń to this day, as the masons' guild house and another one called "United Guilds." Nonetheless, ordinary taverns also took overnight guests. An XVIII century account mentions: "a linden table squared off at the bottom, a bench all along the wall, two couches and four tables;" there was an alcove next door with a door leading to a rest room. This was the guest part of the tavern—the owner occupied the other. When something was in the air or the threat of war hung over the country, the innkeeper was obliged to give the name of each guest to the town office and not to admit anyone without a passport.

It is surprising how many public baths there were in the Middle Ages. They could even be found in the villages, and perhaps for the reason that they were in common use, they became princely regalia of sorts; the prince often granted the heads of villages or hamlets the right to build a bath house to be used by all residents of the given village for a certain price; the residents were not allowed to bathe at home, in barrels or tubs. In practice, however, not only knights and princes, but also peasants and burghers had them. Casimir the Great was so accustomed to the public bath that even during his last illness he could not refrain from using it; he did so against the orders of his physician, and this reportedly contributed to his death. Boleslaus the Brave was also a devotee of the public bath; to this bath, he took with him young men, whom he forgave political offenses, but whom he punished there in a paternal way. During the times of Casimir the Great, the Mazowsze starost, Andrzej Ciołek, had a huge tub at his estate, in which a large number of people could bathe at the same time. Many examples could be cited to show how popular the bath was among the nobility, the princes and the peasants.

Steam baths were also known at least since the end of the XIII century. Red-hot stones were put in a barrel, splashed with water, and the bather sat next to them enjoying a steam bath. After bathing, he dried his body, put on a bathing shirt, rested on a bathing bed and then partook of food. Later bath regulations frowned on eating during the bath as well as directly before it:

"Whoever wants to take a bath for improving his health, should bathe on an empty stomach, never eat or drink in the tub or the bath house, and eat only one or two hours after the bath."

Everyone felt the need to bathe at least once a week. In Germany, a great deal of attention was paid to the day one bathed, or should bathe. There was a proverb that drunkards bathed on Monday, the rich on Tuesday, jokesters on Wednesday, the scabby and lousy on Thursday, the stubborn and ne'er-do-wells on Friday, and important personages on Saturday. Why was Thursday down at the bottom of the bathing scale? It is said that it was because this was the day that Christ was imprisoned and his agony began, since one of the Polish preachers thundered against those who refrained from taking a bath on Thursday, as the memorable day Christ was imprisoned, but did not hesitate to devote themselves to fornication and licentious debauchery on that very day.

Bathing blossomed particularly in medieval towns. In German towns even the tip (*trinkgeld*) was called bath money (*badegeld*). The extensive use the bath was put to in medieval towns is illustrated by the fact that in the XV century 20 bath houses could be found in Vienna, 8 in Nuremberg, and

Cracow, besides the private ones, boasted 11 public baths. The town itself owned three of them, i.e., a Jewish one, one at the tollgate and one at Piasek. At that time, they brought the town a considerable income. There was an abundance of them in other towns as well. In XV century Lwów, besides the royal bath and other public ones in the hands of private entrepreneurs, there existed a town bath house which students could use free every three weeks, on the recommendation of their teachers, and at the beginning of the XVI century the cathedral dean of Lwów, Jan Krowicki, left a sizeable sum to the town with the provision that the town use the dividends from the sum to give all students and six priests a free bath every week, and every beggar every two weeks. Rich burghers often left generous legacies for meals and baths for the poor. "I, Zofia Kropidłowa, in this my last will and testament direct: that after my death my older son Adam should provide baths and meals for the poor, so that they may pray to Almighty God for my soul" (1606). "I, Stanisław Brykner, a Cracow merchant, wish that after my funeral, when my wife finds the free time, she organize a common bath for the poor, for which I devote 415 zlotys" (1646). These are bequests often encountered in the wills of Cracow burghers.

Not everyone in the Middle Ages allowed himself the pleasure of using a bath house. Baths were avoided by those who wished to achieve the kingdom of heaven by mortifying their body, and thus monks of the stricter orders or even laymen who led ascetic lives. They considered the bath a luxury, nearly a sin. Once a lady developed an unholy passion for a certain pious monk, with the result that he could not free himself of her persistent amorous advances. It was only when he showed her his never-washed body that he cooled the fervor of the infatuated woman. And also the chronicler Godysław Baszko, praising the piety of the Great Poland Prince Przemysl I, as a particular proof of his mortification brought up the fact that he punished his body with a hair shirt and for the last four years of his life did not use the bath. Physicians also forbade their patients to bathe during certain illnesses, for instance when someone was bothered with chills, and in times of pestilence they even advised the healthy not to bathe; in their opinion the bath, just as intemperate relations with women, made the body susceptible to disease; through open pores it could easily absorb the germs in the polluted air. In the epoch of the Renaissance, fear of venereal disease (*morbus gallicus*), which just at that time assumed frightening proportions, kept many people from going to the bath house. In 1524 Erasmus of Rotterdam wrote about it as follows: "Twenty five years ago nothing was more favored in Brabant than warm baths, now they are all cold. A new eczema is keeping us from using them." The reason was that public baths were bound to be the main breeder of this disease. It is true that the sick, covered with disgusting abscesses came there with their creams and bathed together with the healthy. Górnicki, comparing the conditions prevailing in the world with what went on in the public bath, said the following in *Dworzanin* (The Courtier): "Whoever goes into the public bath, has to suffer many bad times: while one is rubbing himself with spirits and soap, another with cream against injuries, one is blowing bubbles, and another will flog himself to death."

Despite this, even in the following century the bath house blossomed in Poland, and only the XVIII century did away with it. For instance, of the eleven bath houses that Poznań had had earlier, not one remained in the Saxon times.

The bath attendants and barbers working at the bath houses did not enjoy a great deal of popularity. As a matter of fact, their profession was held in such contempt that in Cracow they could not be members of certain guilds, and even their sons were barred from admission to other trades. In his "Fraszki," Kochanowski compares them to fallen women:

"The bath attendants and the whores live in the same way. They both bathe the good and the bad in the same tub."

Let us pass on to private houses.

In the beginning, houses were not built along a straight line in medieval towns. Some extended into the street, others were set back, resulting in a colorful variety, which was intensified by the fact that the narrow houses with two or three front windows not only extended upwards but also, to gain a little space in their upper floors, jutted out toward the street on both sides. Extensions of all sorts stuck out from these houses, cramping the street even more. This probably presented a colorful picture, but was detrimental to the street, which was thus transformed into a narrow, dark and dirty alley. These houses were mostly made of wood; brick was a rarity. For reasons of health and because of the danger of fire, the town authorities came out against this system of wildcat construction, issuing orders on how building should be done without encroaching on the street. The frequent fires came to their aid, wiping out whole districts of alleys which had to be replaced by brick buildings that conformed to the regulations. There were many such building regulations in Germany from the end of the XIII century; the oldest in Poland date from the second half of the XIV century.

The houses of the townspeople at first were not built with an eye to esthetics or comfort; only slowly, in the XIV century, did any attention begin to be paid to these matters. During this time, and even more in the following century, we see some of the houses built with a certain grandiosity, with murals and sculptures inside and outside the building. It is enough to recall the so-called hetman chamber in Cracow decorated with figurative sculptures from the time of Casimir the Great, or the XV century house of Mikołaj Kreidler which Długosz describes as being decorated with the sculptured portraits of the Polish kings. When Aeneas Silvius visited German towns about the middle of the XV century, he was amazed at the splendor of the houses of Viennese and Nuremberg patricians, which in his opinion could easily have passed for monarchs' palaces. To this day a number of medieval houses have been preserved in the West, dating from the time when intellectual culture and the accumulation of wealth made it possible for the town patricians to furnish their houses in the grand manner. Especially worthy of attention are houses in Frankfurt on the Main, Cologne, Greifswald, Gdańsk and Elbląg. Also, chronicles and descriptions of medieval towns speak of sculptures and painted facades, of their being adorned with the coat of arms of the owners, of various sculpted emblems, some of which have been preserved in Cracow until the present day. These emblems were very necessary at the time. Although the streets of medieval towns were named (usually after the church that was located on them, the locality to which they led, or the craftsmen of some trade who lived on them), the houses were not numbered and thus were designated with the last name of the owner, if he was well known, or with the emblem that hung over the gate or on the facade. Thus, there was a house under the crayfish, the ram, three crowns, the lizard, elephants, bell, Moor, white lion, rhinoceros, peacock, squirrel, etc.

The larger house was closed with a sturdy gate, well fitted with tin plate; through it one walked or rode into a spacious hallway, then to a courtyard, where the merchant temporarily stored his wares, before arranging them in granaries or cellars. Already at that time larger houses had several courtyards, composed of a front (*Vorderhaus, Vordermach*) and back buildings (*Hinterhaus, Hintermach*).

As late as the XIII century, the windows of houses in the West were extremely small and without glass panes, closed with shutters. One could encounter glass panes only in the magnates' houses. While glassworks were known earlier, they produced the more costly dishes and stained glass for houses of worship. A glassworks that existed near Poznań from at least the end of the XIII century, worked exclusively for the Poznań cathedral, and other XIV century glassworks in Little Poland supplied the royal castle and churches with glass. In Cracow at that time, glaziers belonged to the painters' guild, painting pictures on glass and providing stained glass for the churches. Only slowly, perhaps already in the XIV century, and surely at the end of the XV and early XVI, whole windows of glass, usually colored, were used in rich houses. These were generally of a large size, in the Venetian fashion. Such a house with varihued windows must have looked very colorful. As shades were not in use yet, these colored windows kept the curious from fathoming the secrets of the house, but failed to let in enough light.

Even in later times not every house could afford glass windows; the poorer people used animal membranes, and that is why the glass window pane was sometimes referred to as a membrane.

Rooms in the house were divided into chambers (*stuba, stube*), having a stove (*stufa*) from which they derived their name, chambers with fireplaces (*komenate, caminata*) and unheated rooms (*camera, kammer*), then kitchens, coal bins (*kohlkammer*), privies and ordinary bathrooms. The ground floor of the house was usually occupied by stores, workshops, counters and warehouses—this depended on the size of the house and to whom it belonged—a rich merchant, peddler or craftsman. Under it were vaulted cellars with entrances straight to the street or inside the house, for instance near the stairs. The ground floor was connected with the upper stories by a winding staircase leading to a spacious hall (*Vorsaal*), from which doors led to the various rooms, front living rooms, kitchens and bedrooms. A balcony connected these rooms with the outbuilding. Naturally, things were arranged differently in some houses, since some of them had an entrance to the courtyard through a hallway, and others, especially if the owner worked at farming, had separate entrances straight to the courtyard; others still had bedrooms or parlors (*Staatsaal, saal*). In broad outline, however, the house of the urban patrician was about as described above.

One thing must be pointed out. It is generally accepted in the West that urban houses followed the archtype of the country houses since, like them, they centered around a spacious hall with two rooms and kitchen. This was undoubtedly true of small, one-story houses belonging to burghers who also ran farms. But the rich patrician modeled his house rather on the knightly castles. The main residential building of the knightly castle in the Romanesque style—as well as in the Gothic to a certain extent—was called a palace and also served to denote the main chamber of the castle. It sometimes occupied a whole floor, with an open staircase, but most often bedrooms and the palace chapel were adjacent to it. We do not have detailed descriptions of the houses of German patricians, but in one of the first patrician houses in Cracow, now called "Pod baranami" (Under the Rams), stairs led to the *palatium,* and here we see a chapel extended like a bay window into the square and other residential chambers. In this Cracow house, *palatium* probably meant the space on the second floor above the hall, what is called *Vorsaal* in Germany, since the term *palatium* is most often encountered in Poland as meaning the hall, and sometimes even the courtyard. In Cracow we also have a number of descriptions of houses from the end of the XV century and the beginnings of the XVI, before the Renaissance style put its mark on them. Let us look at a few of them.

On Grodzka Street, there were houses of all kinds, large and small, brick and wooden, with one or two stories. Some of them, surrounded by a wall together with all their farm buildings, formed something in the nature of a suburban cottage. We know of a tiny 1505 five-room house on this street. It belonged to two sisters, one of whom was married to a shoemaker and the other to a tailor; both sisters lived there with their husbands and children, but they had to divide the property to avoid strife. It was difficult to partition the property, since the house had one large room, one little one with a closet, a chamber and a kitchen. They arranged it in such a way that the large room belonged to both sisters, and each placed her table by a window. The kitchen also remained common property; only the little room with a closet became the exclusive property of one sister, and the chamber of the other. This house did not even have a privy.

Another house was much larger, since it had two shops at the entrance, then two chambers, one larger and one smaller, three rooms, two kitchens and a vaulted cellar divided by a grating, since it belonged to two owners. There was also a privy serving both occupants. A third house on the same street was considered large for those times, with several stories, an outbuilding and farm buildings, two courtyards, one of which ended in a stable. It belonged to two brothers who were goldsmiths, Jan and Pawel Fetter. It had 26 rooms, among them two shops, two goldsmith workshops, a huge chamber, a great parlor, a number of dark rooms on the ground floor, six on the second, with a great deal of room for expansion. Besides a privy and coal bins, it also had a bath, and vaulted wooden cellars under the house. Judging by the description, these were not comfortable apartments—there is direct reference to dark rooms.

Let us go to the market place. In the year 1488 the tenement house on the corner of Floriańska Street and Mariacki Square belonged to the family Igielek. It was a smallish, brick house with vaulted cellars, brick and wooden rooms, with a bath and an oven for baking wafers nearby, a garden in the back. Counting the kitchen, it had 10 rooms, among them a spacious room with three windows, next to it a "white room," a chamber and other rooms. And thus one of the corner houses of Cracow's main street, the later "Pod murzynem" (Under the Moor), turns out to have been a small house. Across from it on the market place, another house was built at the beginning of the XIV century, referred to as a huge tenement: *lapidea magna.* At the end of the XIV century the mint was located in this house, but unfortunately we have no description of it, just as we know nothing about another great house which was known as the grey tenement (*lapidea grisea*) from at least the XV century, in which the famous Wierzynek received his royal visitors, nor do we know about the so-called "old mint," later called the Hetman tenement, or other houses which still have the Gothic vaulted cellars from those times, or even from an earlier day. But a description has been preserved of a tenement that was famous in later times, in the following centuries called "Pod barany" (Under the Rams). In the second half of the XV century it belonged to the family of Lang, the branch that was called Karniowski, so that it was also called the Karniowski tenement. In 1486 it was a two-story structure, with a main building and outbuildings. Through a great gate from the market place one entered a spacious hall beyond which was a courtyard with a free-standing house and stables. A long approach led to it from St. Anna Street. Under the main house and outbuildings were built vaulted cellars with entrances directly to the market place, St. Anna Street or the courtyard. The ground floor was occupied mainly by shops, but also had a few residential rooms, among them a great chamber with four windows facing the street and the courtyard, further another room near the stairs with windows facing St. Anna Street and again a large room with another small one adjoining it. The stairs led upstairs to the *palatium,* with brick rooms on either side, one ending in a balcony extending to the market place in the form of a chapel, and other side rooms. As one of the largest houses in town, it accommodated four tenants.

The descriptions given still do not provide us with a precise idea of the burgher house in medieval Poland. In the XIV and XV century, there were no houses larger than two stories, and along the streets there were many one-story and even wooden ones. The situation was the same even in the rich Netherlands, where the system of single-story, one family houses prevailed; if they were of wood, they were not connected with one another. But already in the XV century, some towns in Holland forbade the building of wooden houses because of the danger of fire. New brick houses not only were adjoining, but might share a common wall. They were meant for a larger number of families, for instance three, and thus were rental properties. But this happened only in the XVI and XVII centuries, and even the largest houses at that time were not built higher than three stories, i.e., a ground floor and two others. A normal one-story house was 8 feet high (2.52 meters). Similarly in Polish towns, primarily in Cracow, Lwów and Poznań, from the XVI century on, larger, two-story houses were built. In the XVI and XVII centuries, Cracow had mostly brick houses, although still in the XVII century one could see many wooden houses in midtown. In 1621, a "new wooden house" was built in back of the "Pod Krzysztofory" house, i.e., right near the market place. Things were even worse on streets further from the market place. They were lined not only with wooden houses, but also ordinary clay cottages woven from brushwood. We read of such clay cottages in Poznań at the end of the XVIII century; it is small wonder, since conditions were similar in German towns, such as Augsburg and Wetzlar, where at the end of the XVII century there were clay cottages with thatched roofs.

Naturally, things were bound to be worse in the borderland towns of the east. At the end of the XVI century, in the capital of Lithuania itself, Wilno, could be found many pine cottages or chimneyless huts in which the occupants lived in constant smoke, *in domibus suis perpetuo fumo appletis*. This was said to have a terrible effect on the eyes, so that a certain foreigner, describing conditions in Wilno at the time, blamed the smoke for the fact that he had never encountered so many blind men as in Wilno.

There are no reports of houses in Poland during the Middle Ages with lead or copper roofs; only a few churches and synagogues were covered with lead plates in the XIII century, and from the end of the XV century with copper as well. As late as the beginning of the XVI century, however, a rich Cracow burgher, Fogelweder, a relative of the Augsburg Fuggers who had shares in a Hungarian copper mine, covered his house on the market place with copper plates, and that is why the house was called "Copper" for nearly two centuries. But this was an exception; in the Middle Ages houses were usually covered with wooden tiles. Later shingles also came into use, but throughout the whole existence of independent Poland wooden tiles were used more prevalently than shingles even in the towns. Even at the beginning of the Prussian rule, the chimneys on the roofs of Poznań houses were made of wood and only under the iron Prussian fist did they give way to brick, just as wooden tiles gave way to shingles.

In the Middle Ages, as in later times, entrances to the cellars led straight from the street; this did not add to the cleanliness of the sidewalks and of the houses themselves. In various towns, including Cracow itself, this architectural relic has been preserved to this day; in Poznań, however, the Prussians removed cellar entrances of this type, moving them inside the houses. Some houses had balconies, occasionally made of stone, but as a rule wooden, so that they did not add to the beauty of the street. A town representative made fun of a certain houseowner during a lawsuit, when the latter claimed that the balcony had adorned his house from time immemorial, since "wooden balconies on a brick wall—what kind of adornment is that!" It was not only the wooden balconies that disfigured the town houses, but also buttresses supporting walls that threatened to crumble, especially if they were irregularly added, did not add to their charm; the houses were also disfigured by stone benches driven into the ground floor or the facades. In Cracow these appendages could be seen not only on side streets, but right on the market place. They created a small-town atmosphere in the city. When buildings underwent alterations in the Poznań region, the Prussian authorities did not allow such decorations to remain.

Did the burgher houses in Poland during the Middle Ages have arcades? We doubt whether the Cracow market place was completely surrounded by them in the XIV and XV centuries, but there was no shortage of them. The building code of 1367 clearly speaks of arches (*Schwiebogen*). We also encounter houses built in the Italian manner, with recesses in the shape of cupboards, and so surely with arcades. At the end of the XIV century, we see such a cupboard house on Rzeźnicza Street, today called Mikolajska, and at the beginning of the XV century on a street crossing it, Świńska (now St. Krzyża). Such houses were called cupboards (*almaria*), and it seems that a whole complex of houses near Rzeźnicza and Swinska Streets derived their name from them: *In Almaria*. What is more, in 1422 there is clear reference to the construction of a vaulted arch on one of the houses of Swinska Street. It is even more likely that wooden houses had arcades similar to those that have been preserved to the present day in various smaller Polish towns, although these, of course, are from a later period. Lwów and Wrocław had them as well. They probably contributed to the colorful look of the town but, filled as they were with craftmen's benches and vendors' stands, they made it difficult to keep the street in a decent state of cleanliness, especially since this obligation fell to the property owners. The slightest carelessness in these arcades provided fuel for fire, which was a real scourge of those times and, coming at short intervals, often turned whole districts into piles of rubble. In 1494, a fire in Lwów destroyed the whole Jewish and Ruthenian districts, together with their suburbs, and ten years later almost the same part of town once more burned to the ground, until finally in 1527 a fire that again began in this section lay the whole city in ashes. Nearly at the same time, Cracow suffered a similar fate, when a great part of it went up in flames in 1494, and in 1528 Cracow, Kleparz and Kazimierz burned down. These fires destroyed the medieval, Gothic character of all these towns. From that time on, new houses were built, or old ones reconstructed—if the fire spared any part of them—in the style of the Italian Renaissance, with attics that were to protect the roofs from fire. It was then that the old arcades finally disappeared, since the new building codes removed them precisely because of the danger of fire. The Renaissance times created the type of house in use to the present day. However, not all cities followed the example of Cracow and Lwów. Some, rebuilding under Italian influence, introduced arcades at least on the market place, as for instance Tarnów and Sandomierz; other, newly-created towns built by Italian architects, modeled themselves in this respect on typical arcaded towns, such as Padua or Bologna—as for example Zamość, Żółkiew and others.

3

Nicolas Copernicus

Alexandre Koyré

The year 1543, the year of the publication of the *De Rev-olutionibus Orbium Caelestium* and of the death of its author, Nicolas Copernicus, marks an important date in the history of human thought.

One is tempted to consider it as that of the "end of the middle ages and the beginning of the modern times," because, much more than the conquest of Constantinople by the Turks or the discovery of America by Christopher Columbus, it marks the end of a world and the beginning of a new one.

Yet, perhaps this would still be a misvaluation: the cut made by Copernicus does not mark the end of the Middle Ages alone. It marks the end of a period which embraces both the Middle Ages and Antiquity; for it is with Copernicus, and only since then, that man no longer stands in the center of the world, that the cosmos does not revolve around him.

It is rather difficult for us, today, fully to understand, to realize and to appreciate, in their overwhelming greatness the intellectual effort, the daring and the moral courage embodied in the work of Copernicus. In order to be able to do so, we would have to forget the spiritual development of subsequent centuries; we would have to force ourselves to go back to the naive and unquestioned certitude with which common sense accepts the immediate evidence of the immobility of the earth and of the motion of the skies.

Even that would not be sufficient. To this evidence we should add the influence of a threefold teaching: scientific, philosophical, theological. A threefold tradition, a threefold authority of calculus, of reasoning, of revelation. Then, but only then, would we be able to render to ourselves an account of the boldness of the Copernican thought, which tore the Earth from its foundations and hurled it in the skies.

If it is difficult for us—or even impossible otherwise than in imagination—to realize the liberating effort of Copernicus; it is just as difficult to grasp the depth and the strangeness of the impression that the reading of his work could not fail to make on men of his time: the destruction of a world in which science, philosophy, religion were represented as centered upon man and created for him; the crumbling of the hierarchical order which, opposing the sublunar world and the skies, united them in an apparently cohesive system. . . .

The New World conception seemed too crazy to be taken seriously. Besides, the book, as a whole, was much too difficult for readers not trained in mathematics and astronomy.

As Copernicus expressed it himself: *mathemata mathematicis scribuntur.* His theory seemed to be only a new hypothesis, not more important than those of other astronomers till then. This opinion was commonly adopted for about half a century or so. The Church did not stir; Melanchthon (and Luther) alone realized at once the bearing and the meaning of the work.

Only later, much later, it became obvious that the work of Copernicus was not a matter for "mathematicians" alone. It dealt a mortal blow to the geocentrical and anthropo-centrical world. When, in the works of Giordano Bruno, it developed some of its metaphysical and religious implications, the old world reacted. A twofold reaction followed: the condemnation of Copernicus and of Galileo, the attempt to suppress the new world conception; the *Pensées* of Pascal, and endeavor to reply.

It would be of priceless value for the history and the phenomenology of human thought to be able to follow the development of Copernicus' thought. Alas, this is an impossible task. Copernicus left no intellectual autobiography; the biography by his pupil Joachim Rheticus, is lost; the few indications he

gives us in his proud and beautiful letter to Pope Paul the
Third, which constitutes the foreword to *De Revolutionibus,* are
very scant and, moreover, not very reliable. As for the *opus*
itself, he presents it to us—even in the *Commentariolus*—in a
state of perfection that is the despair of the historian.

Still, if we have to abandon the hope of writing the history of
Copernican thought, we must, at least, make an attempt at
grasping its historical meaning and truth . . . to bring it nearer
to our own thinking while avoiding its modernization. And, in
order to do so, we must try not to see in Copernicus the
forerunner of Galileo and of Kepler and not to interpret him in
the light of later developments.

This is a very important task—a task which, in my opinion,
has been rather neglected until now. As a matter of fact,
whereas we have a number of good expositions of the astronomy of Copernicus, and whereas treasures of ingenuity
and erudition were spent on the problem of his biography,
whereas innumerable efforts were spent in order to prove
Copernicus to be a Pole or a German (an interesting, but still a
subordinate problem)—the study of his physics has seldom
been seriously attempted. And yet, as Schiaparelli has already
stated with his habitual insight, the Copernican problem was
above all a problem of physics and of cosmology.

Nicolas Kopernik was born at Toruń, in Polish Prussia
(Pomorze), on February 19, 1473. His father, whose name, too,
was Nicolaus, was a burgher of Kraków; his mother, Barbara
Watzelrode, a daughter of an old patrician Toruń family.

As both of them died when Copernicus was twelve years old,
he, as well as his brother Andreas, was adopted by his uncle,
Lucas Watzelrode, his mother's brother, who later (in 1489)
became prince-bishop of Warmia. Was Copernicus a Pole or a
German? This question, or rather the importance attached to it,
appears somewhat anachronistic. Copernicus lived in a time
which, with some exceptions, was not yet poisoned by
nationalism and nationalistic passions, which still enjoyed the
blessings of a common culture and of a common scientific language. Besides, he lived in an Empire (medieval Poland was not
a national state, but an Empire) whose multinational subjects,

united by and through common allegiance to the State (Res Publica), happily ignored minority problems and rights (which, by the way they fully enjoyed), frequently intermarried and, generally speaking, got along pretty well.

If we were able to put to Copernicus himself the question, "Are you a German or a Pole?" he certainly might not have understood us, and probably would have answered that, of course, he was a *Polonus,* meaning that he was a burgher of Toruń, son of a burgher of Kraków, a good Catholic, a canon of Frauenburg in Warmia, a faithful subject of the Kingdom of Poland, and a bitter enemy of the Teutonic Order. For his scientific work, as well as for intercourse with his peers, he used the language of science and culture, i.e., Latin; but of course, when he had to deal with common people, he used their speech, Polish in Kraków and German in Frauenburg.

If we insist and try to make him understand that we intend to interpret his work and his genius by his "nation" or his "race," he probably would be embarrassed.

On the other hand there is no reason whatever to suppose that Copernicus was anything but a Pole. Besides, until the middle of the nineteenth century, nobody ever doubted it. And it is only since the growing nationalism of European and especially of German thought and historiography, that some German historians, eager to serve the aims of German imperialism, have made a claim on Copernicus. A claim just as futile as analogous claims with regard to Leonardo da Vinci, Dante, Michel Angelo and so many other giants of the past.

In 1491 we find Copernicus studying in Kraków. We need not speculate about the reasons which guided his choice. The University of Kraków enjoyed a very high reputation at that time. It was, as a matter of fact, since the downfall of Prague, the most important of the Eastern Universities, a famous center of learning and humanistic culture. Besides, Kraków was not far away from Toruń, and it is safe to assume that Copernicus still had relatives in the birthplace of his father.

Although it is obvious that he made a thorough study of astronomy there, there is no reason to doubt that he followed the habitual curriculum of the Faculty of Arts, including dialectics and philosophy. Copernicus was not a narrow specialist, an "astronomer" as Peurbach or Regiomontanus, but a man deeply imbued with all the rich and complex culture of his time, an artist, a classical scholar, a scientist, a man of action: a *humanist* in the best sense of this word.

Because of his astronomical studies, the biographers of Copernicus assume that he enjoyed, quite particularly, the teaching of Albert of Brudzewo (Brudzewski). However, Albert of Brudzewo, who indeed taught astronomy for a long time with great success and distinction (in 1482 he wrote for his pupils a commentary on the *Theorica Nova Planetarum* by Peurbach), was by no means the only professor of astronomy in the University of Kraków. On the contrary, there were as many as fourteen of them. Besides, since 1490, Albert of Brudzewo did not teach astronomy anymore, but lectured on Aristotle's *De Coelo*. He left Kraków in 1494, and the biographers of Copernicus usually admit that Copernicus abandoned it too about the same time.

In 1496 he went to Italy to study law at the University of Bologna. On January 6, 1497, we find his name inscribed on the roll of the *Natio Germanorum* of the University. This, by the way, does not imply that Copernicus was, or even considered himself, a German. "Nationes" of a medieval university have nothing to do with nations in the modern sense of the word; the German Nation (in Bologna), on the rolls of which there was quite a lot of non-German names, was the "smart" one and, as such, was usually joined by young Polish noblemen. Copernicus was not a nobleman but a commoner; yet as the nephew of a bishop he could hardly join a socially less prominent "nation."

Copernicus stayed in Bologna for about three years. He did not abandon astronomy. He seemed already to have known enough of it to be received by the famous astronomer, Domenico Maria Navarra, *non tam discipulus quam adjutor et testis observationum* (not as a pupil, but as an assistant and witness of the observations). At the same time, he studied a lot of other things: law, medicine, philosophy; he learned Greek; he read Plato . . . Once more, it becomes obvious that Copernicus was not a mere "astronomer" but one of the most universal minds of his time.

In 1500 he went to Rome (1500 was the year of the Jubilee

which attracted thousands of pilgrims to the capital of Christendom). As his pupil Rheticus informs us, he gave a course of lectures on mathematics; unfortunately it remains unknown what specifically he lectured about.

It seems that Copernicus did not crave going home. However, he was compelled to take possession of a canonry at the cathedral church of Frauenburg, to which he had been elected owing to the protection of his uncle, Lucas Watzelrode.

In 1501 he went to Poland. After his formal installation in the canonry he asked for leave, and, having obtained it, returned to Italy. This time he settled in Padova, famous for its schools of medicine and law. In 1503 he moved to Ferrara, but did not stay there and having received *Doctor utriusque iuris* (on May 31st) returned to Padova.

Copernicus seemed to be well pleased with his life in Italy. Alas, all good things—even leaves of absence—come to an end. Chapters do not like non-resident members and Copernicus, though nephew of the Bishop, had to abide by the rule. In 1506 he rejoined his diocese, never to leave it until his death.

The life that awaited Copernicus at home was not the quiet and easy life of thought and of prayer. Quite on the contrary, it was a life of action. A mediaeval bishopric, and quite particularly such a one as the bishopric of Warmia, was a political as much as an ecclesiastic institution and had to do with worldly as much as with religious affairs. For years, until the death of Lucas Watzelrode, Copernicus acted as his secretary (and his doctor), entrusted, among other things, with the economic administration of the bishopric; we owe to this activity his treaty on money. He did not have much time left for meditation, for study, for calculations . . . So it was only gradually, bit by bit, that his immortal work grew and took shape.

I said: meditation, calculus . . . , not observations. We must not think of Copernicus as spending his nights scrutinizing the skies in order to discover some new facts, some new positions of the heavenly bodies. Copernicus was not a practical astronomer. He was not Tycho Brahe. He made, of course, some observations, but they were neither numerous nor very important. The greatness of Copernicus—and I would like to stress that point—consists in his having framed and developed a new theory, not in having provided us with new facts. Indeed his theory or, better to say, his system is based entirely on data already available then, chiefly on those of Ptolemy. And, to say the truth, his system—a new interpretation of these old data— at least insofar as we are concerned with calculation of observable phenomena—is no more in accordance with them than that of Ptolemy which it endeavors to replace.

Those of us who are not very well acquainted with the history of astronomy will, probably, be slightly astonished. And yet it is a fact that, for all practical purposes, the Ptolemaic astronomy gave a most satisfactory account of the observational data. Mathematically speaking, the astronomy of Ptolemy was one of the most wonderful achievements of the human mind.

It is only from the point of view of cosmology, i.e., only when the astronomer tried to treat his circles and orbs as real objects in real space, that he encountered some difficulties; the circles and orbs pertaining to different planets sometimes intersected and embraced each other.

The central idea of his system seems to have been conceived by Copernicus rather early, perhaps even before he left Italy. In the prefatory letter of the *De Revolutionibus* Copernicus says that he kept his work secret not for nine years (as the Pythagoreans prescribed), but four times nine years, spent in the elaboration and perfection of the theory. Copernicus understood that it was of no use to formulate a new idea, or even, as it was in his case, to try to revive an old one. He was perfectly aware that if he was to succeed, he had to present a complete theory of movements, just as workable as that of Ptolemy or his medieval commentators and followers.

We do not know exactly when Copernicus completed the elaboration of the *De Revolutionibus*. Certainly not before 1530, perhaps even some years later.

It seems that sometime before completion of his system Copernicus wrote and circulated among his friends a short and schematic exposition of the new astronomy, the so-called *Commentariolus*, which remained unpublished till 1876.

From the point of view of astronomy, i.e., of the concrete arrangement of the movements of celestial bodies and orbs, this work differs somewhat from the *De Revolutionibus*. It reveals at least some of the reasons which guided and moved the thought of Copernicus.

The author begins by pointing out that the astronomy of Calippos and Eudoxos did not succeed in explaining the observable and indubitable variations of the distances between the Planets and the Earth. The system of Ptolemy, though much more successful concerning this point, failed in another respect, namely, it did not succeed in presenting the movements of the planets as composed of *uniform* circular motions; and in order to save some kind of uniformity, he was compelled to introduce into his calculations the rather dubious concept of "equant." This proceeding constitutes, from the point of view of Copernicus, a somewhat dishonest device. Consequently, astronomy had to try out something else.

Seven "axioms" or "petitions" (*axiomata vel petitiones:* it is interesting to note this Euclidean and Archimedian terminology) present the chief characteristics of the new system.

The first and foremost of these axioms or petitions states the necessity for building up a system of celestial movements "in which everything would move uniformly around its proper center, as the rule of absolute motion requires."

The second asserts that "the center of the Earth is not the center of the Universe, but only of gravity and of the lunar sphere."

The third assumes that "all the spheres revolve around the sun as their mid-point, and therefore the sun is the center of the Universe."

The fourth and fifth "axioms" contend that the common motion of the celestial phenomena is due not to the motion of the firmament but to that of the Earth.

The sixth "axiom" claims that the Sun remains still and that its apparent motion is only the projection of the motion of the Earth; the seventh argues that the retrogradation and other peculiarities of the motion of the planets are only apparent, not real motions, and that these appearances are due to the projection on the firmament of the annual motion of the Earth.

Seven small chapters describe the mechanism of the planetary movements (the Moon, the superior planets, Venus, Mercury, Earth) and give an account of the dimensions of the

epicycles and orbs. The statements are made without demonstrations and proofs of any kind, the latter being reserved to the
larger work.

Although Copernicus persistently and obstinately opposed
the publication of his *opus magnum*, he nevertheless made no
secret of his views. The *Commentariolus* seems to have been circulated fairly widely. Not only was it known to the author's
friends, but, according to Tiraboschi, it found its way even to
Rome, where the Austrian Chancellor Johann Widmanstadt
presented it to Pope Clement VII in 1533 and explained to him
the principles of the new astronomical system. In Rome neither
the Pope, nor anybody else seemed to be impressed by the new
theory. It is possible that the title of the text and the use of the
term "hypothesis" gave an impression that it was only a new,
and somewhat extreme, mathematical construction, which did
not pretend to give a description of the real world. It is also
possible that this was the interpretation which Widmanstadt
gave to the new theory. Probably the Pope and the cardinals did
not grasp its implications.

In any case, nobody raised any objections whatever.
Moreover, some three years later one of the members of the
Roman curia, the cardinal archbishop of Capua, Nicholas
Schonberg, wrote to Copernicus (November 1, 1536) a letter
suggesting the publication of his discoveries, and asked in advance for a copy (for which he offered to pay the expenses).
The Cardinal of Capua was by no means the first one who
urged Copernicus to publish his work. Quite on the contrary,
many of his friends, and above all, "his very dear Tiedeman
Giese, Bishop of Kulm" had, for a long time, insisted on publication, as a duty toward science and mankind. But Copernicus
could not make up his mind. He feared *calumniatorum morsus*
(bites of calumniators). And, at 60, he obviously valued nothing
more than tranquility.

In the year 1539 Joachim Rheticus, a young professor of the
University of Wittenberg, came to Frauenburg. He had heard
about the new theories of Copernicus. He wanted to find out
the truth about them.

Well received by Copernicus, he stayed with him for about
two years, studying the manuscript of the *De Revolutionibus* and

working with the old man whom he always called his Dominus Doctor Praeceptor.

Long before he completely mastered the new astronomy, he wrote a short outline of the Copernican doctrine. He sent the script to his master, Johannes Schöner, who had it printed.

The publication—the famous *Narratio Prima*—later was reprinted in nearly all editions of the *De Revolutionibus*, as an exposition of the Copernican astronomy, containing also some very precious biographical data.

For Rheticus the new astronomy was the revival of an old philosophical lore. According to him, it was following Plato and the Pythagoreans, the greatest mathematicians of that divine age. He pointed out that "the ancients, not to mention the Pythagoreans, were sufficiently clear about the fact (that) the planets evidently have the centers of their deferents in the sun, as the center of the Universe."

The *Narratio Prima* met with considerable success. A new edition was published in 1541 *cura et studio* of Achille Ganarus, a Basler physician. The learned world was thus in possession of the basic elements of the doctrine.

The first reactions were rather favorable. Erasmus Reinhold, professor of the University of Wittenberg, who in 1542 issued a reprint of the textbook of Peurbach, expressing in its preface the hope to see astronomy restored by Copernicus, whom he called "a new Ptolemy."

The publication of the *Narratio Prima* made further withholding of the *De Revolutionibus* senseless. At last Copernicus yielded to the urgings of his friends. The priceless manuscript was entrusted to Rheticus, who had it printed by the famous Nuremberg typographer, Johannes Petreius. The author received the first copy of his work on his deathbed on May 24, 1543.

Rheticus, appointed professor at the University of Leipzig in 1542, left the supervision of the printing to his friend Andreas Osiander, an unorthodox Lutheran follower. Osiander realized that there was some danger in the thesis advocated by the new astronomy. He tried to shield it against the ire of the theologians and the Aristotelians, and to take some precautions. As a matter of fact, the boldness of Copernicus troubled Osiander.

Obviously the new world conception was contrary to the Scriptures, and he was himself a good enough—though heretic—Christian to doubt their divine inspiration.

Osiander's prefatory letter intimated that the goal and aim of the astronomer is not to find out the real movements of the heavenly bodies (which he is unable to do), but to connect his observations by means of hypotheses enabling him to calculate the positions of the stars and the planets. Such hypotheses, that of Copernicus no more than those of others, make (or need not to make), therefore, any pretension (or claim) for being true or even verisimilar or probable. They are nothing more than calculatory devices, and the best of them is not the truest, but the simplest and the most convenient.

This very interesting and very modern looking piece of epistemology, curious and valuable from the point of view of the history of philosophy and science, had nevertheless the misfortune to be very severely judged by the friends of Copernicus.

It is probable that Joachim Rheticus saw the preface in a more favorable light. He did not assail Osiander, nor contradict him; moreover, he allowed his foreword to be reprinted in the second (Basle 1566) edition of the *De Revolutionibus,* to which his own *Narratio Prima* was added as introduction.

As to Copernicus, he took very few, if any, precautions. He inserted in this book the letter he had received from the Cardinal of Capua some years before. He dedicated his work to Pope Paul III. But in his own, very noble foreword (which Osiander did not publish), he insisted proudly and unflinchingly upon the rights of science and philosophy. *Mathemata Mathematicis scribuntur,* he proclaimed; the ignorant should better keep silent. Copernicus also explained why he tried to elaborate a new theory of planetary movements. It was the disagreement among the mathematicians, the variance that prevailed among them, the multiplicity of the astronomical systems (Copernicus quoted the systems of homocentric spheres, of epicycles, of eccentrics), as well as the failures of all of them to represent exactly the apparent movements of celestial bodies. That made him think that the "mathematicians" had either neglected some essential principle or, on the contrary, had introduced some false assumption into their constructions.

Among the philosophers dealing with this question some believed in the movement of the Earth. This gave Copernicus heart to try out such a hypothesis himself, and to see if it did not furnish a better explanation of the celestial phenomena. This was precisely the case; moreover, one obtained in this way a perfectly well ordered image of the universe.

M. Dreyer, the author of one of the best modern histories of astronomy, remarked in this connection that Copernicus first noticed how great was the difference of opinions among learned men as to the planetary motions. Next, he noticed that some had attributed some motion to the Earth, so he considered whether any assumption of that kind would help matters. We might have guessed as much even if he had not told us.

The account of Copernicus is somewhat reserved and reticent. And yet, even if he does not reveal the full history of his ideas, he gives us, nevertheless, some precious, though scanty indication about their incentives and motives.

He speaks very clearly of his objections to all other systems of ancient and medieval astronomy: first of all, they violated the principle of the uniformity of the circular motion of the heavenly bodies, which in Copernicus' opinion meant that they were physically impossible. They provided a disconnected and irrational picture of the Universe.

Copernicus objects to the astronomy of his time because of its great complexity. It is better to admit the movement of the Earth, says he (though it may appear absurd), than to let one's mind be distorted and torn asunder by the nearly infinite multitude of circles and orbs of the geocentric astronomy. As a matter of fact, when we look at the schematic picture of his system of the universe, we are taken in by its apparent simplicity and beauty. Yet this impression is not quite correct. The number of circles in the astronomy of Ptolemy was not as large as he says. And they were by no means absent in that of Copernicus. There were 42 cycles in the system of Ptolemy. And there are 34 in the Copernican; eight cycles is all we gain. Those who thought that the gain was not big enough for the price involved cannot be blamed.

Strange as it seems, Copernicus does not particularly insist in the *De Revolutionibus* on the real gain of his system: on its physical systematization and simplification, on the fact that a great number of particular movements of the celestial bodies are, from now on, explained as the apparent result of one and only one real movement, namely the movement of the Earth. Nor does he insist on the fact that the role of the Sun or of the solar period in all of the planetary motions is from now on explained in a perfectly easy and natural way.

If Copernicus fails to do so, his pupil does it for him. Rheticus not only criticizes the Ptolemaic system for its endless invention of spheres, but opposes to it: "the remarkable symmetry and interconnection of the motions and spheres, as maintained by the assumption of the foregoing hypotheses, are not unworthy of God's workmanship and not unsuited to these divine bodies." Rheticus does not stop with that. He sees a deep meaning and a confirmation of the Copernican astronomy not only (as Copernicus himself) in the fact that the speed—or the slowness—of the planetary movements corresponds to their distance from the Sun, but also in the fact that this astronomy reduces their number from seven to six: There are, in the Copernican world, no more than "six moving spheres which revolve about the sun, the center of the universe." And Rheticus adds, "Who could have chosen a more suitable and more appropriate number than six? By what number could anyone more easily have persuaded mankind that the whole Universe was divided into spheres by God, the Author and Creator of the World? For the number six is beyond all others in the sacred prophecies of God and by the Pythagoreans and other philosophers. What is more agreeable to God's handiwork than that his first and most perfect work should be summed up in the first and most perfect number?"

Another objection of Copernicus to the Ptolemaic astronomy—a philosophical one—appears at first glance to be very strong. Copernicus says—and, of course, he is quite right—that it is absurd to want to move the *locus* and not the *locatum*, and that, therefore, the starry sky which, according to Aristotle, is the *locus* of the Universe, must be considered as unmoved.

This seems to us a perfectly well reasoned out argument. Indeed, we feel that it is contrary to reason (and even, perhaps, to common sense) to let the whole immense (or, for us, infinite)

Universe revolve around a tiny speck of dust. We feel convinced. But the Aristotelian (or Ptolemaic) is not. His Universe, though pretty large, is by no means immense (and he objects to its allegedly motiveless extension by Copernicus); he feels that there is a fundamental, qualitative opposition between the heavy, inert Earth and the imponderable heavenly spheres: to move the first, an external, material motor of a tremendous power would be needed; the motion of the latter, on the contrary, is a sequel of their perfection, of their nature itself. Therefore, concludes the Ptolemaic from the same premises as Copernicus, the mobile sphere is *not* the *locus* of the Universe, so we must admit above it another one, which is the true, immobile sphere (the eighth, or ninth, or tenth . . .)

The proofs that Copernicus advances for his system are curious. In fact, they do not *prove* anything at all. From the point of view of his adversaries they are worthless. His refutation of the physical objections of the Ptolemaics against the motion of the Earth are, too, rather feeble. Withal, they are of a tremendous historical importance.

Copernicus shows us that, from the optical point of view, it is impossible to decide whether it is the observer or the observed who are in motion. Quite right, would the Ptolemaic answer; the well-known relativity of motion implies doubtlessly that the motion of the Earth is optically *possible*. But it implies at the same time—always from the optical point of view—that it does not present any advantage as compared with immobility.

To the physical objection that the rotation of the Earth would engender a tremendous centrifugal power which would blow it to pieces, Copernicus replies that the same objection could be raised against the motion of the skies, the more so as the velocity of their motion is infinitely greater than that of the Earth.

As a matter of fact, from the point of view of the Ptolemaic, Copernicus is wrong, because the motion of the heavenly spheres, considered as imponderables, is of a quite different nature from that of the ponderable Earth, and could not give birth to a centrifugal force. Besides, the revolution of the skies, being a natural motion, cannot be the cause of an effect which would endanger their conservation and being.

We must not smile at these arguments. From the point of

view of the Aristotelian physics they are perfectly valid. Besides, Copernicus himself makes use of them in order to show that, if the Earth revolved around its axis, it would be a *natural* motion, wherefore none of the effects deduced (hypothetically) by Ptolemy, *on the assumption that this motion would be a violent one* and *contra naturam,* would take place.

We see that Copernicus—as everybody until Galileo and Descartes—admits the distinction between *natural* and *violent* motions; he only asserts that the same laws apply to the Heavens and to the Earth and, by doing this, he lays the ground for that deep-reaching transformation of human thought to which History has given the name of *Copernican Revolution.*

But this we shall see more clearly by glancing at the Copernican dynamics.

The dynamics of Copernicus is by no means "modern." Nevertheless, an abyss separates it from that of his contemporaries, because, spontaneously and unhesitatingly, he applies the geometrical point of view to the Universe. Even his esthetics is a geometrical one—the esthetics of geometry, or more exactly, of geometrical optics. His physics, too—though he never says so *expressis verbis,* and perhaps does not even recognize it clearly and distinctly—is a geometrical physics.

Not quite, of course. Copernicus still uses a "physics," that is a theory of nature, or better to say, a theory of natures; and yet the geometrization of his thought is deep and strong enough to transform completely the fundamental Aristotelian notion of *form* itself. Thus, when and where medieval and classical physics talked about *form,* they usually meant: substantial forms; Copernicus, on the contrary, has *geometrical form* in mind.

The implications, as may be seen readily, are numerous and far-reaching. For instance, whereas for ancient physics it was the specific nature of a definite substantial form (and, of course, of the corresponding matter) which determined the kind of *natural* movement pertaining to a body (rectilinear for the sublunar, circular for the heavenly bodies), it is its geometrical form which plays that role for Copernicus. If the celestial bodies move around themselves, it is not because they have a specific nature, it is simply because they are spherical.

Copernicus seems to believe that the spherical shape—geometrically the most perfect form that all natural bodies seek for this reason—naturally engenders the most perfect, the most *natural* movement, i.e., the circular one. Thus (a) the same reasoning enables and even obliges us to ascribe to the Earth the same circular motion with which the planets are endowed (and this is the reason why Copernicus dwells at such length and with such a profusion of arguments upon the sphericity of the Earth which nobody in his time doubted, and which—if it were not so tremendously important—could therefore be treated as a matter of common knowledge); (b) the same laws of motion which apply to the planets, are valid also for the Earth; (c) partaking of the same circular form, and following the same laws of motion, the Earth no longer stands in opposition to the moving heavenly bodies as a world apart—an Underworld—but forms *with them* a single and unique Universe.

The geometrization of the concept of form placed the Earth among the stars, and, so to say, lifted it into the skies.

We understand now why Copernicus attributes such an importance to the rule or principle of the *uniform circular motion* and considers it as the basis of his whole celestial mechanics.

For him it was the only means to put the *machina mundi* into motion. In the dynamics of Copernicus . . . the (circular) movement is caused by (or due to) the (spherical) form of the bodies. The bodies turn around because they are round, without an external (or even internal) motor. Put a round body (a sphere) into space, and it will turn around. Place an orb into it: it, too, will revolve around itself, without having any need either of a motor to keep up its movement, or of a *physical center* which would support it. And this is the dynamical reason why, having expelled the Earth from the center of the movements of the World, Copernicus can leave it empty.

Although Copernicus places the Sun in the center of the Universe, he does not place it in the center of the celestial movements. The sun does not play any role in the celestial mechanics of Copernicus. Its role is quite different. It is purely optical. It lights, or gives light, to the Universe—and that is all.

Yet I am quite wrong in saying: that is all. For the function performed by the sun, the function of illuminating and lighting the Universe, is, for Copernicus, of extreme and supreme importance. It is this function which explains and secures the remarkable central place that it holds in the World. It is in order to give light to the Universe that the sun, this *lampada pulcherrima* (the most beautiful lamp), is placed in its center—a position that is, obviously, the most fitting for this end. And this is the reason, the true reason, which inspired the thought and the soul of Copernicus. It is not a purely scientific reason. It is much more than that.

Old traditions, the tradition of the metaphysics of light (metaphysics which during the entire Middle Ages bears and accompanies the study of the geometrical optics), Platonic and Neoplatonic or Pythagorean reminiscences and revivals (the visible sun representing the invisible one, the sun being the master and king of the visible world and thus representing God) can alone—at least in my opinion—explain the emotion with which Copernicus speaks about the Sun. He adores it, and almost deifies it.

People who, like Digby, Bruno, and others, have linked the Copernican astronomy with a kind of heliolatry, who at the same time have felt themselves raised into the skies, were by no means infidel to the inspiration of the great Polish thinker.

Copernicus is not a Copernican. He is not a "modern." His Universe is not the infinite space of the classical physics. It has limits, just as that of Aristotle. It is larger, of course, much larger, so large as to be immeasurable (*immensum*), and yet finite, contained in, and limited by, the sphere of the fixed stars. The sun is in its center. And around the sun rise the orbs (which bear and carry the planets), orbs just as real as the crystalline spheres of the medieval cosmology. The orbs revolve because of their form and carry with them the wandering planets, which are set in them as jewels are set in their mount . . .

Such was the splendid order, the luminous astro-geometry, the magnificent cosmo-optics, which replaced the astro-biology of the Ancients.

4

The Polish Reformation in the Sixteenth Century

Aleksander Brückner

At a time when simony was thriving in Poland, when bishops played politics and enriched their relatives, and the clergy argued with laymen over tithes while dispensing indulgences and various other privileges according to fixed fees, a religious movement exploded in Germany that was to disrupt the religious homogeneity of Europe and give new direction to religious life and thought. At first Poland was indifferent to that movement. The education of the population was at such a low level that the new slogans elicited little response. The religious sense of the better educated classes was so weak that the slogans were ignored. Yet the miracle happened: in an era of religious apathy, religious problems suddenly thrust aside any other questions. An age-long lethargy was now traded for passionate disputes. Man's fearful conscience, having lost faith in its former leaders, sensed its own responsibilities. Problems which had concerned only theologians suddenly became the interest of everybody. In fact, the Polish people could not ignore the movement, for they were situated close to its origins in Central Europe. Eventually the gentry, if no one else, became so inflamed with religious zeal, that they even abandoned the faith of their forefathers.

The clergy had become quite worldly, however, and could

not produce anyone who could espouse the cause of the Reformation in Poland. John Łaski, alone, might have; he had become famous for his wisdom, dignity, and accomplishments. However, he had exhausted his energies outside Poland in Friesland and London and returned physically spent to die prematurely at a time that was particularly decisive for the future success of the movement. Not one of the bishops except Kiev's Pac and Samogitia's Pietkiewicz—both men of uncertain quality—came out openly for the movement. Neither did those on whom the dissenters had counted: Leonard and Uchański. From among the canons (besides Łaski) only Lutomirski dropped away from the Church.

The more prosperous burghers in the larger cities did adopt the "German" faith, but they were not the class which set the tone of Polish life. The gentry were the people who brought about the change in the religious life of Poland. At first, however, they were rather reticent and did not take part in the movement. But gradually the gentry in the north began to accept the Reformation and spread it from Albrecht's Prussia, from Gdańsk and Toruń. This first phase, the Lutheran-German-Urban phase of dissent, was influenced especially by association with Frankfurt and Wrocław, where religious faith was changing very rapidly since 1521.

A further stimulus was provided by the university professors. They influenced the young sons of the gentry to hurry to Melanchthon and Luther rather than taking the beaten path to Italy; later the students were attracted to Königsberg by the renown of the poet Sabin.

King Sigismund the Old took some energetic action to forestall the spread of the Reformation in Gdańsk, but later he limited himself to writing edicts forbidding the import of Luther's works and recalling the young people home from Wittenberg. Church authorities tried to discourage the movement, but they did so only in those rare instances when they were provoked by such obvious indiscretions as Hogendorfer's public appearances at the Lubrański School or the behavior of the Dominican monk Andrew Samuel, who was forced to leave Poznań. During the fourth decade of the century, or even as late as the death of the old king (1548), the rumbling of the approaching storm was generally ignored.

Then, the young people returning home from Wittenberg gradually, quietly started to spread the new faith and gain new adherents, albeit warm rather than fervent ones. They were joined by Nicholas Rej (1505–1569), one of the most prominent writers of his day, and other members of the gentry. The burghers and the lower clergy began to read the many books which were being imported in spite of Church censorship. The country began to teem with religious faddisms.

Next, the people began to demand that the national language be used for the Mass to replace the unintelligible Latin; they demanded the abolition of celibacy to put an end to the immoral conduct of the clergy; they wanted the Holy Sacrament to be received in both species as practiced by the priests and by the ancient Church. All this was made available to the Polish people: the Old-Church Slavonic language of the Eastern Orthodox Church, Orthodox clergy with wives, and the sacrament in the form of wine and leavened bread. The clergy hoped that the disputes would end with these concessions. And if Rome did not concede, they hoped that a national council of some kind would settle the whole matter, and this would finally lead to the desired unity. (The more prominent Catholics, Hosius for example, did not oppose the changes, but required that the Catholic Church and not just the "national" Polish Church should give consent to these changes.) By that time, matters had progressed much beyond the matter of the people's demanding that the Church make the changes they had requested.

Poland, having slept through the first three decades of the Reformation, was now confronted with its total split. What Luther began was now being continued by Zwingli and Calvin, and intoxicated Polish heads grasped at the new religious fads. This time the women did not lag behind. They got hold of popular brochures—of Seclucian in Königsberg, his satires, dialogues and songs; they hurried from manor to manor, spreading the printed propaganda by word of mouth. Meetings roiled with arguments about religion, arguments so passionate that the original concerns no longer sufficed; everyone wanted so much to reserve for himself the freedom to decide about his own conscience and salvation that he tried to impose on others what he himself had just achieved. But, for the moment, the Catholics remained silent.

What were the real reasons for the growth of the Reformation movement? The strong antagonism against the clergy, a heritage from the Middle Ages, had grown considerably. Already in the first decades of the century the gentry, particularly from Great Poland, that is, from Wielkopolska, the western part of Poland, became indignant about the clergy's privileges, about the fact that the wealthiest Cistercian abbeys (Bledzew, Ląd, Obra, Węgrowiec, Koronowo, Paradyż) as well as the Miechów rector did not like to admit Poles; that the clergy did not pay taxes; that the ecclesiastical courts—considerably more efficient than the civil courts—made judgements in accordance with foreign law, expanding their activity and disturbing the gentry: people were indignant because the clergy was unyielding—especially the Bishop-Chancellor Tomicki who was to have said that he would rather see Poland perish than allow Church property to be jeopardized.

The clergy, quite satisfied with the king's edicts of 1520 and 1523 (forbidding the sale and distribution of Lutheran books) and with the bloody suppression of the Gdańsk revolt, extorted an edict in 1535 which recalled Poles from Wittenberg. Still, the Reformation was able to penetrate quietly into Poznań and Cracow, and after 1540 there was increasing and troubling evidence of this. The clergy, sure of the Old King and the "keystone" faith of the people, adhered to its old pattern. "I believe like the Universal Church."—"And how does the Universal Church believe?"—"As I do"—that was the way a popular philosopher would dispose of the question. But this was only the calm before the storm.

Gradually, the proponents of the Reformation began to reach more and more of the people. They attracted first the most educated, the magnates such as the Ostrorógs and Górkas in Great Poland and the Radziwills and Kiezgajlos in Lithuania, then their courtiers, more of the wealthier gentry, and then the poorer gentry. Young people continued to return from German schools with books on the new faith and the "heretical" teachings, which rejected all the past. They ridiculed the tonsure, images and saints, the Mass and purgatory as human inventions, inspired to gain profit for the church. As a result, many Catholics began to ask for reform. An ecumenical council was demanded, in union with the dissenters if possible, for the purpose of reconciliation. People deluded themselves with the hope that Rome would bow to inevitable concessions, and even ignored the danger that any concessions might jeopardize the national-state order.

Meanwhile the gentry, men like Jan Tarnowski, withdrew from Lutheranism in the face of the extreme demands of the people, particularly the "servants of the Divine Word," and turned towards the more radical religion of Calvinism. The ministers moved further still, some joining the Anabaptists, others the Tritheists, the Ditheists, or ultimately the Antitrinitarians.

THE EXPANSION OF THE REFORMATION

The apostasy of the gentry was general. When, according to ancient custom, the 1564 diet at Parczew opened with a Mass to the Holy Spirit, barely two temporal lords attended it with their King; in the Chamber of Deputies, however, there were plenty of the believers of the new faith, while still others remained at home.

> Now the king went to church, but the majority of the senate and court . . . ran off to their forests or meeting-houses. . . .

Thus wrote Rotundus, the town mayor of Wilno in 1564. In his youth he had admired the Lithuanian piety which was now destroyed by the heresy from Poland, and he asked in indignation: From what gallows did these scoundrels drop?

The factors which contributed to the sudden growth of the Reformation included not only the old controversies with the clergy, but also the radical thought disseminated by German schools; the oral propaganda of youths studying at German universities, and the printed propaganda of Prussian books. It was stirred by an eagerness for faddism, irresistible even to the ladies and their daughters sitting at the communion table of the meeting house, and finally by fashion and blind imitation.

Meanwhile, however, Luther died and no one took his place, least of all Melanchthon, against whom orthodox Lutheran opposition was increasing. As a result, the Lutherans became involved in dogmatic controversies over trifles, which soon undermined their unity. With this, Calvin looked even more impressive; he zealously broadened his activity and propaganda and, more and more, became the obvious leader of the whole movement. He drew the attention of many Poles, who valued his more extreme and rational teaching. They established contact with him, gave themselves completely to his influence, undeterred even by the Lutherans of Albrecht and Königsberg (who had strong disputes with him).

What did the Reformation contribute? In its initial phase the most striking effect was the moralization of the individual. It may not have permeated the whole man, nor rid him completely of the old Adam. However, in comparison with his previous carefree and thoughtless trend, it displayed a greater dignity, concentration, renunciation of every wickedness and a zealous concern with matters of faith (which hitherto had been only superficial). Humble contemplation and examination of conscience distinguished the person of the new faith. The empty social life and the pursuit of pleasures or affluence made way for a more Christian way of life. It led some individuals to a complete renunciation of the world, to freeing their peasants from serfdom, to ridding themselves of their lands gained by blood, to the renunciation of the state and its courts of law and armies, in exchange for a modest, active, and charitable life imitating the Apostles.

Others, however, seized upon the upheaval of the Reformation to plunder the Catholic churches, robbing the altars, ousting the monks and parish priests, and appropriating the tithes and the parish lands. Some even attacked churches during services, insulted the priests, and desecrated the Host. In a few instances they also took vengeance on Catholics for injustices they had experienced from the Church in the past.

But many of the converts to Lutheranism or Calvinism did not change their habits, even if they had changed their faith.

They often continued to pursue an unevangelical style of life, of luxury and pleasure; they neglected the congregation, the minister, and the school. The Evangelical gentry exploited the peasants just as the Catholic did. The exhortations of the evangelical ministers were no more effective than the sermons of Skarga (1536–1612), a prominent Jesuit preacher and writer whose *Lives of the Saints* were greatly valued. And yet, although the initial zeal cooled off, life took on a new, deeper tone; it became more earnest and oriented toward heaven and truth. The intellectual culture eventually attained considerable depth by the very fact that the new faith required a knowledge of the Scriptures, for which there had been such fierce struggles, an understanding about what one believed and why; the Protestants could not remain illiterate.

The intellectual life of Poland was most affected by this trend. The members of each of the new denominations avoided the Catholic school. They set about to provide for the training of their youth in their own spirit, and for the preparation of their own ministers. The followers of the Reformation developed their polemical, apologetic, doctrinal literature in the Polish language, and the gains beneficially affected the literature and the intellectual life of the nation, not simply the religious life. The first *Book of Gospels* in Polish was published and the task of translating the entire *Bible* was undertaken. Larger and smaller catechisms appeared in print, with the alphabet, with songs and hymns and prayers. The Protestants translated or compiled instructive texts to teach the young the meaning of penance, of the baptism (which the Anabaptists refuted), the divinity of Christ (which the nonbelievers opposed), governmental authority (against the Arians). The Reformers struggled against Catholic doctrine, defending their own creed. Krowicki, Giłowski, Czechowicz, Budny, Wiśniowski, Farnowski, and Niemojewskis (both James the Calvinist and John the Arian) published a great variety of works of popular literature, poetry, comedies, tragedies, satire, and allegories, more or less effective, all aimed at harassing the Catholics and ridiculing them. They also gained a respectful place for the Polish books and enhanced the prestige of the native tongue, compelling their Catholic adversaries to use the vernacular.

The people also imported foreign books. The influence of foreign literature was attested by Andrew Modrzewski in a letter to his old classmate, Paul Głogowski:

Books were being brought here from Germany [Lutheran] and were even being sold publicly at the Cracow Academy itself. They were read with approval and praise by the many who love everything that is new. Neither did our theologians condemn them. Then suddenly, the pope (Leon X, 1520) forbade their reading under penalty of excommunication. Overcome by fear, our masters not only stopped reading the banned books, but even burned them, being afraid to keep them.

Bookstores were ordered to be searched, confiscations were made, bans issued. Open sales of heretical books were forbidden, but the Poles continued to smuggle books from Frankfurt, and particularly from Königsberg after the Seclutian printing press of Lutheran texts in Polish was established there.

The Reformation, however, had a less desirable effect on political life. The initial unity which had favorably distinguished Poland from the East and the schismatic church was dissolved. The intellectuals began to fight for their own interests against those of the state. The existence of a Catholic king forced the Protestant gentry to safeguard their liberties and to curtail the powers of the monarch. However, they did not propose their own candidate for the throne, nor did they consider foreign protection, as they would do in the seventeenth and eighteenth centuries.

THE EVANGELICAL CONGREGATIONS

Only an approximate number of Protestant congregations existing in the sixteenth century can be defined. There were about two hundred and fifty in Little Poland, of which sixty-nine survived to the middle of the seventeenth century, and thirteen to the reign of King Stanislaus Augustus. There were twenty so-called Arian congregations, composed of

Antitrinitarians, Polish Brethren, Socinians, and Unitarians. In Great Poland there were about one hundred twenty Polish congregations. Of these, thirty-two were Lutheran and four Arian. Twenty-one Calvinist and seven Lutheran congregations survived to 1650. By 1764 only eight Calvinist and one Lutheran churches remained. In Lithuania (including Podlasie) there were about two hundred eight congregations, including eight Lutheran and seven Arian congregations. About one hundred forty were still in existence in 1650, but only forty in 1764. In total, there were about five hundred seventy non-Catholic congregations of Poles, of which about two hundred forty were still active in 1650 and about sixty in 1764.

In contrast, three thousand sixty-four Catholic parishes remained in Little and Great Poland, about five hundred in ethnic Lithuania. These congregations of the gentry (the peasants remained invariably faithful to Catholicism) were distributed quite unevenly; the greatest concentration of converts lived in the Chełm region, and in the Lublin palatinate. A few existed in the palatinates of Inowrocław and Bełz and only a very few in those of Cracow and Poznań.

About a sixth of the gentry abandoned Rome, but since 1567 some began to defect from the new faith. Thus, in 1569 there were fifty-eight lay Protestant senators, seventy Catholics, and two Eastern Schismatics. The number of Evangelicals dropped to between twenty-five and twenty-seven during the eighties, and in the nineties it fluctuated between sixteen and fourteen. During the seventeenth century the number first dropped to ten, then from 1614 it fluctuated between three and eight, and in 1659 the last of the Evangelical dignitaries died. Politically, therefore, the Catholics were not seriously threatened, even though many most influential magnates did leave the Catholic Church. Ultimately, the Catholics were saved, because the dissidents disagreed among themselves.

The number of Protestant congregations grew even when some of the gentry began to return to Catholicism, and the need for some kind of Protestant organization became apparent. Ultimately, the Calvinists divided Poland into provinces and each of the provinces into districts; thus, the province of Little Poland, for example, was divided into five provinces.

Each province was headed by a superintendent while each district was supervised by three or more elders chosen from among the ministers or pastors, and the laymen, either gentry or burghers. The elders called the regional synods and the superintendents called the general synod to oversee morality, schools, hospitals, education and publications, and to bar insubordinate members from the Lord's Supper or even from the congregation.

The Protestant organization in Poland acquired a distinctive "gentry" character, whereas the clergy took on the characteristics of the burgher class; there were no members of the gentry among them. At first the gentry excluded the clergy from the administration, limiting their duties to church services. This rule, however, was impossible to maintain, and the gentry eventually had to admit the ministers to the synods. Nevertheless, the gentry continued to hold sway—electing their own ministers for their congregations. (Even the Lutherans were unable to introduce their usual episcopal organization, but had to content themselves with a clerical superintendent, having very limited influence.) The Calvinists rested all the authority with the synod, administered by the gentry (as long as this interested them), being certain that the ministers would never achieve anything hostile to the gentry. The ministers had a free hand only in religious matters.

The power of the clergy was further undermined by the general dissension of all people against any organized religion. A Catholic complained that laymen

> began to preach themselves, and to train their wives,
> so everyone preaches, but nobody listens.

Later an Evangelical wrote:

> . . . your banquets
> Seem to delight in having religious discussion
>   for dessert.
> Those who know nothing want to be the learned
>   doctors, and their wisdom increases when
>   they are drunk to the gills.

"True study" was provided through books, in Poland more than anywhere else, because there were only a few preachers, nor did one ever hear of some mass dissension. Quietly and slowly individuals turned from the Church to the congregation, still others from Luther to Calvin, and their decisions were directed by books. Therefore the Reformation was very much indebted to printing, and especially to books printed in Königsberg and Magdeburg, whether original or adapted from foreign models. Rej's *Merchant* (1549), published in Königsberg by Seclucian (who did not know the name of the author), was eloquent and sincere; it contained many effective barbs, expounding the new teachings and condemning the old creed. The lampoons in verse and prose, the Prussian faddisms poured off the presses so fast that none ever had a reprint and most of them were lost.

The Catholics, of course, tried to ward off these attacks. The priests responded with similar publications, defending tradition, and tried to point out the fickleness and instability of the faddists. Their writings were less numerous and less aggressive, with the exception of Kromer who, it is true, used scholarship (and not witticisms) in the *Monk* to develop an eloquent defense of Catholicism.

In the course of this battle the Polish writers and translators who had published the Psalter, legends, prayers and hymns, even the Apocrypha, finally translated the Gospels. The dissidents came out with their translation, and they were not above making various comments and additions of their own. The Catholics then produced their own version of the Gospels, and soon after surpassed the Protestants by publishing the complete Bible. But this was no real triumph, since they had reproduced an old medieval translation, modernizing the language, yet frequently failing to correct some glaring errors. The Calvinists, in turn, surpassed the Catholics with scholarship and expression and wrote the Brześć Bible, published at the expense of the Radziwills. It was based on the study of the Bible, and resulted from the long and persevering collaborative effort of Polish ministers. In addition, a new version of the Bible was published by Simon Budny who knew the Eastern Orthodox texts and frequently relied on them for the sake of his personal Arian beliefs.

INTERNAL CONFLICTS

Dissension became obvious in Poland, when some of the gentry returned to the Catholic Church. Of course, many also turned from Lutheranism to Calvinism. Laymen took a greater voice in church administration. The Calvinists also split with the Lutherans over the doctrine, especially concerning the sacrament of the altar and predestination; the Calvinists wished to take a more rational approach to these matters. (Lutheranism survived, for the most part, amongst the burghers and a few noblemen in Great Poland.) To confuse the Protestant revolution even more, a third denomination appeared in Great Poland: the Bohemian Brethren. Fleeing the Hapsburg persecution in Bohemia and Moravia, they found the warmest of welcomes among the Górkas, the Ostrorógs, the Leszczyńskis, the Krotoskis; they finally settled around Leszno. They were modest, industrious, simple in their life and teachings, and they expressed an ethical rather than a dogmatic faith. Their strong organization impressed the Calvinist burghers (who, as we have seen, were having trouble maintaining their own organization with the gentry) and they readily turned to the Bohemians to buttress their own position. This only made matters worse for the Calvinist movement, however, because the gentry formed an aversion to the Brethren's quiet, drab lifestyle, the manual labor of their ministers, their avoidance of literary polemic, the very simplicity of these handicraftsmen. Another rift developed among the gentry when John Łaski, who had headed the movement, died. This led to the total destruction of the congregation; the process was hastened by the writings of Servetus and the teachings of the Italians—the physician Blandrata, Ochino, Socinus the Elder, and others. These physicians and jurists first spoke only cautiously against the fundamental dogmas concerning the Holy Trinity and the deity of Christ. They soon found zealous followers, not among the gentry who shied away from the dogmas themselves and any scholasticism, but among the ministers. These people appealed to a pure faith, unsullied by human inventions about apostolic life, and battled with the "tritheists" of all camps. Then they began to advocate a "Christlike" way of life, free of all injustice and wrongdoing, and a rejection of the sinful world with its wars, courts of law, oppression of peasants, affluence and license; mature persons ought to renounce the worldly vanities at the time of their "immersion."

The Protestants in Poland had started out by following Lutheranism; then many turned to Calvinism, and then again they were further divided by the controversy over Anti-trinitarianism. But even this was not to be the end of the splits, either in Poland or elsewhere.

The "minor" congregations broke up into even more extreme sects: Communism, Judaism, and Transylvanian Unitarianism (which recognized God alone, denying the deity of Christ). The final destruction was prevented by Socinus the Younger who subdued the more extreme views. Despite the protests of some, he persuaded most of the Protestants to adopt a creed at the congregational meeting in Raków, which was incorporated in the Racovian Catechism and became famous throughout the world.

Ultimately the Reformation was almost completely undone when the sons of the reformers began to return to Catholicism. They admired the Catholic Church, which seemed to be stable and free of doubt. The more critical people questioned their fathers' faith and the weaker-minded merely succumbed to Catholicism, yielding to the influence of ardent Catholics. It was mostly the burgher children (scoffingly nicknamed the "Augsburg blemish") and the ministers of the congregations and their offspring who persisted in their creed.

LATER ACHIEVEMENTS OF THE DISSENTERS

Polish dissenters attempted to overcome the complete failure of the Reformation in their country by convening at the Union of Sandomierz in 1570 (at a time when religious differences were steadily increasing abroad). But the agreement did not amount to much. Not a uniform worship (liturgy), nor a uniform organization (each denomination retained its own), nor even a common faith was reached (each denomination recognized its own as the only true one). No consent was even reached to receive sacraments from the other denominations.

And a split arose when the members discussed the doctrine of the Lord's Supper: was it a symbol (as for the Calvinists), or was it a real event (as the Lutherans held)? The definition that the dissenters agreed upon brought the denominations together in a way, but because of the somewhat ambiguous wording, they did not satisfy the Lutherans, who even rejected Melanchthon's attempts to mediate.

The agreement amounted to mutual recognition that each denomination was Christian and in no way contradicted the original teachings. It was also guaranteed that the three denominations would not condemn each other and that they would plan general synods to discuss matters of mutual concern, such as the defense against Catholics, maintenance of schools and hospitals, and basic morality.

The last great success of the dissidents, gained almost by a *coup d'état,* was the article on freedom of conscience, that they drew up at the Warsaw Confederation in 1573. The future king was to swear:

To preserve the common peace between separated and differing people in faith and worship . . . and because in our Commonwealth there is a significant *dissidium in causa religionis christianae,* [discord in the matter of Christian religion] to prevent the rise of any destructive *seditio* [mutiny] among the people on this basis, which we have clearly seen to happen in other kingdoms, we mutually pledge this to ourselves . . . that those of us who are *dissidentes de religione,* shall keep peace among ourselves, refrain from bloodshed over differences of faith or changes of churches, nor punish by imprisonment, confiscation, nor abet in any manner and authority or office in procedures toward this end, etc.

This confederation does not abrogate the authority of any lord over his subjects, be he lord temporal or lord spiritual, nor hampers the obedience of subjects to their lords. Indeed, should such *licentia* occur *sub pretextu religionis,* as always, it is still permissible for every lord to punish a disobedient subject according to his understanding.

The dissident gentry had demanded this resolution during the Warsaw Diet of 1570, and almost at the point of adjournment they succeeded in passing it. For the sake of peace, one bishop signed it (Krasiński of Cracow), as well as twenty-five senators and seventy-two members of the gentry. All other bishops protested immediately, as did many laymen, especially the gentry of Masovia.

This kind of "peace" among separate faiths was nothing new. It was preceded by German and French agreements, which at first were limited to two denominations—Catholic and Lutheran or Calvinist—and confined in time. The Polish text went further. It gave freedom to every denomination, and this was why it evoked the objection of many a dissenter, who shuddered at the thought that the Anabaptists, the Antitrinitarians, even the Adamites and the Turks also were guaranteed freedom of worship. However, this law actually applied only to the gentry. It guaranteed them freedom of conscience, while the peasant remained bound to obey his master in spiritual as well as secular matters. The Warsaw Confederation remained in force, although it was constantly attacked and condemned by the clergy, and even anathematized by the Piotrków synod in 1577.

The decrees of the Warsaw Diet also separated the gentry further from the burghers. The gentry were repudiated now because their religious differences with the burghers became linked to their opposition to the state reform advocated by the burghers. The burghers were ready to make political compromises, but they demanded religious concessions in return. The people saw Poland as predestined to become the land of religious tolerance and could not agree to turning the Dissenters over to the Catholics, as the gentry would have wished.

The gradual division that developed between the gentry and the people of Poland and the many splits that took place within the Reformation led to disastrous effects. The movement enjoyed a triumph only for a decade, between 1550 and 1560. It unfortunately attracted many promising talents from possibly fruitful work towards sterile theological pursuit. Thus, James Gorski, a philologist, and Erazm Glicner, an educator, concentrated on theology and defended the faith instead of spreading knowledge. Few remained on they sidelines, fearing relaxation of state and social bonds; most of all, they feared a regression to the "barbarism of the Middle Ages." But the Reformation did enrich the literature and language of Poland by far. Many who otherwise would have been content to tend their lands began to write in defense of their faith. For the first time, the Reformation forced writers to stretch a language that had been suitable enough for the kitchen (as Powodowski had put it) to express the word of God, to proclaim brotherly love, repentance, humility, and study of the plight of the peasant.

THE ARIANS

As the various movements that had been born of the Reformation faltered in Poland, one movement continued to flourish—called the Arians. The members of this group were Antitrinitarians, the Bohemian Brethren, the Socinians, and the Unitarians. They continued to flourish in Poland because they followed a simple way of life that appealed to many of the common people (as I have mentioned above). Polish Arianism was appealing to some of the burghers (and this is its unique characteristic) because it was first, purely intellectual and doctrinal. This trend had originated in Italy and was described by frightened Calvinists (like Beza) as "Poland's doom." Its proponents Socinus (Laelius, and the younger Faustus), Blandrata, Gentile, Gribaldi, Alciato, Ochino, Negri (not to mention Stankar and Lismanin) were rationalists who, in the name of free inquiry, carefully undermined (especially Blandrata during his sojourn in Poland) and then demolished the foundations of Christian beliefs. Arianism also appealed to many other people because it also was not doctrinal. This trend had its origins in Germany (Münster) and with the Moravian communists. It demanded not learning, but a Christian way of life.

In Poland the first proponent of Arianism was Peter of Goniądz, a burgher from Biała Podlaska, who rejected the doctrine of the Trinity, and, to the great indignation of the 1556 Secemin synod, censured the social order. He found his only protector in the person of Kiszka, a Lithuanian magnate who financed the printing of his books and maintained him at his estate in Węgrów. Soon, Gregory Paulus was to surpass his master, and though the synods could condemn him, and the executioner could burn his blasphemous bulletin in the Warsaw Square, the teaching found fervent followers among the burghers. So it was that next to the German faith (Lutheranism) and the faith of the gentry (Calvinism), the faith of the burgher (Arianism) took its place.

Valentine Krawiec, a merchant from Lublin, and Mundius, a member of the city council in Wilno, were untiring propagators of the movement. Mundius became closely related to the Moravian "communists." All of the early ministers were burghers (Krowicki's gentry background is somewhat suspect) including Gregory Paul of Brzeziny (who was expelled from the parish school in Poznań in 1549 for being a dissenter), Martin Czechowic (the son of a Zbąszyń artisan who ministered for a time in Wilno and was perhaps the first to baptize adults by immersion), and Stanisław Paklepka (once a student in Basel and Zurich, after whose death the Lublin congregation ultimately came over to Krawiec).

Although the Arians continued to flourish for a time among the burghers after other groups had faltered, even they met with defeat ultimately. The Reformation finally came to grief in Poland, because the many peasants not only treated Catholicism with indifference, but viewed the new faiths with contempt and hatred. The peasant and the poor townsman were rather dull and without much inclination to mysticism, and accordingly had little interest in any religion. Further, they were not attracted to a new faith that did not do any more than Catholicism had to alleviate their plight in any way, and, in addition, denied them any sensory appeals and failed to stimulate their imagination or even their curiosity. In addition, of course, they had come to distrust their lords and betters and consequently any of their faiths. In brief, most of the population in Poland had no interest in religious beliefs.

A further cause of Protestantism's decline was the mediocrity of its representatives. Jan Łaski alone had prestige that even Orzechowski had to acknowledge, but all the rest were an unimpressive group; they could not even match their own laymen such as Rej. There were active people among them, but when bitter battles arose, their courage quickly failed them. As the Catholics developed more and more eloquent fighters, the Protestants withdrew from the field.

More and more doubts were disturbing the troubled consciences of men, and even the first generation experienced during the years 1567–1570 an almost mass withdrawal of their finest representatives; Olbrycht Łaski (a most painful blow to the ministers—this was the nephew of their hero Jan Łaski), Michael Christopher Radziwiłł (son of the "pillar," however weakened, of Lithuanian Calvinism), Tomicki (son of the "pillar" of the movement in Great Poland), Starzechowski (of the Ruthenian "dynasts"), and others abandoned the new faith even during the reign of Sigismund Augustus. The bitter accusations that Olbrycht Łaski threw at the ministers were no idle fabrication:

> Here you have endless scandals, here you have constant quarrels, here you have the shameless opinions of felonious heretics. There is a never ending battle about religion, a never ending despair for the poor and harassed conscience. Stop to consider what a variety of sects you have, the number of differences among your writers. There is fraud in religion, blasphemy in faith, intemperance in behavior. There is no order, there is no status, there is no authority, there is no dignity in the church. I see nothing among you except confusion: I have experienced nothing but contention. And surely God is not the God of contention, but a God of peace! . . . only now (in Catholicism) has my conscience been relieved, my religion stable and my faith at peace!

These words were written for Olbrycht by a priest, but they contained the truth. It is enough to mention the name of Stankar, a recent authority of the Evangelicals, whose *Canones reformationis* imposed an "order of correction" on both the clergy and the laity, but barely ten years later his polemic on Christ's mediation evoked the greatest outrage and his indignity gave potent weapons to anti-Catholics. The conflict between the

"Major congregation" and the "Minor" one was water for the mills of Rome. The demands of the Calvinists and Lutherans which were made repeatedly since 1564, but most strongly at the Lublin Diet of 1566, that the Arians (the Anabaptists and the Tritheists) be expelled from Poland (for which a proper declaration was already secured from the King), were opposed by the bishops together with the Nuncio (Ruggieri). "If others, the Calvinists and the Lutherans are not to be expelled at the same time—and this would be impossible"—then no resolution should be taken. Strife among the heretics meant peace for the Church. Besides, to take action against only select sects would be tantamount to legalizing the others.

In their search for something stable, people passed from one faith to another. The Calvinist Mielecka, daughter of Radziwiłł the Black, picked through all the sects, even the pagan-Jewish (a Judaic-like group emphasizing the Old Testament over the New), before the Jesuit Herbst converted her to Catholicism. Lew Sapieha abandoned his forefathers' Greek Orthodox faith for Lutheranism in 1570, while yet a boy in Leipzig. Soon (according to his own words) he "sided with the Arians, and later with the Anabaptists, remaining in this error for no little time," until he turned to Catholicism in 1586. The same happened to A. Pociej and others. The universality of the Roman Church, its stability unshaken through so many centuries, the imposing splendor of its ritual (compared to the austerity of the dissenters), the dedicated activity of the Jesuits—these were the impediments against which the delicate dissident bark, swept in all directions, kept crashing. Arias (a Spanish Jesuit) is said to have converted to Rome seventy-seven persons at King Batory's court, while Skarga, Laterna and other Jesuits repeated his achievement so effectively that the dissenters were thrown into a panic.

Unwittingly, the Catholic environment of the Court had its effect, particularly during the reign of Batory and Sigismund III. Earlier, Sigismund Augustus was concerned only about peace, about finding some golden mean on which both the dissenters and the Catholics(!) could agree. This attitude had disastrous effect on those who were rather vacillating, not to mention the effect on the calculating ones. For a while, religious affiliation was no hindrance to promotions to important positions. King Sigismund III in the early years of his reign gave senatorial appointments to dissidents without difference. This tolerance ended under the influence of the Jesuits. However, except for the Jesuits, zealous Catholicism was not the rule. Hosius and Karnkowski were by no means typical examples of the episcopate, and there were a great number of "cold" Catholics, commonly called "politicians." One of these was Jan Zamoyski, among the statesmen. Another, among the writers, was Jan Kochanowski who greeted the marriage of Archbishop Dudycz with a lengthy elegy (*Dudycz himself nulli religioni addictus, sed vago cultu Dei vivens*); he openly mocked the Protestants, but neither was he any more charitable toward the Catholics, and he so carefully avoided any overt display of Catholicism that the Jesuits of the seventeenth century counted him among the heretics. His wife was a Podlodowska, and the Podlodowskis were zealous Protestants, described in Rej's *Zwierzyniec* (The Bestiary).

5

From Radicalism to Humanitarianism

Stanisław Kot

Relation of the ideology of the Polish Brethren to the teaching of the New Testament. From social radicalism to humanitarianism. Evolution of their relation to the state. Moral level of the Polish Brethren. Their significance in Europe.

Among the Polish Brethren the discussion about their relation to the state and to society lasted for a hundred years, from the appearance of Peter of Goniądz (Gonesius) to Samuel Przypkowski. We know only the more important published manifestations; the heated deliberations at meetings and synods and the disputes carried on among members of the Church privately, are not open to us. The chief question which rallied the Church and maintained harmony was not the relation to the political and social order of the time but primarily the Unitarian doctrine; nevertheless, in no other church of that time did matters of life and social morality play such a role as among the brethren, and just for this reason caused so much discussion and excitement. Their ideology may be criticized as utopian, for they were only a handful in a society on which they were unable to impose their views. But it must not be forgotten that despite this their opinions had no merely theoretical character, for it was their principle to live as they thought and believed.

The social and political ideas of the Polish Brethren were

developed on a strictly religious basis derived from the sources of Christianity, which they limited to the teaching of Christ and the Apostles. At first glance, then, it may seem hard to understand why there were so many changes and hesitations, ranging from the social and anti-state radicalism of the "anarchists" of Raków to Przypkowski's complete approval of the state and the social order. Why did Krowicki, Palaeologus, and Budny derive from the same sources different conclusions from those derived by the Moravians and their Polish sympathizers; why did Brenius, Wolzogen, and Stegmann extract different solutions from Przypkowski? Here the same factors were at work by virtue of which the Roman Church, starting from the same religious basis, treated the practical problems of public life so differently from the medieval heretics, or the Protestant Churches so differed from the radical sects that grew out of them.

The teaching of Christ did not set up a program for the social reconstruction of the world.[1] It only commanded absolute love of one's neighbor, including even one's enemy; for only such broad love awakens a real understanding of God and opens the way to Him. One's way of life, one's work, are only important as they are necessary for life, but have in themselves no proper moral worth. The economic life plays no role in it; care for the morrow should be left to God. Wealth is not forbidden, but it is dangerous to the soul. God gives man his work, and in time of need charity will come with help: that is the real test of piety. In order to be able to perform an act of charity, the existence of labor, income, property must obviously be assumed. There is not a word on the question of the state. Imperial Rome is treated as a lawful institution under the providence of God. The faithful are to remain in the existing social and political order and to wait for the Kingdom of God on earth.

The Apostolic Church rallied about the teaching of the Sermon on the Mount and began in the spirit of its recommendations to draw up a certain social order, binding only upon the members of the Church, not upon the whole of mankind. In

---

[1] Cf. Troeltsch, *Die Soziallehren der christlichen Kirchen und Gruppen* (Tübingen: 1912); English translation, *The Social Teaching of the Christian Churches* (London: 1931), Vol. II.

the Apostolic Church, poor as it was, communism based upon community of consumption developed. There is no trace of the organization of community of production, nor in general of an organization of any sort which took account of technical considerations. The existence of private property and income was a condition of mercy and charity. No idea of social equality was expressed. In the Apostolic Church there were also no courts or magistrates. In the poor handful gathered together there appeared no need of defining relations to the state. In this system the germ of revolution was undoubtedly involved, though as there was in it not the least conscious wish to raise a revolution, it passed away without any struggle to maintain the principles on which it rested.

The missionary activity of St. Paul dampens what was revolutionary in the Gospel idea and strengthens the conservative character of Christianity. The idea of equality is defined: it will be an equality of all men before God, not one of claim and pretension, but equality in the sense of uniform littleness and unworthiness, which is fulfilled when all have an equal share in the worship of God and in love. With this religious basis the rationalistic idea of equality, which would fain be extended to earthly relations, has nothing in common. The principle of appointing men to different vocations, or of calling them according to the will of God, stands in the way of bringing these two ideas together. Hence God in his inscrutable purposes has introduced inequality in social and civil life. This inequality is to be the incentive to love one's neighbor, to active mercy and aid for the weak. Nothing is said of reforming existing relations, but of bearing them in patience and of using them for the inner purposes of man. The early Church is the more readily reconciled to this inequality since men attribute unchangeability to the conditions of contemporary Rome. The Christian congregations, organizing their internal life and their new worship, and at the same time rapidly spreading, adapt themselves to the usual demands of social and economic life and reject communism. Missionary work proves impossible without agreement with the state; thus its existence is acknowledged and its value is even raised as an institution concerning itself with law, order, and outward decency. Upon acceptance of the state, the social order bound up with it, with its division of classes and temporal goods, is approved. With the claim to its own laws evangelical resignation is forgotten and the germ of its own jurisdiction is formed.

Thus a conservative basis is established in the Christian world; however, it consists not in an inner sincere attachment to the institutions of the time, but in a combined feeling of contempt for them, submission to them, and relative acknowledgment of them. The souls of the faithful are closed to the ideals of the state, are disposed to be hostile to earthly authorities and to nationalistic and imperialistic tendencies. There is no awakening of understanding for the ethical values of law, the state, and economic life, nor of any desire to transform them to suit their own ends. Social and political institutions are a product of the hated paganism; hence, it is possible to be inwardly independent of them, and alongside them to organize the proper life of the Christian Church, but it is necessary to recognize their outward functions and to adapt oneself to them. So, in the main, primitive Christianity hands down to posterity in Holy Scripture two different interpenetrating currents in relation to the political and social order: the conservative and the revolutionary.

We must remember this in order to understand how the New Testament could furnish food for both conservative and subversive tendencies, depending on which passages were assigned decisive weight and on what was sought in them. If the Racovian radicals relied on the Sermon on the Mount, their opponents looked for support in the epistles of St. Paul. If the communists were provided with the Apostolic Church at Jerusalem, the conservatives appealed to the organization of the churches of a Christianity spreading over the Roman Empire. Even if in discussion (which happened rarely) they took into account the succeeding centuries of the Church, the third and fourth, there also they found the two currents, the one socially radical (Tertullian, Cyprian, John Chrysostom), citing the tale of the rich young man, and the other moderate, trying to reconcile the obligations of mercy with private property and economic demands; one politically hostile to the state, to courts, and to war, the other, with the domination of Rome by the Christians, more and more deeply compromising (the synod at Arles in 314 decreed excommunication on soldiers deserting from the Roman army).

Simpler minds, less keen, less cultivated or one-sided, were blindly attached to those teachings of Holy Scripture which fell in with their inclinations; the opponents of the doctrinaires were compelled to use more subtle reasoning to detect and explain contradictions, to interpret them by external circumstances, by the choice of audience, by the historical factor, thanks to which they sometimes arrived at an acute analysis of the texts and at apt historical criticism.

As in the very beginnings of Christianity the demands of reality called forth display now of a hostile, now of a compromising attitude toward the political and social order of the time, until in the end there ensued a harmonization of religion with life; so in the century of the history of the Polish Brethren we have witnessed a like evolution. The first generation of our Antitrinitarians was distinguished by an uncompromising radicalism. All of them, born in the Catholic Church, swallowed up in the whirlpool of the Reformation, passed through the doctrine of Luther, of Calvin, of Zwingli, or of Łaski, more and more violently withdrawing from the old Church and more and more uneasily seeking realization of the "pure doctrine." There grew up in them an impulse to reject all the compromises that centuries of the Church's history had accumulated, and to put into practice the highest ethical ideals which spoke to them from the Gospel. Keeping to a strictly religious basis, they did not proclaim a revolution either social or political, but wished to apply absolutely the commands of love both with their social consequences, even to resigning privileges, and with their political consequences, even to denying the law of the sword.

Social radicalism very quickly lost force. Various factors tended to quench it. First was its religious origin, which did not favor its transformation into a broad program of social action. It was motivated not by economic misery nor by the social wrongs of the lower classes but by absorption in the command to love one's neighbor. If Jan Przypkowski freed his serfs from servitude, he fulfilled his personal obligation of love toward "creatures of the one Creator," but he did not adopt the notion of abolishing servitude altogether and conferring freedom upon the peasants in the whole Republic. If Niemojewski and Brzeziński sold their fertile estates in Kujawy and used the proceeds in assisting poor brethren, thus satisfying their own consciences by following the advice given to the rich young man of the Gospel, they by no means made a like demand on nobles who did not belong to their group. Subsequently, heroic acts of this sort of renunciation of earthly goods did not prove economically desirable. Even Niemojewski conceded that it was impossible to command charity which swallowed up all the property of a rich man, for it involved the owner in poverty, condemned him to beggary, and even so did not permanently ensure against want the poor who had been given alms, but at most only caused a transfer of wealth to other hands.

They did not know how to develop for themselves a conception of the economic reconstruction of society which would have allowed them to combine the demands of religion with those of economics. They rejected the communism of the Moravians as not strictly answering to the commands of Christian mercy; they saw in it only a proof of the efficiency of "managers," who condemned their brethren to heavy labor and exploitation. Belonging in the main to the gentry, the Polish Brethren could not follow in the footsteps of the radical German or Dutch groups, which were composed of laborers and artisans. Thus the attempts at first made to impose on members of the Church the obligation of manual labor, for which they were fitted neither by education nor by experience, did not gain acceptance among them. Dutch and English sectarians, accepting the Calvinistic doctrine of trade ethics, plunged into work, thrift, and the accumulation of wealth, and in time became a strong pillar of capitalism; in commercial and colonizing lands on the seaboard this was possible. The economic system of the Republic, which was founded on agricultural production and the labor of a feudal peasantry, did not furnish such opportunities, and the Polish Brethren were unable to separate themselves from this system. Thus even by the end of the sixteenth century they had become reconciled to it and practiced active love of neighbor only by making the circumstances of peasant life easier and by refraining from exploiting their serfs. Their radicalism was transformed into humanitarianism.

The following is placed in the mouth of an Antitrinitarian

noble as a characteristic prayer, in a prayerbook composed by Jan Stoiński:

> Let me, O God, set such a watch upon my conscience, that my land may not cry out against me, and its fields also may not weep together for my unjust treatment of my servants, that I put them to labors beyond their duty, heavy and hardly to be borne, or do not grant them what is their due, or withhold their just wages from my hired men. . . .
>
> Let them not work for me like cattle, but let me remember that they are yet men, created in Thine image, in nature like me. Let them have no cause to complain to Thee against me, that Thou hast not heard them and hast not avenged their wrongs upon me.

And as to the common people of the towns, Stoiński put into the mouth of an Antitrinitarian noble this vow:

> May I never encroach on their right, and never abridge that freedom which they have from me or from my ancestors; nay, let me rather enlarge it when there is need. For as I love myself in my greater freedom as a noble, so also do they in their freedom, narrower though it be; and what I do not like, it is not becoming in me to do to another.[2]

Similarly, out of the initially absolute condemnation of criminal judicature there developed in time a more practical humanitarian demand for a relaxation of the extreme severities of the criminal law, and in particular of the penalties for theft. In general the Polish Brethren tried to minimize the wrongs of the social order by Christian mercy and brotherliness. As far as they could, they abolished among themselves all distinctions of class, birth, and property. Within the sphere of the Church, nobles and commoners lived and were recognized as equals. Their restraint of greed, luxury, and display diminished outward differences; the rich, moreover, did not flock to such an extreme confession, and the wealthier members of the Church

---

[2] Jan Stoiński, *Modlitwy nabożne* (Devout Prayers) (Raków: 1633), pp. 695, 393, 389.

distinguished themselves by their great liberality, which made it possible both to aid the poor and to support ministers in the poorer congregations, and to carry on an extensive publishing and missionary work.

If the social ideology of the Polish Brethren soon passed its crisis and reached a basis of compromise, it was more difficult to settle their relation to the state. They began their existence as loose private groups averse to the state, which they regarded as an unavoidable result of the existence of evil in the world, although, by strongly emphasizing obedience to the civil government, they were able to defend themselves against charges of sedition and tendencies to revolution. They did, however, frighten away from themselves all elements that were not willing to renounce active participation in the life of the Republic. It proved that in a gentry state one could not survive without fulfilling certain obligations to the state, especially when it was threatened by the pressure of eastern barbarism. Absolute abstinence from civil life could in the West be practiced only by little groups of sectarians, drawn from the poorest stratum. It was impossible in Poland to imagine the existence of organizations of the common people not based on any guarantee in the public law; it was at most admissible in the case of groups of foreign colonists like the Mennonites on the bottom lands near Danzig. The Polish Brethren, who scandalized all churches by their Antitrinitarian doctrine, could shelter themselves only under the privilege of the rights of the nobility, and it was necessary to pay for their enjoyment of the rights by discharging obligations to the state. As the experience of history shows, every religious group, insofar as it is united in a church organization, acquires a tendency to spread if it does not wish to die out, and hence is forced to enter on the path of compromise with the existing order. Various sects succumbed to this same fate, even those as radical as the Mennonites, Baptists, and Quakers. Among the Polish Brethren the process began with the acknowledgment of elementary duties to the state; then came the turn of warmth of patriotic feelings, and even of patriotic devotion, in proportion as the conviction grew that the State secured them certain values of a higher order. The Republic, which allowed them to enjoy the great treasure of freedom of conscience, aroused, despite all their scruples, a fervent attachment of which we have proofs, for example in the *Poloneutychia* of Andrew Lubieniecki, or in the *Chocim War* of Wacław Potocki (an epic poem on the Polish victory over the Turks at Chocim in 1621).

It is obviously impossible to apply to the political ideology of the Polish Brethren criteria that were not developed until the eighteenth century. They were not striving for the political freedom of the citizen in the sphere of the State, nor for enabling the serfs to influence the course of State affairs. On the contrary, they themselves withdrew from these affairs, seeking no honors or offices. "Having equal liberties with you gentlemen *cum paritate juris,*" said Andrew Moskorzowski, addressing the Estates of the Republic on behalf of the Antitrinitarian nobility at the electoral diet in 1632, "we have left the move to you gentlemen in all honors and dignities. We run after none of them; we do not try to seize anything before anyone else; yet sitting in our solitude we do not hinder others." [3] They asked of the state only that its laws and institutions should not violate the requirements of their religion, asked of it above all freedom of conscience, for all confessions as well as for themselves. Even when they were being persecuted in violation of the law, they did not raise the standard of rebellion. They complained, tried to persuade, protested, and finally, in face of the harshest violence, when forbidden to confess their religion, they left their native land and went into banishment, misery, and exile. Their native land repulsed them; they did not disown it. They placed the cause of God and of conscience above any worldly goods and affections, in this respect true sons of the era of the Reformation, whose spirit the Jesuit Peter Skarga expressed in his memorable cry: "Defend the Church and the souls of men before the fatherland! If the temporal fails, let us hold fast to the eternal."

In Polish society during the sixteenth and seventeenth centuries the Polish Brethren represented not only great intellectual but also great moral values. They gave profound consideration to the commands of Christian ethics and tried in all strict-

---

[3] Ossoliński Ms. 647, p. 39.

ness to conform their lives to them. The moral level of their churches aroused the enthusiasm of impartial observers. The Scotsman Thomas Segeth related [4] that when he found himself at Raków in 1612, "it seemed as though he had been transported into another world, for whereas elsewhere all was full of the noises of war and tumults, here it was quiet; men were so trained to frugality and calm that you might think that they were angels."

In spite of the fact that they were hated and passionately opposed by all the confessions, we find no complaints against their morals whether collective or individual. Even the Jesuit Martin Łaszcz, not at all fastidious in his choice of calumny, found himself at a loss when he desired to render them morally odious. He did not succeed in discovering anything against them, and he had to fasten upon them slanderous lies current about the Moravian Anabaptists. It was just this moral level, based on concord of life with faith, which ensured them such strong solidarity that they were able to endure for several generations, and even the severest test of banishment from their native land resulted in but few desertions among them.

Uniting in themselves a lofty morality with profound knowledge, the Polish Brethren, despite their numerical insignificance, constituted an influential and attractive center. The whole world of that time was interested in them. The Raków prints, though everywhere banned, were in demand and were snapped up, especially in Germany, France, Holland, and England. The pens of theologians of all the churches were sharpened against them. A considerable library could be formed of the literature called anti-Socinian in the seventeenth century. By their doctrine they raised a ferment in distant regions. For want of detailed investigations in this field, it is impossible as yet to pronounce how important an influence they exerted on the history of religious thought and on the intellectual development of the second half of the seventeenth century. It is certain that they placed their mark on the religious movement of the radical Dutch confessions and, in part through them directly, on the English sects. Voltaire in his time was still aware of this

---

[4] Cf. Ruar, *Epistolae*, p. 379.

when, for example, he emphasized in his *Lettres anglaises* the sympathy of Newton for the Polish Brethren. No attention has, however, been called by historians of political ideas to this Polish contribution to the important intellectual work out of which the European Enlightenment sprang.[5]

The Polish Brethren did not live to see the time in which their ideas, principles, and methods of thought began to exert an influence on the intellectual life of the world. They died out while dispersed as exiles, grieving that their own nation had rejected them, although to them its spiritual and moral elevation was of the greatest consequence. Only after centuries of oblivion have students of the Polish past discovered them. But the consciousness is precious to us that in the remote past such an unusual flower grew up on Polish soil, that the nation produced within itself a group of such moral elevation, such critical spirit, and such gravity of life.

---

[5] Troeltsch's fundamental work, *Die Soziallehren der christlichen Kirchen und Gruppen* (Tübingen: 1912), while defining the position of petty German and Dutch groups in the history of the political ideology of Christianity, does not even mention the Polish Brethren.

• 6 •

Helping the Danish Ally

Jan Pasek
Translated by Maria A. Y. Święcicka

ANNO DOMINI 1658

King John II Casimir was with one army near Toruń; another army stayed in the Ukraine; whereas our division under Pan Czarniecki was stationed for three months near Drahim. In August, we went to Denmark to help the Danish King Frederick III, who had launched a diversionary attack during the Swedish invasion of Poland. He surely did not do so out of sympathy for us, although his nation had been favorably inclined toward the Polish nation for a long time, as old documents show, but because of an innate hatred which he cherished toward the Swedes. On account of the bitter hostility between neighbors and in order to avenge the injustice inflicted upon him, he took advantage of the occasion when the King of Sweden was busy in Poland and invaded the latter's country with his own army, attacking, destroying and killing. Gustav, who was a great and lucky warrior, returned from Poland, leaving his garrisons at some Prussian fortresses, and pressed the Danes so violently that he not only took back his own but conquered almost their whole country as well. The Danish King, in an attempt to make his behavior look more justified, then declared that he broke the agreements and made war against Sweden purely out of love for our nation. He, therefore, asked the Poles as well as the Emperor for help. Giving as an excuse his pacts with Sweden in the Peace of Westphalia, the Emperor refused to send troops. The second excuse he gave was that he had no army at the time, since he had allowed the Polish King to hire it. The Polish King sent Czarniecki with six thousand of our army. He also sent in his name, General Montecucculi with the Imperial army. We were ordered to ride there unencumbered by supply wagons. (Wilhelm, the Great Elector of Brandenburg, was representing the Polish King and was, so to speak, the commander-in-chief of these troops.) We left our transport and supply columns in Czaplinek, hoping to return to them within half a year at the latest.

As we were leaving Czaplinek, the military men were alarmed at the prospect of going beyond the sea where no Polish foot had ever stood, at going with six thousand troops into Sweden, whose might we could not withstand with allour strength in our own fatherland. Moreover, no final decision had yet been made as to whether the Imperial army was to go with us. Fathers wrote to their sons, wives to their husbands that they should not go to Denmark even if they were to lose pay and retinue, because all considered us as good as perished. My father, however, although I am his only son, wrote to me commanding me to call upon the Name of God for assistance and not to let myself be disturbed by all this, but to boldly follow the will of the leader with father's and mother's blessing. He promised to beseech the Divine Majesty ardently and assured me that not even one hair would fall from my head without the Will of God.

As we were going toward Cielętnice and Międzyrzecz already near the border, many officers and retainers turned back to Poland, especially those from Great Poland, newly recruited into the regiments organized under the various district banners. From other regiments only two or three men remained. Thus these cowards discouraged even good lads so that many hesitated. After we had already crossed the border, each made his vows to God in his own way. The entire army began to sing in the Polish manner: *Oh Glorious Queen!* The horses in turn began to snort so noisily in all the regiments that all plucked up courage. Everyone took this as a good omen, which turned out to be the case.

From Międzyrzecz we continued along the same road. The army passed a hill from which one could still see the Polish border and some towns. Many a man turned around and thought: "Dear Fatherland, will I ever behold youu again!" As long as we were close to home, some strange longing overcame us, but as soon as we had crossed the Odra, the nostalgia was swept away and after we had gone further, Poland was soon forgotten.

The Prussians received us rather courteously; they sent us their delegates even beyond the Odra. We were given the first provisions near Kiestrzyn and kept receiving them everywhere until we had crossed the land of the Great Elector of Brandenburg. One had to admit that all went smoothly, because a regulation had been issued concerning quarters for the night across his whole country and provisions were brought to these places in advance.

Then the army moved in southwestern Denmark to Nyböl; thence to Apenrade and from Apenrade again to Haderslev to spend the winter. Although the army was to penetrate even deeper into the Danish kingdom, Czarniecki decided that we should take up winter quarters as close as possible to the enemy's border in order to eat more Swedish than Danish bread—and this was the way it happened. Throughout the entire winter our raiding parties would penetrate the Swedish villages and avenge the wrongs inflicted upon our own nation.

A great abundance of provisions was brought back from all the patrols: cattle and sheep in sufficient number; one could buy a good ox worth a whole thaler for two Danish marks. Honeycombs were brought to us in great quantities, because everywhere in the fields there were spacious apiaries where bees were kept in straw boxes, not in beehives.

There were stags, hares, and deer beyond all expectations and not very timid because not everyone was allowed to hunt them. There were no wolves, which was another reason that the game was not timid; it let itself be approached and shot at from close up. We used to hunt it in the following manner: After we spotted a herd of stags in the field—for these wretched creatures used to come up to the village like cattle—we rode down the herd from the side of the open field, then picking up speed and uttering a cry, we drove the stags into the peat pits, which were very wide and deep. The animals fell into these in heaps, and one only had to pull them out and slaughter them. As I had already mentioned, there were no wolves there, because the law was such that whenever a wolf was spotted, all village and city dwellers to the very last man had to leave their homes and pursue the wolf until they managed to starve it to death, drown it, or capture it. Then without flaying it they would hang it by a heavy iron chain from a high gallows or from a tree, and thus it hung until only the bones remained. They not only did not let a wolf propagate, but did not even let it spend the night in their country, whenever it managed to make its way there through the only possible narrow entrance between the seas in search of some cervine meat. There is no access from the other sides, because on one side the kingdom is washed by the Baltic Sea, on the other side, as well as on the north, by the ocean. For all these sides the wolf had no access, unless he were to hire a small smack in Gdańsk from his Honor the Mayor and pay for it well.

For this reason there is a great abundance of game in Denmark. There are no partridges, however, because they are so stupid that they are frightened by mere trifles, fall down into the sea and drown.

The Danish people are good-looking; the women are pretty but somewhat too fair. They dress nicely but in cities as well as in villages they wear wooden clogs. Whenever they walk on the city sidewalks they make such a clatter that one cannot hear one's own words. The upper-class women, however, wear shoes as our Polish women do.

In showing affection, the Danish women are not as restrained as the Polish women are, for even though they show some unusual shyness at first, they fall madly and passionately in love at the first meeting after exchanging merely a few words and they do not know how to conceal this amorousness. They are all too eager then to give up father and mother and a rich dowry, and are ready to follow their beloved even to the ends of the earth.

They have their beds hidden in the walls like closets and they use lots of bedding. They sleep in the nude, just the way their mothers bore them, and they do not consider it shameful to dress and undress in front of one another. They do not even heed a stranger, but take off all their attire by candlelight and in the end they take off their chemises too. Then they hang everything on pegs and in the nude they bolt their doors, put out the candle and crawl into the closet to sleep.

When we told them that this was shameful and that in our country even a wife did not do this in front of her husband, they used to tell us that in their land no shame was attached to this because one should not be ashamed of one's limbs, which were created by God.

As for their sleeping in the nude, they said: "The chemise and other articles of clothing which are of service to us and cover us during the day, deserved a rest and should be allowed to have one at least at night. Besides, of what use are they to us and why should we take fleas and bugs to bed with us and allow them to bite us, thus interfering with our sweet dreams?" Our lads used to pull all sorts of practical jokes on them, but nevertheless, the custom was not broken.

Their eating habits are very peculiar, because they seldom eat anything warm, but cook various dishes all at once for the entire week; then they eat them cold, bit by bit and frequently. They even eat while threshing, since women thresh there with flails just as men; after almost every sheaf which they have threshed, they sit down on straw, take bread and butter, which always lies in a wooden dish, butter the bread and eat it, then get up once again and work. They do this repeatedly.

When they slaughter an ox, a pig, or a ram, they do not waste even the smallest drop of blood but drain it all into a container, mix into it barley or buckwheat groats, stuff the tripe of the animal with it and cook everything together in a boiler. Then they put this stuffed tripe on a big dish in the shape of a wreath around the head of the slaughtered animal and set this on the table at every dinner and eat it as a great delicacy. They do this even in the homes of the gentry, and they kept treating me to this until I finally told them that we Poles should not be eating this because dogs would become our enemies, since this is their dish.

They have no ovens in their homes, with the exception of the great gentlemen, because ovens are heavily taxed by the king. It was said that the tax was one hundred silver thalers for every oven per year. They have spacious fireplaces, however, in front of which they put as many stools as there are people in the house. They sit down on them to warm themselves. Also for better heating of the room, they have a little trench like a trough in the middle of the room. They fill it with coal and then fan it from one end so it glows and heats.

The churches are very beautiful. They were formerly Catholic churches. The services are also more beautiful than those of our Polish Calvinists, because the churches still have altars and paintings. We used to be present at the sermons, since they prepared them in Latin especially for us and invited us to them. They preached very carefully to avoid uttering one single word against the faith; one could have said that a Roman Catholic priest was preaching. They boasted about this and said: "We believe in what you believe, and you call us dissenters in vain." Still Father Piekarski scolded us for going there. To be sure many went there just to see the beautiful Danish girls and to observe their customs. They have a service similar to that of the Germans, during which the men cover their eyes with their hats, the women with their veils and then bend over and put their heads under the pews. On such occasions our lads used to snatch their prayer books, scarves, etc. Once the minister noticed this and burst out laughing so that he could not finish his sermon because of it. Also we who were watching this had to laugh. The Lutherans were astounded that we laughed and that their preacher was laughing with us. He later cited a parable about a soldier who begged a hermit to pray for him. The hermit knelt down to pray; in the meantime the soldier snatched away from him the little ram which carried his little knapsack, and ran away. At the end of this parable, the preacher exclaimed: "Oh piety of all pieties! One prays, another steals!" From that time on, whenever the women had to cover their heads again, they first put away their prayer books and scarves, but they still continued to exchange glances and laugh.

When I questioned them as to why they concealed their heads and covered their eyes, since neither Christ nor the Apostles did that, no one could answer me. One of them did say that this was done in memory of the days when the Jews cov-

ered Christ's eyes and ordered him to prophesy. To that I retorted: "If by this you want to express a remembrance of the
Passion properly, then while you are covering your eyes one
should beat you on the neck with a fist, because this was the way
it was done then." But they would not agree.

The Great Elector of Brandenburg soon learned about these
services and when Czarniecki, the starost of Kaniów, was visiting with him he said: "For God's sake, your Honor, please warn
his Excellency the Voivode on my behalf to forbid the Polish
gentlemen to go to church, for surely many of them will be
converted to the Lutheran faith, since I hear that they have
been praying so ardently that this fervor engorges the scarves
of the Danish girls." The Voivode had a good laugh on account
of this warning.

That same Prince Wilhelm behaved very courteously toward
us, accommodated us on all occaions, entertained us and
dressed in a Polish manner. Whenever troops were passing by,
as a rule some men would deliberately ignore others; he, however, came out and stood in front of his tent—or quarters, if he
happened to be staying in a town—and held his cap in his hands
until all banners had passed. Perhaps he also cherished the
hope of being offered the Polish crown after Jan Kazimierz's
death. As a matter of fact, it might even have come to that if Jan
Hoberbeck, his envoy, had not blundered during the election,
for when one senator said to him: "Let his Highness the Elector
renounce Luther, and he will become our King." The envoy
angrily declared that the Elector would not do such a thing
even for an empire. Prince Wilhelm was displeased when he
learned of this and reproached the envoy for having said this so
categorically without first having asked him about it.

During our stay in Denmark, the Voivode Czarniecki dealt
with him often, because he represented the Polish King and
had command over our army as well as over the Imperial army
whose fourteen thousand troops were under General Montecucculi. The Elector had under him twelve thousand Prussians, better men than the Imperial troops, and we always preferred to go into combat with them. It was also not good to
make camp close to the Imperial forces, because they immediately would send seamstresses to our camp. It was strange

that in such an affluent country in which everyone had plenty of everything in winter quarters, the Imperial troops sent their wives begging to us. A young woman, fair but emaciated, as if after the heaviest siege, would come to the tent with this oration: "Sir Pole, do give me some bread and I shall sew shirts for you."

When one saw such a miserable creature, one had to give alms, and for a week or two she made shirts for whoever needed them. These women came in handy, for it was not difficult to get linen, since enough of it was brought back from patrols, and we had no one to sew for us because we had only one woman in our army, a trumpeter. When their husbands grew weary awaiting them, they would come looking for them from one tent to another. Whoever found his wife, took her home and thanked us for having fed her well. If we still needed her, that is, if she had not finished sewing shirts, we had only to give the husband some biscuits and he would go away, leaving her for a longer time. He visited her only now and then. And so many a wench looked so much better in the course of two weeks that her husband could not recognize her. . . .

[The manuscript breaks off here. The section describing the events preceding the capture of Kolding is left out.]

They debated how to entrench themselves and how to fell the palisade walls; however, they failed to consider with what they were to fell them. Where was one to get axes? Finally the light cavalry sergeant ordered the men to search all the villages in a radius of two or three leagues for axes and even before dawn some five hundred of them were already stacked in a heap. As soon as the clocks struck four o'clock in the morning, orders were given to sound the reveille. Then Czarniecki, who had hardly slept that night, got up and gave orders to distribute the axes among the cavalry banners and the infantry. One hour after the reveille he ordered the trumpets to sound once again, this time to summon everyone to be ready in an hour for assault. Everyone was to carry a sheaf of straw on his chest as protection from musket shots. All were to leap forward together under the battlements and press toward the walls as close as possible to avoid being struck down from above and in order to be able to shoot back.

As soon as it began to grow light, the army sneaked closer to the city and I went to see the army chaplain. Later the Voivode, Czarniecki, said to me: "Lieutenant Charlewski volunteers to be in command of the soldiers. Let him do so then and you, Sir, will stay here." I answered him: "Everyone heard that your Honor had asked me to go. Someone might think that I am afraid, so I shall go."

When we dismounted, Pawel Kossowski and Lecki did the same. With the retainers there were five officers from our regiment, but I was in command, since it had already been delegated to me before these senior officers made up their minds to volunteer. We commended ourselves to the protection of God and His Holy Mother and everyone made a vow to Almighty God. We took leave of our companions as if parting for eternity and then stepped back to a place apart from the mounted men. Father Piekarski, the Jesuit, gave us an encouraging sermon . . .

Even though every sacrifice made sincerely from the heart is well pleasing to God, the most pleasant sacrifice of all is, nevertheless, when one offers one's blood on the battlefield for the Honor of Almighty God. Why did He bless Abraham so that his race should inherit the entire world? Only because, at one single command of God, he had been ready to sacrifice the blood of his beloved Isaac. We are summoned by the injustice which the Almighty has suffered from the Swedish nation; we are summoned by the temples of God desecrated all over Poland by the Swedes; we are summoned by the blood of our brothers and by our fatherland devastated by their hand; we are summoned by the Holy Virgin, Our Lady, whose immaculate name was blasphemed by their nation; they all summon us to intercede sincerely for those inflicted offenses, so that the world should still see in us the unfading glory and courage of our ancestors. You brave knights bring here, as Isaac did, your blood as a sacrifice to God. I assure you, however, in the name of God, that each one of you whom God leads out of this danger safely as He did Isaac, being content with the mere intention, will be rewarded with glory and with all

His blessings. He who will be injured in any way, however, will have the power to wash away even the most mortal sins for every drop of blood shed in the name of Almighty God and His Mother and will assuredly secure for himself an eternal crown in heaven. Sacrifice yourselves then for Him, who today lies poor in the manger and who willingly offers his own blood for your salvation to God His Father. Offer then your deeds of today instead of an early mass, which we usually celebrate at this time to welcome the new guest—the God sent in human shape to the world. I, however, have faith in Jesus whose most Holy Name I utter, and in the intervention of His most Holy Mother to whom I call: "Defend the honor of Your Son." Through Your intercession, oh Holy Mother, bring about that He may bless this undertaking, that He may lead our excellent knightly company successfully out of this tribulation and preserve it for further glory of Almighty God. Such are the commanders, the protectors, the custodians whom I give to you for this undertaking and I have faith that I shall greet all of you on your return in good health.

He then recited with us the act of penitence and all the additional prayers which are customary for those whom death awaits. I approached him more closely and said: "I ask your Reverence for a special blessing." Leaning down from his horse he placed his hands on my head and blessed me, then he took off his relic and put it on me and said: "Go boldly, have no fear!" Father Dąbrowski, another Jesuit, also rode up to other regiments, but he cried more than he preached. He had the habit of bursting into tears as soon as he began to preach, even though he was not a bad preacher, so he could not finish his sermons and provoked laughter.

In the meantime the trumpeter, who had been sent to the Swedes to propose to them an honorable surrender, if they wanted one, had returned. The Swedes replied: "Do with us whatever your knightly fancy bids you; as for us, we were not afraid of you in Poland, so much the less are we afraid of you here." Immediately afterwards they also began to shoot: They esteemed us lightly, since they saw that we did not even have one small cannon, but only one infantry regiment, four squadrons under Piaseczyński and three hundred choice Cossacks. The cavalrymen, they believed, were people not accustomed to assaults and would disperse under the first fire; so their prisoners had told them. Each one of our retainers held his sheaf of straw in front of him. The officers were only in coats of mail but some also had round shields.

Suddenly the Voivode came and said: "May God and His Holy Name grant you His protection. Rush forward, and when you have crossed the rampart ditch leap under the battlements as fast as you can, because under the walls the Swedes can no longer harm you so much." Since the clergymen had told us to offer our deeds of today as an early mass—for this took place on the very dawn of Christmas Day—I began to sing a carol with those who were under my command: "Let us praise the King!" Also, Paweł Wolski, who later became the starost of Lityń, but at that time was an officer of a squadron of cuirassiers and, like myself, a commander of his squadron's retainers, ordered his people to sing the same. God ordained it so that in our squadrons not one man perished, while those who did not sing were decimated.

As soon as we reached the rampart ditch, the sheaves of straw began to steam terribly. Some men got tired and began to throw the sheaves into the ditch; others, who saw those ahead of them do it, did the same and the ditch became levelled with sheaves, so that it was far easier to get across for those who were marching at the end than for us in the royal regiment, who marched ahead. It was hard to climb the slope with the sheaves in the snow; whoever managed to drag his along, however, learned that it helped, for bullets were found in some which had even penetrated to the middle.

When we scrambled up out of the ditch I ordered my men to shout: "Jesus, Mary!" even though others called "Hu, hu, hu!" as I hoped that Jesus Christ would help me more than this Lord Hu. We rushed in with all speed under the battlements. The bullets showered like hail; some men groaned and some fell to the ground. It so happened that by a huge pillar, or rather corner, where I was with my unit, there was a window with a very thick iron grating. I immediately ordered my men to take turns hacking the wall under it; when some got exhausted, others took over. On the second floor, directly above us, there was another such window with the same grating. From that window the Swedes shot at us, but only with pistols. They could not shoot at us with other weapons, because the grating prevented them from leaning out and they could, therefore, shoot only at those further away. I then ordered about fifteen rifles to be pointed at that window and to fire whenever anyone stuck out his hand. This was done and presently a pistol fell to the ground. Now they no longer dared to show their hands and only threw stones at us through the grating; but after all it was easier to take shelter from these than from bullets. Meantime our men kept hacking the wall all around the grating, but we were still unable to get at the Swedes. We were glad indeed when we saw the ends of the grating because bullets were showered on us like hail. We eagerly wished to get under a roof as soon as possible, but since we had nothing with which we could break open the grating we still had to continue hacking. As soon as the opening was big enough for one man, I told the retainers to crawl in one by one. Wolski, a man who always wanted to be the first, said: "I shall crawl in." He barely got in when the Swedes grabbed him by the head. He screamed. I grabbed him by the legs. Those within invited him to join them and we struggled to get him back. We almost tore the man apart. He called to us: "For Heaven's sake, let me go, you will tear me apart!" I shouted at my men: "Fire into the window!" They put several rifles into the window and fired: the Swedes let go of Wolski instantly. We then crawled in one by one.

Already about one hundred and fifty of us had crawled in through that window. Meanwhile, several companies of musketeers came toward us. They had learned of us apparently from those Swedes who escaped. They were just entering the cellar when our men fired into the crowd. Six of them fell; others escaped into the courtyard. We got out of the cellar all right and fell into line in the courtyard. More and more of our men kept coming through that opening. When the Swedes saw us in the courtyard they began to sound the trumpet and to wave a white flag as a sign of surrender. In a short period of time they thus altered a custom of their swinish nation, since they had previously said: "We do not ask for clemency!" I did not allow my men to disperse before a general confusion of the enemy could be seen. Wolski gave his men the same order.

There was nobody in the courtyard, as all men were arrayed and each guarded his own post. Suddenly the musketeers came down the steps from the rooms where the commander himself had stayed. I said to my companions: "Look, we are having company." We ordered our retainers to stand in a semicircular line, not in a crowd, for a line is less vulnerable than a crowd. We also gave orders to attack with swords right after the first firing. Behind the troops the music resounded, the kettledrums banged, there was an uproar and shouting. The musketeers entered the courtyard and immediately took position in a fighting line. We also advanced toward them; firing could commence at any moment. Meanwhile the Swedes began to run away from the rooms close to the gate, as Lieutenant-Colonel Tetwin had already broken in there with his dragoons. We leaped toward those who were facing us. They fired; several men fell on both sides and a fight with swords began. Several of the Swedes reached the stairs from which they came. The remaining ones were immediately cut off from the stairs from the left side and the fighting with swords resumed. Those who ran away from Tetwin came to us as if to a slaughterhouse. We killed all of them.

Now our soldiers scattered hastily, plundered in the rooms, seized and killed everyone that they came across in all corners of the castle, and dragged away the booty. Tetwin also came with his dragoons, assuming that he was the first one to enter the castle. A mass of corpses lay around and only about fifteen of our companions stood by, since the others had already dispersed. Tetwin crossed himself and said: "Who slaughtered these people when only so few of you are here?" Wolski retorted: "We did but there will also be enough for you; they are looking down from the tower."

A youth came leading a fat officer. I said: "Let me kill him." He begged: "Let me undress him first, because he wears beautiful clothes and they would get splashed with blood." He began to undress him when Adamowski, an officer under Captain Leszczyński of a Cossack regiment, came and said: "Pan brother, his neck is too thick for your hand, let me kill him."

We kept haggling over who was to kill him while in the meantime some men rushed into the cellar, where gunpowder lay in barrels. Along with other things, our men also took the gunpowder in their caps and handkerchiefs, each in whatever way he could. One dragoon, the scoundrel, came with a lighted fuse and also took gunpowder; somehow a spark ignited it. Oh Almighty God, what a detonation it was when the walls began to crumble, and the marble and alabaster figures began to fly!

At the very corner of the castle, overlooking the sea, there was a tower. It was roofless and covered with a flat roof of tin, like the floor in a room; its brazen rain-water gutters were gilded; all around stood balustrades with gilded brass statues in the corners, in places also figures of white marble, as if alive. Even though I had not seen them entirely from close up we nevertheless examined them carefully after the explosion. One of them was thrown by the explosion safe and sound to the side where our army was. It looked just like a living woman. To marvel at her, people rode there and told others that the commander's wife lay there, hurled by the explosion. So lay this dummy with her arms spread out, like a beautifully shaped human body which was difficult to distinguish from a living one; only when one touched its stony hardness did one know for sure.

In that tower, or rather in that hall, kings used to indulge in their pleasures, to eat their suppers, to dance and entertain themselves in various ways. From there the view was very beautiful: the king could see almost all the provinces of his kingdom and a part of Sweden as well. The commander and his entire suite had fled to that tower. From there they asked for clemency, although not right away. We might have granted it to them, but the gunpowder which ignited directly under that tower elevated them very high. It blew up all the floors, and, when the impetus seized them, they flew so high upward that they waltzed in the clouds of smoke: one could hardly see them up there with the naked eye. Only after their speed was diminished could one see them better, when they came back and fell into the sea like frogs.

The wretches wanted to flee from the Poles to Heaven, but they were not admitted there. St. Peter closed the gate immediately and said: "Ah scoundrels! You maintain that the grace of the Saints is useless, that their intercession with God is meaningless and unnecessary. In the churches of Kraków you wanted to house horses, to the horror of the Jesuits, so that the poor souls collected ransom for you as for pagans. Now Czarniecki has offered you peace and wanted to spare your lives, but you have contemptuously refused. Do you remember when you treacherously blew up the Poles in the castle of Sandomierz? Even there God saved those who should have been saved. The explosion threw Pan Bobola, a local nobleman, with his horse to the other bank of the Vistula and yet he was safe and sound. Also now you have directed heavy fire at the Poles and yet you did not kill many of them—why? Because they are guarded by the angels and you by the black devils—now you see what their service is like!"

Dear God, how just Your judgments are! The Swedes did such wrong to our Poles in Sandomierz when they treacherously planted mines in the castle, and here they set a trap for themselves. Our men did not do this to them intentionally, because this explosion killed about twelve of our own men. Nobody knew which of our people perished there; we only surmised this, if anyone was not found either dead or alive.

Both the Danish and the Swedish kings saw this, and the entire imperial and Brandenburg armies saw it. They assumed, however, that the Poles were celebrating Christmas. Then the Vice-Chancellor to the Crown, Radziejowski and Korycki told the Swedish king, at whose side they still were, that this was something else, because there is no such custom among the Poles but at Easter.

After this lucky victory, which we attained in three hours, the Voivode garrisoned the fortress with Captain Wąsowicz and his men. We went to our quarters, because one had to attend a Holy Mass on such a solemn occasion. We had a priest, but there was no liturgical equipment. Only when we reached the forest did Father Piekarski receive the equipment for which he had sent during the night. The army came to a halt; the altar was prepared on the trunk of a felled oak and there the Mass was celebrated. Fire was lit to warm the chalice, because it was freezing cold. We sang the *Te Deum laudamus* so loudly that it resounded all over the forest. I knelt down to serve Father Piekarski at Mass. Bloodstained, I began to dress the priest when the Voivode remarked: "Pan brother, you should at least have washed your hands." The priest retorted: "This does not matter. God does not loathe blood shed in His Name." Soon after, we came upon many of our retainers, who brought us all sorts of provisions. Whoever found his servant sat down and ate, compensating for yesterday's hunger.

The Voivode rode along happily, for it was an unusual instance to take such a fortress without cannon and regular infantry. He could have had both from the Great Elector, who was stationed in the vicinity, but he had pride and did not want to bow down to anyone, wishing to draw fame to himself. Trusting in God, he plunged in and he won.

7

The Protection of Jewish Religious Rights by Royal Edicts in Pre-Partition Poland

Isaac Lewin

I

By religious rights we mean the rights of a group of people who belong to a given faith to live according to its rules and to carry out its various precepts in practice. The State, as an organization which connects men of different confessions, does not always permit all its citizens to live strictly in harmony with the rules of their religion. Sometimes, full liberty of confessional practice is granted only to those who constitute the majority of the inhabitants of the State. In some cases even the majority group is restricted by the State in some of its religious practices. There are many cases noted in history when the secular and religious "arms" came into conflict. Of course, restrictions by the State of the freedom of religious customs and ceremonies of the *minority* groups of its citizens occur far more frequently in history. There are various degrees of tolerance or intolerance by the State towards its religious minority groups. They range from the extreme type of intolerance contained in the principle *"Cuius regio eius religio"* (where the majority group forces its faith upon the minority) to unrestricted liberty of conscience for all human beings. All depends on the degree to which the State interferes with the religious life of its minority groups.

Sometimes, although rarely, the State interferes with the religious sentiments of its citizens in a contradictory manner. It gives its support to a certain confessional organization for the purpose of forcing its members to adhere to a specific religious rule or custom. The State then interferes with the religion not by restricting but rather by strengthening its organization. This happens when the State is interested for its own purposes in strengthening the authority of a religious practice. This is described as "lending the 'secular arm' to religion."

I wish to describe the relationship of Polish government in medieval times to Jewish religious rights. Let us state at the outset that some rights were not only protected but also guaranteed by the legal assistance of royal functionaries, which means that the "secular arm" was secured for them.

The royal edicts up to the seventeenth century are considered in the following chapters. The sources for judicial practice, although important for the completeness of the picture, were not utilized, because the framework of this study would, in that case, be too greatly expanded. I hope, however, to do this on a different occasion.

II. THE PROTECTION OF THE SABBATH AND OF THE FESTIVAL DAYS

The different days of rest (Sabbath vs. Sunday) and holidays of the Jewish and Polish populations were, since the very beginning of the common history of these peoples on Polish soil, the cause of much strain in their economic relations.

The first Polish statute concerning the Jews, the edict of 1264 of Duke Boleslaw the Pious of Kalisz, contains an important regulation concerning this matter. It refers to the question whether the Gentile debtor is entitled to force his Jewish creditor to receive on Sabbath the money owed him and to ask for the return of the pawn on the same occasion. The statute of 1264 stipulates in Art. 29 as follows: "We decree that nobody shall force a Jew to return pawns on his holiday." This is the text of the short stipulation of the first statute which was later confirmed several times (for instance by King Casimir the Great in 1343 [1] and by King Alexander in 1505 [2]).

The Latin heading over this article reads: "Judaei non iudicentur die feriata," meaning that Jews must not be tried on holidays. This could therefore be interpreted to mean that the intention of the Duke was not to disturb the holiday of the Jewish creditor by prosecuting him on the Sabbath. But Art. 30 of the same statute proves that the point is quite different. It contains a rule that a Gentile who attempts to take back his pawn from a Jew by force, or who intrudes, for this purpose, into the Jew's house, is to be gravely punished by a fine payable to the government treasury. The connection between both articles is not distinctly stressed, nor is it clearly stipulated that this act of forced securing of the pawn must necessarily occur on the Sabbath. The same applies to the later edicts of King Casimir the Great and King Alexander, both of which copied word for word the statute of Boleslaw. Nevertheless, I am of the opinion that the original intention was to protect the Jew against a Gentile borrower who might invade his home on a Sabbath in an attempt to reclaim his pawn forcibly while simultaneously leaving the money in the Jew's house. A clear proof of this interpretation is to be found in the edict of King Casimir IV of August 13, 1453, in which the previous statutes are confirmed.

Art. 41 of this edict of 1453 reads as follows: "Should a Gentile wish to redeem his pawn from a Jew on the festival day of a Sabbath, or another Jewish holiday, when Jews do not dare to touch the money for the redemption of the pawn, and the Gentile should not pay attention to such a Jewish holiday, but should invade the Jewish home for getting back his pawn, and take it back by force—he must be punished as a robber and a thief." [3] It is evident that the violence does not refer to the

---

[1] Published by Biershadski, *Russko-Yevreyskiy Archiv*, Vol. I, p. 16.

[2] *Volumina Legum*, I, 314.

[3] *Codex Diplomaticus Maioris Poloniae*, Vol. III, No. 1368, p. 88–94; Bloch, *Die General-Privilegien der polnischen Judenschaft* Poznań, 1892, p. 102 ss.; Gumplowicz, *Prawodawstwo polskie względem Żydów*, p. 161 ss.

pawn but to the Sabbath or the other holidays. The Jew refuses
to accept the money for religious reasons, because it is not in
accordance with his faith; the debtor, however, is anxious to
redeem his pawn without delay. In this case the law protects the
religious feelings of the Jew and threatens to punish the Gentile
severely, should he use force in taking back his property. The
Jew does not suffer any material damage, because the debt has
actually been paid off on the Sabbath; nevertheless the violator
of his religious feelings is punished like a thief. The protection
of the Sabbath is obvious.

The principle of safeguarding the Sabbath progressed later
to such an extent that no Jew could be summoned to or tried
before a court on Sabbaths and holidays. King Sigismund August stated it clearly when he confirmed in 1571 the rights
granted by his predecessors to the Jews of Poznań: "They (i.e.,
the Jews) must not be summoned into court, according to the
law, on Sabbaths, or be tried then." [4] A Jew could apparently
deny the judge the right of sitting in judgment upon the case on
the Sabbath, should the Jew have been forced by the plaintiff to
appear then before the judge. The rule extends equally to the
litigant adversary of the Jew (*in iudicium non vocat*), as well as to
the judge (*neque iudicet*).

In some edicts of King Stephan Batory the norm concerning
the protection of the Sabbath was repeated and based on the
precepts of the Jewish faith. The royal edict of 1576 stated
briefly that "on holidays and Sabbaths they must not be tried." [5]
On the other hand, King Stephan's edict of 1580 for the Jews of
Poznań stated parenthetically that the Jews must not be summoned into a court by a Gentile on Sabbaths or other holidays,
as well as tried on those days, because "this is forbidden them by
their superstitious law" (*eorum superstitiosa lex prohibet*), and because it had explicitly so been ordained by the statutes of the

---

[4] Bersohn, *Dyplomataryusz dotyczący Żydów w dawnej Polsce*, No. 138:
"Praeterea ut illos diebus sabbatorum iuxta ius commune in iudicium non
vocat, neque iudicet . . ." Kraushar, *Historya Żydów w Polsce*, Vol. II, Warsaw,
1866, p. 64, writes, concerning the conditions of Jews in Poland during King
Władysław Jagiełło's reign (fifteenth century): "Święta żydowskie sprawę
przerywały."
[5] Bersohn, *loc. cit.* No. 152: "Item, w święta i sabbaty ich, od żadnego są-
dzeni być nie maja."

Kingdom (*statutorum regni dispositione disertis verbis id cautum est*).[6] It is significant that the King appeals first to Jewish law, even before mentioning the previous statutes of Polish law which protected the Sabbaths and other Jewish holidays. It seems that by this means he desired to clarify the reasons of the norm concerning the protection of the Sabbath; he stressed therefore that the "superstitious Jewish law" forbade touching money on Sabbaths and holidays.

King Sigismund III, when renewing Jewish rights in his edict of May 27, 1592, confirmed the protection of the Sabbath but changed the order of the reasons. He appealed first to the statute-books, and then to the prohibitions of the Jewish faith.[7] The edict of Sigismund III can be given an even wider interpretation; it could mean that the King sanctioned the keeping of the Sabbath, "because it is an inhibition of their (i.e., Jewish) superstitious law." Thus the Jewish law in general was to a certain degree protected by the law of the State.

King Michael Wisniowiecki returned in his edict of 1671 to the original form of the protection of the Sabbath contained in the already mentioned edict of King Casimir IV of 1453. It confirms some points of the common edict of King Sigismund III.[8]

It can be assumed then, that in the seventeenth century Jews in Poland could not be tried before the courts on Sabbaths, although the edict of King Michael Wisniowiecki does not mention it (and knows only of that form of the protection of the Sabbath which consists of forbidding the Gentile debtor to take back by force his pawn from the Jewish creditor on Sabbaths and other Jewish holidays). It seems that the heading over Art. 29 of the Statute of Kalisz of 1264, *"Judaei non Iudicentur Die Feriata"* ("Jews should not be tried on a holiday"), derives from a later period, when the safeguarding of the Sabbath had just this form; and it was therefore possible to put such a

---

[6] Bloch, *Die General-Privilegien der polnischen Judenschaft*, p. 99.

[7] The document has been published by Pazdro, *Organizacya i praktyka żydowskich sądów podwojewodzińskich*, Lwów, 1903 (Doc. No. 8), p. 169; and by Bałaban, *Żydzi lwowscy na przełomie XVI i XVII wieku*. Lwów 1906 (Doc. No. 33), p. 34 ss.

[8] Bersohn, *Dyplomataryusz*, No. 306.

superscription on an article which dealt not with trials on the Sabbath but with the redemption of pawns on those days. Both norms had the same practical meaning. The common law protected the Jews from being forced to profane their holidays.

Proof for this can be found in some local ordinances of the governors which were based on the royal edicts. In the ordinance, for example, of Wladyslaw, Prince of Ostrog, the governor of Cracow, of 1659, Art. 5 runs as follows: "It has been granted by the law to the Jews that they must not be tried on (their) holidays, as well as on the nine Mourning-days, during the famous fair of Jaroslaw and the Gromnice fair." [9]

Having protected their own holidays, the Jews intended to work on Sundays and Christian holidays. Some ecclesiastical councils (e.g., that of 1542) complained that "Jews are working and trading publicly on Christian holidays." [10] It must, however, be stressed that some of the royal edicts in which kings granted to the Jews the safeguarding of the Sabbath simultaneously stated that they were not entitled to work on Christian holidays. King Stephan Batory (in his edict of 1576 mentioned above), after stipulating that the Jews must not be tried on Sabbaths, stated plainly: "They are entitled, at all other times, to work and to trade, except on Sundays, on Easter and holidays, on Christmas, on Ascension Day and All-Saints-Day, when they are obliged to comport themselves, with respect to work and trade, like Christians." [11] The juxtaposition of both norms in this edict is most significant. It proves, first, that keeping the Sabbath included freedom from forced work on Jewish holidays; second, that in consequence of the protection of the Sabbath it was necessary to stress compulsory rest on Sundays and Christian holidays.

---

[9] This document was printed in the Polish original by Gumplowicz, *Prawodawstwo polskie względem Żydów*, p. 113–114.

[10] Kraushar, *Historya Żydów w Polsce*, Vol. II, p. 215. See also Gumplowicz, *Prawodawstwo*, p. 51. Both refer to the resolution of the ecclesiastical council of Piotrkow under the chairmanship of Piotr Gamrat, in which it was stated that Jews worked and traded publicly on (Christian) holidays, contrary to the canons and prescriptions of the common law. Cf. also Gumplowicz, *loc. cit.*, p. 103.

[11] Bersohn, *Dyplomataryusz*, No. 152. See also Gumplowicz, *Prawodawstwo*, p. 65.

It is interesting that in some agreements between the Jews and the Polish municipalities it is openly stipulated that the Jews were allowed to trade amongst themselves on Sundays. King Wladyslaw IV confirmed in 1645 the agreement between the municipality and the craft guilds of the city of Przemyśl and the Jews of that town; Art. 15 of this agreement provided that on Sundays and Christian holidays the Jews were not allowed to open their stores or to offer their merchandise for sale at the market, but "they may sit on their street" (i.e., trade amongst themselves). They were also permitted to trade everywhere, should a fair be held on a holiday; the only condition was that business could not begin before Mass was celebrated in Church.[12] This agreement was concluded only after a long struggle; as early as 1610 the municipality of Przemyśl accused the Jews of doing business on Sundays and Christian holidays,[13] and it therefore took twenty-five years until they came to the above mentioned agreement. Trading on Sundays by the Jews was apparently practiced during this period.

According to Dubnow, King Sigismund August forbade in some places the holding of the weekly market day on Saturdays, "to safeguard the commercial interests of the Jews, who refuse to do business on their day of rest." [14]

III. THE PROTECTION OF RITUAL SLAUGHTER

The precept of the Jewish faith which requires a special form of animal slaughter caused then the following twofold complication: (1) The Jews tried to obtain royal permission for their method of slaughter; and (2) they wished to acquire the privilege of selling Gentiles meat which they were not allowed to eat themselves. (A misstep in the ritual of slaughter, for example, makes meat unfit for eating according to Jewish law.)

King Casimir IV in his edict of August 13, 1453 (later confirmed by King Sigismund I) settled this matter with the follow-

---

[12] The document in extenso has been published by Schorr, *Żydzi w Przemyślu*, Lwów 1903, p. 147–152.

[13] *Ibid.*, p. 107.

[14] *History of the Jews in Russia and Poland*, Phila., 1916, Vol. I, p. 85.

ing regulation: "Wherever the Jews have their residence in a city or town of our Kingdom, they may slaughter for their use big and small cattle; and should a kind of meat, according to the custom, not correspond to their purpose and desire, they may sell it to the best of their ability, as they may wish." [15]

The statute of 1453 plainly mentions unfitness of the meat "according to the custom" (*secundum morem*), which means, of course, the Jewish faith. By this regulation, both questions connected with religious slaughter of animals were settled favorably for the Jews. They obtained permission to practice ritual slaughter, and simultaneously the King allowed them to sell to Gentiles meat which would be of no use to themselves.

In the "Articles of Good Order" which were granted to the Jewish community of Lwow by King Sigismund August in 1569, the following stipulation is included: "They [the Jews] may engage in butchery and sale of meat to Christians, as well as to other people, according to the custom of other Jews such as of Cracow, Poznań and Lublin." [16] The expression "custom" in this regulation must not be exclusively interpreted as meaning religion; it could also refer to a *commercial* custom of Jews in Cracow and the other two towns. Nevertheless we see here the development of an original permission to trade in meat corresponding to the specific requirements of ritual slaughter.

King Stephan Batory confirmed similar Articles of Good Order to the Jews in Przemyśl in 1576.[17] King Sigismund III confirmed them in 1591.[18]

It seems again that in the time of Stephan Batory the meat trade was in some places concentrated in the hands of Jewish butchers. The Christians of Lwow complained to this King that the Jews slaughtered more cattle than was necessary for the meat consumption of the Jewish population, and that they would sell the excess meat to the Christians. Stephan Batory

---

[15] *Codex Diplomaticus Maioris Poloniae*, Vol. III, p. 88–94 (No. 1368); published also by Bloch and Gumplowicz (see note 3); cf. also Maciejowski, *Żydzi w Polsce*, etc., p. 21.

[16] The articles have been published by Schorr, *Organizacya Żydów w Polsce*, Lwów 1899, p. 81–82, and Pazdro, *Organizacya i praktyka żydowskich sądów podwojewodzińskich*, Lwów 1903 (Doc. No. 4).

[17] Schorr, *Żydzi w Przemyślu*, Lwów 1903, p. 85.

[18] Bersohn, *Dyplomataryusz*, No. 200.

therefore issued on March 4, 1581, an ordinance addressed to the governor of Lwow, in which he admonished him to find a reasonable solution to the problem. By no means, however, did the King limit the right of ritual slaughter in this ordinance; this is good evidence, of course, that the right in principle was not subject to doubt.[19]

We also discover royal protection of ritual slaughter in a different form. Sometimes the king patronized a Jew and secured for him various privileges; he then protected him against the possibility of being refused some important rights either by governmental agencies or by the Jews themselves. In documents of this kind I have found explicit orders that the purchase of meat must not be refused to the individual concerned; this proves, of course, that the sale of meat produced through ritual slaughter was generally protected by the law. As an example let us quote the privilege granted by King Stephan Batory on July 31, 1578, to his personal physician Solomon Calahora: "The Jews shall not dare," ordered the King, "to refuse him [Calahora] the sale of meat or other ceremonials, as well as all things prepared according to their custom, rites and religious practice, under penalty of a fine of 2,000 florins." [20]

In this way, ritual slaughter was indirectly protected by the State law, because the King, in compelling the Jewish communities to sell to someone meat "prepared according to their custom," ipso facto granted his sanction to the custom itself.

IV. THE PROTECTION OF FUNERAL PROCESSIONS, CEMETERIES AND SYNAGOGUES

The religious form of the funeral procession and the sacredness of synagogues and cemeteries required the protection of governmental authorities, because they could become objects of assault. The statute of Boleslaw the Pious of 1264 gave this protection.

---

[19] The ordinance of March 4, 1581, has been published by Bałaban, *Żydzi Lowowscy*, Document No. 15 (p. 16).

[20] The document was published by Bersohn, *Dyplomataryusz*, No. 165. A study of its significance is contained in my book *Fun Amool un Haint* (Past and Present), Lodz 1939, pp. 36 ss.

The following three stipulations are included in this Statute (and its later confirmations):

(1) The arranging of Jewish funeral processions, "according to their custom," from town to town and even from province to province, was allowed, and no taxes could be exacted. Any tax collector taking payment for funeral processions was to be treated as a robber;

(2) A Gentile damaging or invading a Jewish cemetery would be punished "according to the custom and the law of our country," and his entire property was confiscated for the governmental treasury;

(3) Someone throwing [stones] at a Jewish synagogue was to be punished with a fine of two talents of pepper for the governor of the district.[21]

When King Casimir IV confirmed Jewish rights in 1453, the provisions concerning the protection of funeral processions, cemeteries and synagogues were broadened. Throwing stones at a Jewish cemetery was made a punishable act; removing tombstones, too, was severely forbidden. Furthermore, the King stated that jurisdiction in such cases was to be according to the privileges granted to the Jews, which meant that no legal pretext could be used in order to save the violator of a cemetery.[22] The provision for the protection of synagogues in particular was strengthened.[23]

In 1633 King Wladyslaw IV confirmed the privileges of the

---

[21] *Vol. Leg.*, Vol. I, 312 (also in many other documents, e.g., Bersohn, *Dyplomataryusz*, No. 1).

[22] Gumplowicz, *Prawodawstwo*, p. 167–8. It is interesting to compare the following Latin text of the edict of 1453 with the above quoted text of the statute of 1264 (in its later confirmations); the progress is evident. "Item si aliquis ex Christian ipsorum Judaeorum cemeterium, ubi sit sepultura illorum lapides ibidem violenter ejecerit, seu amoverit, aut alia loca in dicto illorum cemeterio quomodo destruverit, ille quicunque taliter fecerit, res et bona ejus super cameram Nostram Regiam devolvi debebunt. Quo volumus fieri, et debere firmum, secundum jurisdictionem ipsis Judaeis per Nos datam." Bersohn (*Dyplomataryusz*, No. 2), in his edition of the same document, omitted this stipulation.

[23] Besides the expression "temerarie et praesumptuose" with regard to the violator, it is remarkable that the governor ("Palatinus," i.e., the "Voievoda") has been called "ipsorum tutor," which means "their protector." Obviously, the synagogues were then placed under the direct protection of the governors.

Jews in Poland and Lithuania and plainly declared that they might use their synagogues and cemeteries without hindrance. The King mentioned in this edict that in various towns of the Kingdom assaults had taken place on Jewish synagogues, and that he therefore forbade this strongly; he exhorted his governors, as well as the district offices, to protect synagogues against any possible attacks in the future, and to punish all violators severely.[24]

V. THE PROTECTION OF THE JEWISH OATH

In the Middle Ages imposing an oath upon a Jew involved practices intended to humiliate him. Regulations frequently aimed to deprive the Jews of this most important way of giving evidence in legal proceedings.

Duke Bolesław the Pious in his famous statute of 1264 and later King Casimir the Great in his edict of 1364 enacted the basic provisions for the Jewish oath, repeated in many subsequent edicts. It was modeled on the edict of Duke Frederick II of Austria (the "Fredericianum"), and possibly also on the edict of the Czech King Ottakar II of 1254 for the Jews of Prague.

The statute of 1264 distinguishes between two kinds of Jewish oaths. One type was to be used in major cases, the second in minor ones. Major cases were those concerning at least fifty talents of silver or those being judged by the king himself. The other cases were considered minor. The oath in major cases was to be taken *super rodale ipsorum* (on their scroll), while in minor cases *ante scolas, ad hostium dictae scolae* (at the door of the synagogue).[25] These words were so interpreted that in the course of time the oath "more Judaico" developed, offensive to human dignity and to the religious feelings of the Jews. In a

---

[24] The document was published by Bałaban, *Żydzi lwowscy,* Doc. No. 85 (p. 113 ss.) The same king granted in the same year (1633) special confirmation of rights to the Jews of Przemysl, and specifically mentions the right of using synagogues and cemeteries without hindrance. (". . . usum synagogae et loci sepulturae vulgo Kirchow.") Schorr, *Żydzi w Przemyślu,* p. 133.

[25] Biershadski, *Russko-Yevreyskiy Archiv,* Vol. III, Doc. No. 1; *Volumina Legum,* I, 313.

number of edicts, therefore, the Polish kings made clear their opposition to the degrading character of the oath.

No doubt had existed earlier. When Grand Duke Witold of Lithuania granted rights in 1388 to the Jews of Brześć (in a document whose prototype was the statute of Kalisz), he added to the stipulation on the Jewish oath an explanation of the words *super rodale ipsorum.* The explanation read as follows: *hoc est super libris Moyse* (it means on the books of Moses). Clearly the oath had to be taken on the Scroll of the Law.[26]

In the edict of King Casimir IV for the Jews of Greater Poland (1453) the following was added in the stipulation on the Jewish oath: *decem preceptorum secundum consuetudinem ipsorum judeorum.*[27] That meant that the oath had to be taken on the Ten Commandments "according to Jewish custom." The same edict of 1453 also explains the exact form of the oath in minor cases as follows: *ipsi judei super feruncam alias colcze circa scolam in hostio pendentem debebunt jurare secundum morem ipsorum.* These words mean that the oath was taken by seizing the chain on the door of the synagogue; this chain is the *ferunca alias colcze.* The Jew had to touch it and to say thereafter "So help me God." Beside that, Jewish custom had to be strictly observed (*secundum morem ipsorum*). The sexton was called to administer the oath by virtue of a subsequent stipulation in the edict of 1453.

Another edict of King Casimir IV that year used the expression *ad rotulam scolae* (which apparently referred to the door handle of the entrance to the synagogue) when speaking of the oath in minor cases.[28] Practically, there was no difference; the oath in minor cases had to be taken not *in,* but *before* the synagogue, while the oath in major cases had to be taken in the interior of the synagogue, before the Ark with the Holy Scrolls.

A quite different interpretation of the word *"rodale"* de-

---

[26] Bersohn, *Dyplomataryusz,* No. 1.

[27] *Codex Dipl. Maioris Pol.* Vol. III, p. 88 ss.; Bloch, *Die General-Privilegien,* p. 102 ss. Gumplowicz, in his edition of this document (*Prawodawstwo,* p. 163), quotes the expression: "super *fornicem,* alias kolcze."

[28] Bałaban, *Żydzi lwowscy,* p. 316, writes that he was formerly of the opinion that a "rotula" means "mezuzah" (religious scripts for every doorpost), but he found a proof in the "Akta Grodzkie Buseckie," Vol. V, p. 623–4, that the true meaning of "rotula" was a door-handle at an entrance.

veloped under influence from abroad,[29] at the beginning of the sixteenth century. When in 1505 King Alexander fixed the various oath forms, he stipulated concerning the Jewish oath that a Jew had to take it in the following way: he had to turn toward the sun, to stand barefooted on a stool, to put on a coat or a dress, and to have on his head the Jewish hat; then he had to recite a long formula, abundant with imprecations and maledictions against himself should he not tell the plain truth. A few stammers in reciting the oath could cause his condemnation.[30]

Two edicts of King Sigismund August—one of 1551, concerning the Jews of Poznan, and the other of 1553, concerning the Jews of Lwow—deal with the interpretation of *rodale*. The courts were apparently by this time of the opinion that it meant a tripod or a three-legged stool; the oath *super rodale* had, therefore, to be taken *super tripodem*. It was required that a Jew stand with one foot on a tripod or on a three-legged stool; he was not allowed to move when he took the oath, which was, of course, almost a physical impossibility. As a result, a Jew was likely to lose every law-suit when having to give evidence by taking an oath. King Sigismund August explained, therefore, that the expression "rodale" in the statute of Kalisz meant "the Ten Commandments of the Mosaic Law," and thus the oath in major cases had to be taken on the Bible. Sigismund August subsequently specified the reasons for his edict, saying that it was his custom to show grace not only to Christians, but to infidels as well; it seemed to him not fitting that one should be required to perform an act impossible to perform. Therefore, he interpreted the stipulation of the statute of Boleslaw dealing with the oath in a manner favorable to the Jews, and he did so *ex certa scientia* (i.e., on the basis of exact knowledge of the matter); his plain decision was that no Jew should be in major

---

[29] Czacki, *Rozprawa o Żydach,* Chapter VI, stresses that Poland took from Czech law the regulation that a Jew who faltered three times, when reciting the oath, would lose the case.

[30] *Volumina Legum,* I, 337. In the summary ("Inwentarz") to the *Volumina Legum,* s. v. "Przysięga żydowska" (in the Petersburg edition of 1860, p. 390), is published the authentic Polish translation of the oath "more Judaico" which was used in Poland.

cases forced to take any oath other than on the Ten Commandments.[31]

King Stephan Batory, like his predecessors, stipulated in his
edict of 1576 (concerning the Jews of Luck) that in cases in
which the dispute concerned at least fifty pieces of pure silver,
the Jewish oath was to be administered "in the Synagogue, on
the Ten Commandments of God delivered by Moses." On the
other hand, the oath in minor cases was to be taken "on the
chain, before the Synagogue, according to Jewish law." [32] In
addition to this general statement on the form of the Jewish
oath, Stephan Batory had to deal with this matter more than
once in some of his subsequent edicts.

In his edict of 1580 (concerning the Jews of Poznan) he vigorously forbade administering the oath to Jews in an insulting
form not in accordance with "the precepts of the statutes and
the Magdeburg Law." He mentioned in this edict that he, as
well as his royal predecessors, had already stated the right form
of oath: *supra rodale,* when larger amounts are involved (without saying exactly what that greater amount was), and *ad valvas
sinagogae* (at the entrance to the synagogue), in a minor case.
Furthermore, the King detailed the insulting form of the oath
which he forbade in his edict. "Some sly people," he wrote, "are
deterring the Jews from taking an oath and explain the word
'rodale' as the 'skin of a swine'; they force them to swear while
standing on it." This was, according to his opinion, not appropriate. *Rodale* meant the Book of Moses or the Ten Commandments, and on it the Jews should swear, as the King had already
stated in his previous edict.[33]

To force the Jews to stand on the skin of a swine while taking
an oath had long been established in German legal practice.
The law book of the thirteenth century, the "Schwabenspiegel,"
laid down this form as a rule in Art. 263. Other insulting forms

---

[31] The edict of 1551 has been published by Bloch, *Die General-Privilegien,* p.
95–97; the edict of 1553, by Pazdro, *Organizacya i Praktyka,* document No. 3.

[32] Bersohn, *Dyplomataryusz,* No. 152.

[33] The edict was published by Bloch, *Die General-Privilegien,* p. 97–100.
Pazdro, *Organizacya i praktyka,* p. 171, is of the opinion that, although only the
Jews of Poznan were mentioned in this edict, it nevertheless applied to all
Jews in Poland.

of the Jewish oath are of German origin, too. The Silesian Code ("Schlesisches Landrecht," 1422) and especially the "Red Book of Loewenberg" require of a Jew to stand barefooted on a three-legged stool while swearing. The Statute of Dortmund (a code of the thirteenth century) stipulated that should a Jew falter while reciting his oath, he was to be punished by the judge. All those law practices penetrated into Poland and influenced the various interpretations of *rodale* contained in the Polish statutes.[34] King Stephan obviously aimed at eliminating these misinterpretations in his edict of 1580.

It appears, however, that this edict was not sufficient; because in spite of it, when a Gentile placed a Jew on oath, he endeavored to win his case by requesting an oath *more Judaico,* with all its annoying forms. On July 31, 1585, therefore King Batory issued a new edict. He stated that many conflicts would arise between the Jews and the Gentiles concerning the real meaning of the oath *super rodale* in major cases. The Gentiles demanded that some ceremonies once practiced be carried out and that if a Jew failed to perform them he lost the case. What these ceremonies were, the King did not explain, but he stressed that they stood in contradiction to the principles of justice. It seemed to him wrong (*alienissimum esse animadverteremus*) that anyone should lose even the most just case only because of a mistake in a ceremony of no importance and with no bearing on the matter. He probably had in mind the ruling that a stammer or a mistake in reciting the oath by a Jew was cause for losing the case. It is, of course, also possible that he was referring to the aforementioned insulting forms of the Jewish oath (standing on a three-legged stool, or on the skin of a swine). The King emphasized that what he would decide after careful consideration should be strictly observed in actual instances of a Jew's oath. The edicts concerning the form of the Jewish oath were

---

[34] See Scherer, *Die Rechtsverhältnisse der Juden in den deutsch-österreichischen Ländern,* Leipzig, 1901. p. 297. See also Kisch, *Studien zur Geschichte des Judeneides im Mittelalter,* Cincinnati, 1939, p. 441. The Polish historian Czacki in his famous study on the Jews (*Rozprawa o Zydach*), chapter 6, stresses that the stipulations concerning the insulting form of the Jewish oath originated in Greek and Roman law. He reminds us also that Hungarian law knew of a similar regulation; finally, he states that some stipulations were taken over from the Czech law.

obligatory on all authorities as well as on private persons.[35] It appears from the edict that in a few actual cases the King himself had been approached; he decided therefore to stress again the principle of the inadmissibility of annoying Jews while administering the oath.

Stephan Batory's successor, King Sigismund III, stated in his edict of May 27, 1592, that an insulting form of the Jewish oath had been practiced (*supra sedecem seu scabellum in pelle suina*); after quoting his predecessor's edict, he confirmed it on all points.[36]

A year later, on August 31, 1593, King Sigismund III had to deal with this matter once more. "The Jews of Poland," the King wrote (in an edict devoted exclusively to the question of the Jewish oath), "have complained that they are being greatly and heavily molested by the Gentiles, whenever they have to take an oath." The King declared that it was a grievous ancient custom to annoy the Jews with various superstitions and "superfluous and unnecessary ceremonies" when they would take an oath. His predecessor, King Stephan, had forbidden that practice; nevertheless the Jews were still suffering, because the illegal form of oath had not ceased to be required. King Sigismund again explained that *rodale* meant the Ten Commandments, and enjoined all the offices and judges in the Kingdom to protect the Jews against the illegal practice of insulting during the oath and to ensure that the Jews swear only on the Bible.[37]

VI. THE PROTECTION OF JUDICIAL DECISIONS OF JEWISH AUTONOMOUS AUTHORITIES

The kings gave to the judicial decisions, and especially to the sentences of excommunication, of the Jewish autonomous offi-

---

[35] The document was published by Pazdro, *Organizacya i Praktyka*, Doc. No. 7, p. 168 ss.; also by Bałaban, *Żydzi lwowscy*, Document No. 19 C (pp. 22–23). According to Bałaban, this edict was confirmed by King Sigismund III on March 10, 1588.

[36] Pazdro, *Organizacya i Praktyka*, Document No. 8, pp. 169–171; Bałaban, *Żydzi lwowscy*, Document No. 33, pp. 34–36.

[37] Published by Bałaban, *Żydzi lwowscy*, Document No. 35, p. 40. This edict is written in Polish.

cials (rabbis and community leaders) extraordinarily vigorous protection. In many edicts judicial power was granted so extensively to Jewish decisions that these religious regulations carried weight even in local Polish law.

King Sigismund I, in two edicts concerning the designation of Jewish community leaders (as well as in a general statement which laid the basis for all activities of the Polish and Lithuanian rabbis), stipulated clearly the legal consequences if a Jew would be excommunicated. According to these edicts, the State could not be indifferent to insubordination on the part of a Jewish individual towards a decision of his religious authority; it was obliged to use the "secular arm" against him, should he persist in his disobedience. The three edicts are dated August 6, 1527; December 12, 1541; and August 13, 1551.[38] They have been more fully analyzed in my book on *The Jewish Excommunication* (Lwów, 1932).[39] I shall, therefore, only point out some new observations which I have made in connection with the subject of this paper.

It is significant that in the edicts of King Sigismund I it was emphasized that any excommunication executed by the government must be performed in due form according to Jewish law; it must be ordained *iure et legitime Iudaeorum* (in accordance with Jewish law, edict of 1541), or *iuxta ritum et morem legis illorum Mosaice* (in accordance with the ritual and custom of the law of Moses, edict of 1551). In this way, of course, the King protected Jewish law and customs in general. Any defect in excommunication according to Jewish law automatically meant the cessation of sanctions by Polish law.

These sanctions were very grave. In one of the three mentioned edicts (1541) it was stipulated that a fine had to be paid by the excommunicated and disobedient individual; one-half of it to the royal treasury, and one-half to the governor of the district or to the governor of the province concerned with the matter. The other edicts go on much further; they provide

---

[38] The documents have been published in: (1) *Graetz-Jubelschrift*, p. 205–206 (see also Lewin, *Die Landessynode der Grosspolnischen Judenschaft*, Frankfurt a.M. 1926, p. 28); (2) *Archiwum Sanguszkow*, Vol. V, p. 334–337; (3) Biershadski, *Russko-Yevreyskiy Archiv*, Vol. III (Petersburg 1903), No. 153; also Bersohn, *Dyplomataryusz*, No. 57.

[39] Published by Prof. Przemysław Dąbkowski, as Volume X/4 of the series *Pamiętnik Historyczno-Prawny*.

the death penalty together with the confiscation of all of the property of the individual, should he persist one month in his excommunication. It was enough for a denunciation to be made to the executive power that one was stubbornly persisting in his sin for the sanctions of the Polish law to be put into effect.

Let us stress in this connection that the analogous institution of the Catholic Church, ecclesiastical excommunication, was not provided with equal power by the State, although the great majority of the population belonged to the Catholic Church. Royal edicts of 1453 and of 1468, which dealt with the legal consequences of ecclesiastical excommunication, stipulated that not till after an individual would have persisted a whole year in being excommunicated, was the secular power to apply sanctions, and even then the penalty to be imposed was not death but a fine.[40]

The reason the Jewish excommunication was favored has been explained in my aforementioned book. King Sigismund I, who granted to the Jewish excommunication-sentences such a vigorous *bracchium saeculare,* had commanded (in three edicts of 1514) the rabbis of Poland to excommunicate those refusing to pay taxes. The King was therefore extremely desirous that the excommunications should be respected and produce their effect upon the individuals, i.e., they should make the excommunicated Jew pay his taxes. Thus it seemed right to the King to threaten excommunicated Jews with the death penalty and with confiscation of all property for refusing obedience to the decisions of the religious authorities.

Furthermore, several important rights were granted to Jewish officials because of the government's vested interests. King Sigismund August in his edict of 1571 ordered the governors of the provinces not to object to Jewish community leaders, should they punish according to their custom (*iuxta morem suum*) violators of Jewish law (*in legem Judaicam peccantes*). The King stated in the same edict that the Jewish community leaders were entitled to punish their coreligionists with death or banishment from the city. They were therefore given the *jus*

---

[40] *Volumina Legum,* Vol. I, 193–197. See also Dąbkowski, *Litkup,* Lwów 1906, p. 65–66, and Bandtkie, *Prawo Prywatne polskie,* Warsaw 1851, p. 215.

gladii (the right to kill with the sword), and the only condition was that the procedure be in conformity with "Jewish custom" and that the guilty individual should have violated the Jewish law.[41] The protection granted by Polish law to the decisions of the Jewish religious authorities had reached its extreme.

In the royal edicts of the seventeenth century, the prerogative of the Rabbis and community leaders to dispose of the life and the property of their coreligionists was maintained either by granting them the *jus gladii* or by securing the *bracchium saeculare* for the decisions of the religious authorities. King John III Sobieski confirmed in toto (April 28, 1676) the edict of King Stephan Batory in which it had been stipulated that should a Jew be stubbornly disobedient to a decision of a rabbi, he was to be denounced to the king and that he would subsequently be executed and his property confiscated.[42]

Since such strong protection of the excommunication-sentences and other decisions of Jewish authorities had been provided by the royal administration, it occasionally happened that the king felt obliged to interfere in an opposite direction. Sometimes he defended individual Jews against the consequences of an excommunication, or even declared that they should not be excommunicated at all. There are edicts of King Sigismund I, as well as of his successors, named *Litterae exemptionis* (privilege of exemption), by which people singled out by name are exempted from jurisdiction of the rabbis and community leaders. The King stated in these edicts that he did not wish that the privileged person be compelled to do anything "by the law and the custom of the Jews" (so, for example, in the edict of 1507 in favor of the physician Izaczko),[43] or that he forbade proceeding against the privileged person "either by excommunication or by other customs of your law and sect, whatever name they should bear" (so in the edict of 1518 in favor of Abraham Bohemus;[44] similarly in the edict of 1524 in favor of Franczek and Falka of Cracow).[45] King Sigismund I

---

[41] This document was published by Bersohn, *Dyplomataryusz*, No. 138.
[42] Schorr, *Organizacya Żydów w Polsce*, Lwów 1899, p. 19.
[43] Bersohn, *Dyplomataryusz*, No. 11.
[44] Biershadski, *Russko-Yevreyskiy Archiv*, Vol. III, No. 104.
[45] Bersohn, *Dyplomataryusz*, No. 469.

stated in greater detail in his edict of 1528 in favor of Dr. Moses Fishel and his wife Esther: "You (i.e., the Jews) may never compel the above mentioned Moses and his wife by excommunication or by other customs of your Jewish sect, or by laws, or by any other means whatsoever." [46] The King, in enumerating (in addition to excommunication) Jewish customs and laws, plainly acknowledged them; in special cases he nullified their effectiveness, but he did not deny, simultaneously, that in general they were obligatory upon the Jews.

Exact knowledge of Jewish law is to be found in the edict of Sigismund I (1530) in favor of Simon of Korczyn.[47] In this edict the King nullified with respect to the privileged person the effectiveness of any major or minor excommunication based on the law or on a community regulation; he forbade excommunicating him as well as publicizing the excommunication-sentence; finally, he removed the basis of *possible* excommunication, were the privileged person to perform any act automatically setting in motion a sentence of excommunication.

The protection and the safeguarding of the precepts of Jewish law here are quite clear. Individuals were exempted from the large sphere in which Jewish law, by the will of Polish kings, had full power with respect to the Jewish population. The exception proves the rule.

---

[46] Bersohn, *Dyplomataryusz,* No. 480.
[47] Biershadski, *Russko-Yevreyskiy Archiv,* Vol. III, No. 145.

8

Seventeenth Century Padua in the Intellectual Life of Poland

Henryk Barycz

I

Three definite phases stand out in the historical development of Polish-Paduan relations. The first period is the medieval era, whose dominant feature was that it gave Poland cadres of professional intelligentsia, mainly lawyers and physicians. By the XVI century or, to be more precise, from the year 1530, the framework of intellectual influence changed, with wide infiltration of values of general, humanistic culture (philosophy, classical philology, rhetoric and history) through Padua, and the sidetracking of professional studies. This was a period of the most animated contacts and the peak of their intensity in the intellectual life of Poland, coinciding with a basic change in the organization of studies and education in Poland, i.e., the beginning of mass migration in search of knowledge, or the so-called scientific peregrinations to foreign lands. Padua played a dominant and unique role in this movement, and for a short time even held a monopoly on educating the élite of Polish nobility. And although soon (the middle of the XVI century), it had to relinquish its exclusive position, since some of the youth were drawn to the fashionable Protestant universities (Wittenberg, Königsberg, Strasbourg, Basle, Heidelberg, Altdorf), it managed to maintain its attraction and primacy also for people of different religious beliefs.

This second period created a type of Polish "Paduan," a man of broad education, exquisite manners, high social culture, a man who rose above narrow sectarian bounds, devoting himself to service and the public good. The Paduans stuck together, forming a distinct, lofty fraternity, close to each other in spirit, acting in unison to achieve political and cultural aims. It is small wonder that this provoked biting remarks by non-Paduans about "pates cut out of the same Paduan cookie mold."

The third period, the "seicento," created in turn another phase in the history of the "Polish Padua," which was a reflection of the newly developing historical situation. The growing sectarian divisions and rigidity destroyed the cultural syncretism so typical for conditions in XVI century Poland. Now a choice of university was made in keeping with criteria of religious affiliation. For Catholics, the chief places to study became Louvain, Paris, Rome, and for Protestants, Basle, Heidelberg and primarily Leyden.

Padua held an unusual and unique position in this new topography of Polish studies abroad. From the beginning of the XVII century, it clearly became a bridge between the two warring camps, to a certain extent a supra-denominational or inter-denominational center, in which both religious groups met freely and could devote themselves to intellectual endeavors without restrictions. This Utraquist position—from the denominational point of view—was very much strengthened by the foundation of two institutions, which barred Church interference into granting academic degrees: the Venetian College of Artists and Medics (1616), and the Venetian College of Lawyers (1635). The creation of these two colleges—an expression of the wisdom and farsightedness of those at the helm of the Republic of St. Mark—negated the denominational exclusiveness in the field of culture and learning prevalent in the Western world. It confirmed the earlier liberalism and tolerance of the Paduan environment, its independent stand, and finally settled the knotty problem of the flight of non-Catholic students. It is enough to mention that at the College of Artists and Medics alone, forty students from Poland, nearly all dissenters, got their doctoral degrees (including surgeons, forty-four persons).

It is not by chance that the first person to be granted a

doctorate at this College was a Polish citizen from Gdańsk, Daniel Fabricius (June 1, 1616). Among these candidates for doctorate degrees were not only Protestants, but also a handful of Ruthenians who were followers of the Eastern Rite, and a sizeable group of Polish Jews from various parts of the country: Cracow, Poznań, Lublin, Lwów, Brody, Zamość and Wilno.[1] These degrees, no longer achieved only by "barons and earls" were a crucial and momentous phenomenon: they broke the cultural and religious barrier for the Polish Jews, drawing them into the orbit of Western culture and formally gave them an equal status within the student community.

Religious freedom was an important, but not the only factor that attracted the Poles to Padua. At least as decisive was the high scholastic level of the university, its unequalled brilliance and irreproachable renown. It was based on three great fields of learning: mathematics and astronomy (G. Galilei, G. G. Gloriosi, B. Sovero, D. Guglielmini), philosophy (C. Cremonino, C. Berigard), and medicine (B. Selvatico, G. Fabrizio d'Acquapendente, A. Spigel, St. Santorio, G. Vesling, C. Patin). The study of law, in which Padua had excelled a short time earlier, now declined, bowing before such centers as Rome, but even law still continued to have distinguished representatives in Padua (Marcantonio Otellio, J. Gallo, G. Pace).

Among the Poles, the university of Padua continued to enjoy an unshaken fame and authority, as has been confirmed repeatedly by documents from that time. The opinion expressed about Padua by Jerzy Radziwiłł at the end of the XVI century: "Scholae Patavinae, quae non tam pulchrae sunt quam celebres ob clarissimos viros, qui ibi legerunt et legunt," [2] was repeated with the same respect during the following century. Maciej Vorbek Lettow, a man who had attended various universities, wrote as follows: "It would be difficult to enumerate all (the professors), *in omnibus facultatibus* there is a great number of them. So, with the exception of the Paris academy, I do not see

---

[1] The first Jew—a doctor of medicine—to receive his degree in Italy was, it seems, one who was noted in the middle of the XVI century, "Spect. Moises med. doctor Iudaeus de subcastro Lublinensi"; cf. A. Wadowski, *Kościoły lubelskie* (Lublin Churches), Cracow, 1907, p. 29.

[2] The Paduan schools are not so beautiful, but they are renowned for outstanding men who have lectured there.

its equal *in Europa.*" "Celeberrima per universum orbem Universitas Patavina," some high Polish dignitaries called it in 1635. "Virtutis et eruditionis dominicilium . . . quo se omnium Polonorum coniiciat fortuna"—thus was its role defined somewhat later by a representative of the academic youth.

Naturally, the mechanism or myth of tradition also played a part in this admiration for Padua, along with strong attachment to the university responsible for broad intellectual horizons, an institution that since the XIII century had given Poland so many distinguished men in diverse fields of community life. The seventeenth century followers and representatives of the "Polish Padua" still felt this spiritual union with the "lofty" past. Krzysztof Warszewicki, who had spent a great deal of time in Italy, stressed this affinity in his speech to the Republic of Venice at the very beginning of the century, when he again found himself under Italian skies after forty years: "So many foreign peoples and nationalities, especially the Polish youth, owe their intellectual refinement to you."

Another reason for the wholesale influx of Poles to Padua was its international atmosphere—in the full meaning of the word—already a rarity in university circles during that century. Owing to its fortunate geographic position, its independence of thought and its academic renown, the University of Padua managed to maintain the tradition of an international center, the role of a bridge between different worlds—between the West and East, between the Catholic and Protestant camps. Padua was a unique place in the academic community of the time, where the nationalities of all of Europe met, from England and Ireland down to Greece and the Grand Duchy of Muscovy; various denominations and cultures existed side by side. Thus, the saying of that time, that the Padua professors "profiteri in conspectu gentium omnium et nationum" [3] was not a paradox.

This variety of nationalities, denominations, cultures and customs, also apparent in the faculty (it was probably the only university during this century at which representatives of different nationalities taught: French, Portuguese, Germans,

---

[3] "Profess in sight of all tribes and nations," A. Favaro, *L'Università di Padova*, Venice, 1922, p. 55.

Dalmatians, etc.), and even more so in the student body, was most attractive to the Poles who always craved something new. It made possible for them a broad cultural exchange with representatives of various nationalities, enabled them to observe and compare, and drew them out of the isolation and national sequestration in which they found themselves elsewhere. This gave Padua a privileged position in the life of the Polish colony by the Bacchiglione. The Padua students and other visitors from Poland met under various circumstances, at public lectures and private lessons, at university graduations and holidays, in the animated and rich social life with colleagues of other nationalities, forming friendships and scholarly and comradely relations with them.

An example of how close these ties could become was the friendship that developed between the Polish scholar K. Buczacki and the Livonian D. Ricquese at private lessons with Galilei, expressed not only in the correspondence between Ricquese and Buczacki conducted from Constantinople, where the former had gone from Padua, but also in the expedition of Ricquese together with an itinerant Scottish poet, Thomas Seghet, to Poland (in 1611). This was not an isolated event. There were more such trips to Poland as a result of foreigners' contacts with Poles abroad, to mention only one—the visit of the Cretan Jewish physician, Solomon Joseph Delmedigo.

Finally, Padua created unusually favorable living and learning conditions, which also served as a magnet. "A great . . . ancient . . . city, only not so populous, not so large, but fertile and convenient to live in"—this is how a keen observer, later a high state dignitary, Jakub Sobieski, father of King Jan III, characterized Padua. "If anywhere in Italy, then at this academy, a great multitude of students is gathered, particularly foreigners, partly because of the reasonable board, partly because of the quiet and modest lodgings, not so expensive as in other Italian cities." This opinion of "smaller outlay" was fully confirmed by a contemporary impecunious burgher. And actually, as we know from the diary of one of the scholars from the year 1665, forty gold zlotys sufficed for a whole year's board in Padua.[4]

---

[4] B. Wojciechowski, *St. Wosiński, lekarz XVII stulecia* (St. Wosiński, Physician of the Seventeenth Century), Warsaw, 1897, p. 11.

To this were added other financial and scholastic amenities offered by the Paduan Athenaeum. Naturally, it was very significant that both public lectures and private lessons were given free of tuition. The arrivals from the north were pleasantly struck by the close, affectionate attitude toward the students, borderin on familiarity, the easy access to the professors and the custom of collectively escorting them to the lectures and back home, the fine, effective presentation of scientific material at the lectures. The faculty's quest for popularity among the students and obvious desire to win them over were partly caused by the great competition that existed among the Paduan professors . . .

These conditions constituted quite a lure for the ultramontanes who arrived at this ideal place to study already "exhausted by the long journey and sufficiently crushed by its expenses," as one of these peregrinators noted, or as the poet Stanisław Serafin Jagodyński wittily put it, "with a lofty disposition, but with an empty, rather than ample purse, either fleeced by robbers, or bamboozled by money changers." Because this was a constant affliction—the instability of currency, frequent monetary fluctuations, "(their) price, sometimes smaller, sometimes greater, on which we had to lose a little at the exchange in Venice"—complained one of the travelers.

The mirage of financial relief granted by the university meant a great deal, especially the relative ease with which exemption from the fees for taking the doctoral degree or a reduction in the fees was granted, on the basis of an oath sworn by witnesses concerning the limited means of the applicant. And the fee was large, amounting to 50 gold złotys, or the equivalent of the cost of a year's stay in Padua.[5] While the reductions offered were tied to an obligation of the doctoral candidate to return this sum after achieving his financial equilibrium, who would worry about the future! And there probably were not many who treated this obligation too seriously. But they did retain this benevolent arrangement in their

---

[5] The conferments of doctors' degrees in theology were somewhat less expensive; a preserved record of conferment of a doctor's degree in theology on Augustyn Zegart, dated September 23, 1649 (Archivio antico dell'Università, manuscript No. 426), contained a detailed account of fees for conferment of a doctor's degree amounting to 272 lire in all, i.e., 18 ducats.

grateful memories as *"mater omnium,* particularly *pauperum,* used to *ultramontanis inopia laborantibus succurrere hac singulari gratia et liberalitate,* that she *promovet* them for free, without any payment, if only they were *digni."*

Besides all of these virtues of Padua—scholastic, cultural, the favorable living conditions—there was still another: the proximity of Venice, which held an irresistible allure for Polish students and travelers. The city of lagoons enticed them by its big-city chic and gaiety, the splendor and grandeur of its private life, the magnificent pomp and ceremony of public life, the possibility for interesting encounters. The famous Venetian carnival with its merry-making and frantic fun made a tremendous impression and is reflected in the memoirs of Polish travelers of the time. "They have strange *voluptates* in masquerades, in which even staid citizens take part during this time; it is a period when ladies have a great deal of freedom, loose conversations are carried on in the most cavalier fashion during these days . . . Most of the carnival is spent in music of all kinds at the piazza San Marco. They also have *Caccie* here in a few places, where they bait oxen and bears with mastiff dogs and cut off the head of the ox *uno ictu in praesentia* of the prince in front of the palace."

Apart from all these amusements (theaters, spectacles) and exotic atmosphere, the unique fascination and incomparable charm of the capital of St. Mark also played a vital role. Already at the beginning of the century, K. Warszewicki stressed this when he said: "The city of Venice is considered a wonder of the world; everywhere, in all sorts of places, it enjoys an established fame as a city strong in military resources and excelling in affluence." "Venezia, chi te non vede, non te pregia" (Venice, those who do not see you, do not fully appreciate you), another Polish traveler noted in 1663 in his travel diary.

These Venetian excursions and contact with the city of lagoons were facilitated by the ease of communication, a kind of water stagecoach travelling between Venice and Padua two times a day, in the morning and the evening: namely a bark drawn by horses through the canals. The cost of the trip was two lire, i.e., a little less than one eighth of a ducat.

II

Organizationally, the Poles gathered around the Polish students guild. At the end of the XVI century (1592), it underwent a basic reorganization. Then a new statute (later supplemented) was approved, and a register was introduced (a similar register was adopted by the English guild a little later, in 1616), along with a record of the minutes of the meetings. This was a period of regeneration of Polish student organizations in Italy generally: in Bologna in 1600, and a little later in Perugia.[6] Rome, which had a Polish national home, did not establish a separate guild.

The great influx of Polish travellers to the town of Antenor, not only students, but also state dignitaries, diplomats, Church dignitaries and habitués of all sorts, who stopped there for cultural reasons, for the atmosphere of the place, for their health (the Abano thermal baths), rest or recreation, produced a characteristic change in the organizational structure of the guild. From a medieval, purely academic association, formed to represent Polish students before the university authorities, it now became an organization covering all Poles visiting Padua, students and non-students, a kind of mutual aid and custodial fraternity, and at the same time an administrative organ of the university.

The Polish guild was a national-state organization in Padua with full autonomy. However, it did have a so-called protector, or as we would say today—faculty adviser, elected for life, in the person of one of the professors of medicine. The first of these was B. Selvatico, then H. Frizimeliga, H. Spinella (from 1692), the Frenchman Charles Patin (elected in March 1693, he died at the end of that year), and finally Alexander Borrhomaeus. But this was an honorary patronage in the full meaning of the term. The protectors practically did not interfere in the affairs of the guild; what is more, some of them were protectors of several other guilds at the same time. To remind. Pro-

---

[6] M. Bersohn, *Studenci polscy w Uniwersytecie Bolońskim w XVI i XVII w* (Polish Students at Bologna University in the XVI and XVII Centuries), part II, Cracow, 1895; about the Polish guild in Perugia, see G. Ermini, *Storia della Università di Perugia*, Bologna, 1947, p. 377.

fessor Frizimeliga of his duties, the association ingeniously resolved to hang the guild emblem on his house. His predecessor, the renowned physician Benedetto Selvatico, was remembered more kindly, and it was probably because of his patronage over the guild that he received the title of court physician to King Władysław IV.

The only people to remain outside the guild were the Polish Jews, who as a rule lived in the Padua ghetto and, since they did not belong to the guild, enrolled in the general university roster on the strength of permission granted (*ex ordine*) by the Paduan chief magistrate. Students hailing from Royal Prussia and also some from Ducal Prussia enrolled either in the Polish or the Germanic guild; as did the Livonians and the Kurlanders. Some Ruthenians indicated their distinctness by signing their names in Cyrillic (in 1616, Jeremonah Jezechiel Kurczewicz, with his own hand), or by the addition of Roxolanus, Rutenus, Muschus. Others, like the three Wiśniowieckis: Jeremi Michał, Aleksander Korybut and Jerzy Korybut, did not emphasize their membership in the Eastern Church or their Ruthenian origin. Sometimes, people also joined the overseas (*ultramarina*) guild. Once even (in 1690), the Ruthenian Rusianowicz, after defeating the Armenian Jakub Minasowicz in the elections, achieved the office of "councilor," i.e., the head of the Polish guild; but he was elected on the condition that he would not enter the Greek College and would not enroll in its register. The fact that more than a dozen or so Silesians joined the Polish guild is also significant.

During the XVII century, the Polish guild had exactly 1946 members. Of these, 1329 joined in the first half of the century, and the rest in the second. Among these 1946 [7] there were about 1627 matriculating students, while the rest were short-term visitors or personages not connected with studies. The number of 1946 matriculated students does not cover all visitors from Poland (here, of course, we exclude Polish monks), both students and non-students. An example is the renowned

---

[7] For comparison it is worthwhile to add that the album of the English guild in Padua for the years 1618–1700 shows 1124 entries, H. F. Brown, "Inglesi e Scozzesi all'Università di Padova dal anno 1618 sino al 1765." *Monografie storiche sullo Studio di Padova*, Venice, 1922, pp. 143–182.

alchemist Mikołaj Sedziwój, who was in Padua in 1623. Some 25–30 percent of matriculated students did not join the guild. In any case, Padua was among the most populous Polish student centers abroad in the XVII century. To illustrate the strength of the Polish element in Padua, it is worth noting that at Leyden University, so popular among the Polish cultural élite, 557 Poles, 749 Lithuanians and Prussians (from both Prussias) and 149 Livonians studied during the entire century. Their participation was even more modest in Basle University, fashionable until a short time earlier, at which only 124 Poles (together with their retinue, not all of Polish origin) and 53 students from Western Prussia [8] enrolled by 1654.

At that time, the Polish guild was one of the strongest student associations in Padua, and it tried to take advantage of this situation accordingly. In 1615, it undertook intense action, modeled on the German guild—the most powerful one in Padua—to acquire the privilege of enrolling its members in the general university register entirely through its agency, and received initial permission from the Venetian doge. This resulted in energetic counter-action by the university authorities. The guild returned to this matter years later in a completely changed situation (in the years 1658 and 1671), passing the necessary resolutions.

The power of the guild at the beginning of the century was manifested in positions secured in the general-university management. In November 1604, Paweł Boym of Lwów was elected syndic (legal adviser) and pro-rector of the University of Artists and Medics, receiving all votes save one. An even more important achievement of the guild was the acquisition of the presidency of this university in 1605—a distinction that fell to Samuel Słupecki, an individual of high culture who hailed from an intellectual Protestant family with ties to French and Dutch culture.

The Polish guild, composed of four strata, was an interesting association from the social and sociological points of view. Its

---

[8] As the album of the Polish guild in Bologna indicates, only 389 persons joined it in the first half of the XVII century—we have entries only for this period.

nucleus was formed by two groups: students of noble origin, who constituted the majority of the guild, and a sizeable part of burgher intelligentsia (professors and doctors of Cracow University and a few from the Zamoyski Academy). The third group was composed of ecclesiastical and lay dignitaries, whose "exotic splendor of purple dress" entranced the eyes of the locals and the visitors; among these must be included a considerable group of the king's courtiers, especially secretaries who came in particularly large numbers during the reign of Władysław IV (1633–1648). The fourth element, especially numerous in the second half of the century, was composed of the monks.

The attachment of many families—senatorial, noble and burgher—to Padua is astounding. They sent their sons there from generation to generation. In various periods we find whole clans of Opalińskis, Leszczyńskis, Ostrorogs, Działyńskis, Weihers, Denhoffs, Ossolinskis, Zamoyskis—the son of the Grand Chancellor Thomas (1617) spent time here, then on two occasions (1643 and 1645) Jan, his grandson called Sobiepan, Adam Zółkiewski, then the mighty Lithuanian families of Pac, Sapieha, Naruszewicz, Wołłowicz; among the burghers we can cite the example of the Boyms—three generations of this family were represented during this century: Paweł, vice-president in 1604, his son Paweł Konstanty (1636), and grandson Michał Mikołaj (1677)—and the Alempeks, Szolcs, Wolfowiczs, etc.

A reflection of the peaceful coexistence of the two groups: the plebeian and noble, was the frequent exercise of the function of councilors, assessors and librarians by the burgher intelligentsia. Neither did the Church and State dignitaries stay away from the guild. Not only did they add splendor to the guild meetings by their presence and take the floor at such gatherings, but in case of need, when the normal life of the guild subsided because of the lack of leadership, they assumed patronage over the property and possessions of the guild, as well as its interests and affairs (for instance the Bishop of Poznań, Andrzej Opaliński did this, and so did the long-time representative of Poland to the Venetian government, the Bishop of Samogitia, Mikołaj Pac). In exceptional cases, such as the time of the expected arrival of the king's son, Władysław Waza, in Padua in March 1625, they formally took over the vacant councillor's office (e.g., Aleksander Deodat Sapieha, Oszmiany subprefect). Some senators felt it to be their duty to watch over and take under their protection the activities of the guild. In August 1635, at the annual meeting of the guild members, there appeared two dignitaries, the Bishop of Kujawy, W. Sokołowski, and the castellan of Poznań, W. Tuczyński, who drew up the basic code of behavior for the guild and its members, consistent with national honor.

Like all associations, the Polish guild in Padua had its periods of flowering and vigor, and then periods when it subsided and even died altogether a few times (1631–1633, 1671–1674). This depended on various circumstances, namely on the personal enterprise and energy of the representatives of the guild, (Michał Mikołaj Boym of Lwów, and Felicjan Łukasiewicz were such councillors), on the flux—the ebb and flow and sometimes total lack of members caused by local factors (plagues, wars) and also the political situation in Poland. In all, despite its inevitable shortcomings, the guild formed a vital and basic element in the development of the Polish colony in Padua, around which all of its life centered.

III

What were the course and the results of studies at Padua like?

Of the humanities, which a century earlier had been the main interest of the Polish Paduans—such subjects as rhetoric, classical philology and history—disappeared entirely from the curriculum. Nor did the study of politics, fashionable in the XVII century, take hold there. Only the renowned Paduan school of philosophy, which played such a significant role in the creation and shaping of the Italian "seicento," did not lose its vitality. Cesare Cremonino exerted a particularly strong influence here; his personality left a distinct mark on the intellectual development of his Polish followers and worshippers. Cremonino's popularity was heightened by his sincere Polonophilism and the benevolence he displayed toward Polish scholars. There was no graduation, dispensation from tuition, or presentation at which this philosopher did not appear in support of his pupils from the north.

Cremonino enjoyed great popularity both as a man and as a professor. "Among philosophers, Cremoninus was *primus.* He *philosophiam discipulis dictabat* not from notes made at home, but from memory, as sometimes the priest preaches from the pulpit, a wonderful *ingenium!*"—wrote one of his students. It was certainly under his guidance that Jerzy Ossoliński prepared *Questiones ethicae,* which he planned to publish and which he kept in manuscript form for a long time among his papers (even when he was chancellor). A particular admirer and devoted listener to his lectures for the whole four years of his stay in Padua (1620–1624) was Jan Brożek; he even attended some lectures twice. Cremonino was an ideal to Brożek and a model of scholarly bearing. Brożek was familiar with everything that the beloved master did and wrote, including his last will and testament, in which Cremonino clarified his scientific position and conduct.

The influence of Cremonino was apparent not only in philosophical views, but also in inculcating the spirit of open-mindedness and independent thought. His anti-Jesuit interventions to the government of the Republic of Venice crystallized and confirmed the anti-Jesuit stand of Brożek and finally inspired him to write his incomparable anti-Jesuit lampoon entitled *Gratis* (1625). Obviously, the writings and activity of Cremonino were not the only source of libertinism. Events that took place in the Republic of St. Mark, such as the expulsion of the Jesuits and the conflict of Venice with the Pope, the activities of the herald and theoretician of the idea of the separation of Church and State, Fra Paolo Sarpio (echoed in the writings of Brożek), also strongly influenced the position of some of the Polish Paduans. An interesting manifestation of this atmosphere of religious liberalism and anti-Jesuit tendencies is a work preserved in one of the Paduan collections dated 1606, *Due discorsi sopra la libertà ecclesiastica* by Giovanni Simone Sardi, with an interesting anti-Jesuit annex by a Pole, *Condoglienza di St. Prz(e)vvovski Lublinese, studente in Padova col Padre Antonio Possevino Giesuita.* So far it has been impossible to identify the author. Most probably, he used a pseudonym.

At the turn of the XVI and XVII centuries in Padua, relations developed between the Poles and Galilei.[9] This is an important page in the history of Poland's scientific culture, one that brought a breath of fresh air to Polish thinking, putting it in contact with crucial discoveries and conquests of science, broadening horizons, but one that unfortunately was not exploited, owing to the specific Polish social and intellectual situation.

Quite early the Poles were fascinated by Galilei's scope and sweep of mind, and cognitive inquiries, and thus they sought to get closer to him. The meeting ground of the Poles with Galilei was not so much his formal lectures devoted to the interpretation of the traditional astronomy of Ptolemy, as private lessons taken individually or in small groups in various fields of mathematics, physics, mechanics, geodesy, cosmography together with the study of the sphere, or physical geography, military engineering (*architectura militaris*) and astronomy with the use of instruments. We know of nearly twenty Polish pupils of the great scholar from the years 1601–1609; some of them sons of magnates, such as Rafał Leszczyński, Krzysztof Zbaraski, Marcin Zborowski, some sons of the wealthy and influential nobility, and finally some representatives of the higher clergy (the abbot of Trzemeszno, Wojciech Mileński), but among them there were also members of the intelligentsia, such as the physician and poet Daniel Naborowski, tutor to Leszczyński, or a student by the name of Doniec.

The scope of study was manifold; depending on the interests of the student, the amount of time and money at his disposal, he either confined himself to the basics of the given subject, or delved into it more deeply. To facilitate the financing of the lessons, groups of four, composed of various nationalities, were formed. Exceptionally, in 1607, the study of the sphere was undertaken by as many as seven Polish students.

Among the most enthusiastic students of Galilei was Rafał Leszczyński, a man of keen and creative cultural interests. Krzysztof Zbaraski was also an eager pupil, who studied here

---

[9] The account of relations of the Poles with Galilei has been based on material contained in the publication: G. Galilei, *Opere,* Ed. nazionale, vols. I–XX. See also A. Wołyński, "Stosunki Galileusza z Polską" (Relations of Galilei with Poland), *Tygodnik Ilustrowany* (Illustrated Weekly), 3, V 1878.

intermittently (1602, 1604–1605), taking lessons together with the study of astronomical instruments. He rewarded the master generously, paying him 820 lire in all. After his return to Poland, he retained Galilei vividly in his memory, and recalled affectionately *la sua dolcissima conversazione.* He read with emotion the news sent to him by a friend from Padua about Galilei's discovery of four moons, satellites of Jupiter (the so-called Medicean stars), entitled *Sidereus nuntius,* from the year 1610 . . . When he came to Italy at the beginning of 1611, Zbaraski stopped in Padua to see Galilei. Discovering to his sorrow that the master had left the Paduan Atheneum, he tried to establish contact with him in Bologna. But at that time all efforts to reach Galilei turned out to be futile. When Zbaraski returned to Italy the following year, he renewed his efforts, and set a date to see the master in Florence.

The future secretary of Zygmunt III, Marek Lentowicz, also remained under the irresistible spell of Galilei's genius. He took private lessons with the master (mechanics), and then became his lodger. After he returned to Poland in May 1604, he soon wrote Galilei an adulatory letter expressing his deep admiration for "giving a direction to his education and sharing his home with him for a few months, as well as for tried and true love and good will." He also wrote of his desire to greet Galilei in Poland.

The most fervent follower of the teachings of Galilei was Stanisław Lasocki from Glew. He already came across the modern problems of the science of mathematics during his studies in Würzburg with an outstanding professor in the subject, Adrian von Roomen. After his arrival in Padua, he continued his studies in the years 1602–1603 with Galilei, taking a course in mechanics, the use of astronomical instruments, and military engineering. He devoted the considerable sum of 675 lire to these studies.

The most convenient way for getting close to the master and taking advantage of his learning was lodging with him. Maintaining lodgings by outstanding professors and scholars was common in the West since the XVI century. The most famous intellectual potentates, even the great Erasmus of Rotterdam, received students into their homes for board and lodgings, thus considerably increasing their meager professorial salaries or authors' royalties (and miserable they were, indeed!). It was a

costly undertaking, without doubt, but had undeniable intellectual advantages. It was a great distinction, and gave the opportunity to boast later at home of having been a pupil and protégé
of such a celebrity. Finally, it was a conscious patronizing ges-
ture. The *dozzimenti*, i.e., lists of accounts of Galilei, preserved
for the years 1602–1609, indicate that the boarding house was
the most profitable venture of the great astronomer, in which
his Polish pupils prominently participated. It is enough to say
that during two "fat" years—1602–1604—the Polish lodgers
brought 5725 lire into Galilei's budget, while lessons given during the years 1601–1608 to Polish pupils brought him an income a little under 3000 lire (exactly 2769 l.). The monthly cost
of room and board (*le spese ordinarie*) came to 80 lire, to which
were added small sums for *le spese straordinarie*. Stanisław
Lasocki (commonly called signor Stanislao Polacco), together
with his companion Paweł Palczowski, well-known author of
Status Venetorum (A Description of the Venetians) spent the
longest time as Galilei's lodger, i.e., 21 months. The cost of this
stay, from the beginning of December 1602 to the beginning of
September 1604, came to 3752 lire. Shortly after Lasocki and
Palczowski, Marek Lentowicz arrived at the boarding house
(from January 8 to September 8, 1603). In May of that year,
Giovanni Lituano, i.e., Jan Pac, stopped briefly at the house of
Galilei, for 18 days. At the end of that year, signor conte di
Zator—Paweł Leśnowolski—with an imposing retinue of three
noble companions and five servants, crossed the threshold of
Galilei. He spent two months in these lodgings, paying the sum
of 1279 lire.

The scientific influence of Galilei also was expressed in the
fact that his pupils bought the mathematical and astronomical
instruments produced under the guidance of the great scholar
since 1597. Their sale constituted a certain part in the income
of the great astronomer (518 lire). The diffusion of these instruments, coupled with the necessary oral and written explanation, was a source of pride for Galilei. He stressed this fact in
his polemics with Baldassar Capra in 1607; boasting of this
form of scientific propaganda, he named, along with titled and
sovereign Italian and foreign princes (German, French), as
many as three Polish dignitaries who owned his instruments:

Jan Tęczyński, Kryzsztof Zbaraski and Rafał Leszczyński; [10] W. Mieleński and M. Zborowski also purchased them.

Although these Polish contacts with Galilei and his scientific thought were—let us not deceive ourselves—of an amateur-dilettante character, and in the final reckoning did not give impetus to independent research in Poland, nevertheless undoubtedly they brought a fresh breath and gave people the opportunity to find out about the newest scientific discoveries at the source. They proved useful to Galilei himself, bringing him from his Polish followers and admirers—for lessons, lodging and instruments—the considerable sum of more than 9000 lire.

With Galilei's departure from Padua, easy access of Polish students and intellectuals to this great mathematician ceased. But Galilei's tradition remained, and J. Brozek referred to it in 1621, when he wrote from Padua in June 1621 his well-known letter to the author of the *Sidereus nuntius* (The Silver Messenger) with the news of the monograph on Copernicus he was preparing and expressions of homage. A few years later, because of this tradition, another outstanding Polish physicist and mathematician, Stanisław Pudłowski (1625), stopped in the city of Antenor.

Enthusiasm for the mathematical-physical sciences and the study of these disciplines by Polish scholars were not confined to relations with Galilei. This was still apparent in the second half of the century, as indicated by the fact that a professor of mathematics, Stefan degli Angeli, one of the favorite pupils of Cavalieri, introduced into his five dialogues *Della gravità dell-ariae flendi esercitato principalmente nelle loro homogenei* (Padua 1671–1672), an interlocutor in the person of "Count" Leszczyński.

A characteristic feature of the general studies of Polish youth, particularly those of a noble or aristocratic background, was the frequent combining of various, usually quite diverse fields of knowledge (e.g., the study of law with mathematics and anatomy). This is how Bogusław and Jan Leszczyński and the

---

[10] *Difesa di Galileo Galilei, Nobile fiorentino . . . contro alle calumnie et imposture di Baldassar Capra Milanese* (Defense of Galileo Galilei, a Nobleman of Florence, against all Calumnies and Frauds of Baldassar Capra of Milan), Venice, 1607.

castellan's sons Wojciech and Andrzej Radoliński (1663) chose their subjects; the latter two were especially interested in anatomy. "*Anatomiae lectiones* were given here in our time, at which *librum naturae* was explained; we were *praesentes* every day, observing in the human body the strange disposition from God and nature."

The strength of the intellectual influence of Padua was not only in the tuition-free general education studies. It was just as strongly pronounced in professional training. Of all foreign academic centers in the XVII century, two universities were in the forefront as suppliers of professional intelligentsia for Poland: the Roman Sapienza, which rendered nearly two hundred doctors of law in the years 1601 to 1690 (exactly 184); and Padua, which educated nearly the same number (at least 163) of medical doctors. The Sacro Collegio dei Artisti e Medici graduated 124 persons in the field of medicine or medicine and philosophy, while the Collegio Veneto dei Artisti, 39 doctors of medicine and philosophy, 2 of philosophy and 2 surgeons. The education of so many physicians makes Padua absolutely the greatest supplier of the Polish health service of that century. Let us also add an indirect, but nevertheless important contribution of the Paduan Atheneum—that these graduated physicians were 100 percent of burgher origins. Most of them came to Padua already with doctorates of philosophy (104 of 163), and often also with teaching experience from one of two Polish universities—mainly Cracow and the Zamoyski Academy.

The domain of the medical arts was wholly taken over by the plebeian element, which really created for itself the possibility of social advancement. It was not a vain boast on the part of the former Paduan vice-rector (and doctor of medicine himself). Paweł Boym when he declared in his last will and testament: "Because for us, people *plebeiae conditionis* (*medicina*) is *honorifica, utilis* and *gloriosa*." Declassé representatives of the nobility also undertook the study of medicine, as e.g., Wawrzyniec Braun (in 1649), the court physician of three kings: Jan Kazimierz, Michał and Jan III; a little earlier (1644–1646), the well-known writer Aron Aleksander Olizarowski studied medicine in Padua.

Via the Paduan physicians, progressive medical ideas seeped through to Poland. The popularity of Paduan medical studies was based (along with the possibility of obtaining great reductions in tuition fees), primarily on the modernity of its medical school, which combined theoretical studies with practical observations and demonstrations, including surgical procedures.[11] Especially anatomy, which from January 1595 had the first permanent amphitheater in the central building of the university *al Bo,* enjoyed great favor and even students who did not devote themselves professionally to medical studies participated in experiments in dissection. In contrast with the XVI century, anatomical studies made great strides and formed the basis of medical education.

Enthusiasm for surgery and anatomy soon brought the Polish medical students together with a distinguished representative of this branch of science, "more than a professor-in-ordinary"—Hieronim Fabrizio d'Acquapendente, the creator of the first Polish anatomy school. The following people took part in this school: Joachim Olhafius, the city physician of Gdańsk, whom the historians of medicine credit with the honor of performing the first human autopsy in Central Europe in the West European manner (Gdańsk, 1613), Jan Ursinus, the publisher of anatomical and embryological works of the master (*De locutione et eius instrumentis liber,* Venice 1601, *De creatione,* 1601, *Opera omnia anatomica,* 1603), Dominik Hepner, Szymon Birkowski, Maciej Vorbek Lettow, later court physician to Władysław IV, the first professors of anatomy at Cracow University— Piotr Mucharski and Maciej Woniejski. They spread the fame of the master throughout the country. Even the leaders of the Polish government curried his favor: Chancellor Jan Zamoyski and King Zygmunt III himself sought his medical counsel. After the death of Fabrizio, anatomical knowledge was sought from his equally renowned successors, the Belgian Adrian Spinela, the German Johann Vesling and the Frenchman Charles Patin.

The medical studies of Polish physicians in the XVII century, in contrast with earlier centuries, were thorough, and as a rule

---

[11] In this connection, the holder of a fellowship from J. Zamoyski, J. Ursinus, of whom we already know, asked his protector on March 23, 1601 to send him money for the purchase of the surgical instruments he needed. (Manuscript of the Zamoyski Library.)

lasted from 3 to 5 years. They included an extended post-graduate internship in practical medicine in Padua or Venice, or else in Roman hospitals (in the famous S. Spirito in Sassia hospital). Thus they returned to Poland with a good preparation and familiarity with the newest medical discoveries. Two salient facts throw light on this modern approach. Marcin Leszczyna of Cracow, graduated October 10, 1658, had William Harvey's work, *De motu cordis*,[12] in his library.

Another Cracovian, Stanisław Wosiński, who graduated exactly eight years later (October 19, 1666), in the years 1671 to 1689 conducted the first, naturally still very primitive, anatomopathological dissections in Poland. Eleven reports of these autopsies, conducted on both men and women, some of them prominent personalities (Prince Ostrogski, Starost Morsztyn), have been preserved. It is small wonder that the Paduan doctors enjoyed great esteem; most of them achieved the position of court physicians or royal secretaries.

But it must be admitted that this group lacked greater creative talent of the caliber of J. Struś in the preceding century; in all fairness, we have to add that conditions in Poland were not conducive to original research. The awakened interest and enthusiasm slackened, and instead of pure research, people succumbed to the prevailing trend of writing mediocre panegyrics or else kept silent. Some switched to theological or legal studies and acquired new doctorates in them. Others remained with their favorite science of mathematics (J. Brożek, M. Żórawski, J. Toński, doctor of both laws), and could not be persuaded to try for medical teaching positions.

Jan Ursinus, diligent and devoted student of Hieronim d'Acquapendente, professor and several times president of the Zamoyski University (died in 1613), did not rise to the occasion and was not very active in the field of medicine in Poland. A classical philologist rather than a biologist and physician, he was noted for the publication of only one short treatise in the field of the anatomy of the skeletal system (*De ossibus humanis tractatus III*, Zamość, 1610), which is most interesting in the parts in

---

[12] J. Lachs, *Krakowskie ksiegozbiory lekarskie z XVII w.* (The Cracow Medical Libraries of the Seventeenth Century), Lwów, 1930, p. 92.

which it introduces a Polish nomenclature for bones (among other things, he initiated the use of dialectical terms, e.g., the Mazovian dialect word "mozgokryjka" for skull). His companion at the Zamoyski University, Szymon Birkowski, also demonstrated his devotion to philology; the domain of philology, particularly the study of Plutarch, was also the initial field of interest of Maciej Woniejski, until the lucrative possibilities of the medical field induced him to seek a medical doctorate in Padua.

However, the rejection of the study of law by the Polish scholars in Padua, which still in the XVI century enjoyed a great success among them, is clearly evident. Rome now became the most popular place to study law, breaking all records in this respect. That is why in the XVII century, Padua could only boast of a trifling number of 27 doctors of law. Of these, only two doctor's degrees are of any historical interest, namely that of Jan Markiewicz (1635), later a well-known anti-Jesuit polemist, and Bogusław Leszczyński, a Cracow canon and rector of Płock, the last member of this powerful clan, already converted to Catholicism, to attend the university of Padua. Leszczyński received his doctor's degree in accordance with the new ceremonial *more nobilium cum immunitate argumentorum* in 1666. Theological studies remained rather insignificant: during the whole century only eight doctor's degrees were conferred in theology. The only interesting personality in this field who contributed to the culture of his time was Mikołaj Słowikowski (graduated in 1654), the archpriest of the Church of Our Lady of Cracow.

IV

The normal university studies were not the only stimuli, inspiration and cultural values gained in Padua. Other important fields, not in the university curriculum, also came into play, such as theater, familiarity with the life, economy, customs, culture and form of government of the Republic of St. Mark, knowledge of written and spoken Italian, book collecting, an increase in artistic sensitivity. This is not the place to examine in detail this other, extramural cultural side of the stay in Padua, as it would require extensive research. But it is hard to resist citing a few examples of the importance of these phenomena for the intellectual climate of the Paduan environment and the extent of their influence. It is also absolutely necessary to correct the harsh and unfair judgment of the monographer of XVI century Polish Padua, S. Windakiewicz, about the pedestrian atmosphere and alleged corruption, the exterior pomposity and refinement that supposedly were characteristic of the mentality of the Polish Paduans.[13]

The stay in Padua was indissolubly connected with the command of the Italian language, which in the XVII century was considered a programmatic and vital element of a higher intellectual cultivation. Thus, even students who spent years of study at university centers outside of Italy, once they arrived there, learned Italian in a hurry, either in the city of the most beautiful Italian pronunciation—Siena—(like Jakub Sobieski), or in Padua (like Jerzy Ossoliński, "practising his knowledge of the Italian here"). The Polish guild maintained a special teacher for this language. One of them, Giovanni Rassin, dedicated his textbook of the Italian language—*Elementorum linguae Italicae*—to Bogusław and Jan Leszczyński in 1663. It must be added that just the stay in Padua, lasting for several years, moving in Italian circles, brought a thorough written and verbal knowledge of the language, as evidenced by many sources.

But it is more difficult to establish the degree of native or acquired familiarity with belles-lettres or scientific writing. We know that XVII century Polish writers, Padua students or residents such as Piotr Kochanowski, Stanisław Serafin Jagodyński, Krzysztof and Łukasz Opaliński, were expert in Italian literature. Inventories of XVII century Polish libraries also indicate that Italian scientific works dominated, ensuring Italian thought vitality and a lasting influence in Poland.

It is worthwhile to add that the Venetian-Paduan center represented the ideal reservoir of book collections, especially tempting for Polish bibliophiles of the period. Jan Brożek was such a passionate book hunter. Throughout his stay in Padua, he lived under difficult financial conditions, counting every

---

[13] S. Windakiewicz, *Padwa, Studium z dziejów cywilizacji polskiej* (Padua, A Study from the History of Polish Civilization), Cracow, 1891, p. 3.

penny. He gave lessons, gave up trips to Rome and Naples, just so he could buy as many books as possible. He bought them not only for practical use, but equally for their artistic or documentary value. He rummaged out incunabula, beautifully illustrated manuscripts (e.g., a well-known copy of the cosmography of Ptolemy from the year 1472, now in the Jagellonian Library), Italian *polonica,* paying huge sums in relation to his possibilities. He made some mysterious exchanges, and generally managed to ferret out the specimen he desired from friends by whatever means he could, even hounding Paduan professors for books (e.g., law professor Aleksander Synglitico for a copy of Diophant's arithmetic). And although he left some of the books he collected as a gift to the guild library, he also took away from Padua in his travelling bag a sizeable collection of interesting publications. At the turn of the XVII century, the medical student (and physician) Jacek Łopacki displayed a similar bibliophilic acquisitiveness. Neither one of the hunters was an egoist, and both in time donated their collections for public use: Brożek to the main library of Cracow University, Łopacki to the city of Cracow for the formation of a municipal public library.

An important, little known until now, field of contacts of the Paduan student with the culture of the time was the theater, especially exuberantly developed in the Venice-Padua district in various scenic forms (literary comedy, *commedia dell'arte,* etc.) during the first half of the XVI century. In recent times Polish scholars (M. Brahmer, T. Ulewicz) [14] have been devoting a great deal of attention to the importance of this center for the development of Polish Renaissance and baroque drama, and especially emphasized its role in the creation of the first Polish humanistic drama—*Odprawa posłow greckich* (The Dismissal of the Grecian Envoys) by Jan Kochanowski (whose connection with the theatrical milieu of Padua extends to the bold attempt to identify the Paduan Lidia extolled by him with the famous Paduan actress Vinzenza Armini).

---

[14] M. Brahmer, *Z dziejów włosko-polskich stosunków kulturalnych* (From the History of Italian-Polish Cultural Relations), p. 53 n.; *Id., W galerii renesansowej* (In a Renaissance Gallery), Warsaw, 1957, pp. 116–189; T. Ulewicz, "Wstep" (Introduction) to the new edition of J. Kockanowski's *Odprawa posłów greckich.*

Fragmentary source material indicates irrefutably that theatrical presentations enjoyed a great popularity among Polish scholars, who had no opportunity to satisfy their craving for the theater in their own country. It must be added that theatrical spectacles in general were a very vital element in the every-day life of Paduan scholars. The theater was attended by the whole student body, up to the distinguished presidents. It was a place for entertainment, social meetings, forming friendships; it took the place of cafes, which did not yet exist at that time (including the famous Pedrocchio cafe!).

A classic example of the powerful opiate of the theater was the behavior of Polish counter-Reformation Bishop Jerzy Radziwiłł. When he found himself in Padua on a visit in 1576, he passionately attended all kinds of ballet and acrobatic performances, and above all went to the theater every day. Soon an unpleasant incident befell him: the servant who walked behind him was robbed of the prince's purse containing 37 Hungarian ducats and a silver seal worth 5 thalers.

This enthusiasm for the theater even increased in the XVII century. It was exhibited by all social groups represented by the Polish community in Padua. Theatrical spectacles were attended by such a representative of the higher clergy, as the Abbot of Tyniec K. Pudłowski, as well as the politically oriented Jakub Sobieski, and the serious Jan Brożek, engrossed in scholarly research. Sometimes amusing incidents occurred at these theatrical spectacles, such as at the meeting of J. Sobieski with two of his countrymen, Royal Equerry K. Zbaraski and Tyniec Abbot K. Pudlowski. "Neither one recognized me; although they spoke with me and I with them in Italian at the comedy, they took me for a Roman, an Italian,"—wrote Sobieski, much amused at the occurrence.[15]

The *commedia dell'arte* variant of the Italian theater was certainly familiar to Polish scholars, although it has been doubted

---

[15] *Dwie podróże Jakuba Sobieskiego* (Two Journeys of Jakub Sobieski), p. 185. This passion for the theater and spectacles is confirmed by *Diariusz podróży odbytej w r, 1661–1663* (Diary of a Journey Made in 1661–1663), p. 33. "We saw beautiful comedies in several theaters (in Venice), where there is a great deal of joy in music. They also present wooden comedies here (marionettes), with a lot of fun. There were also a great many magicians with strange tricks; we saw a woman without hands as well, who wrote, sewed, and played music of all sorts with her feet."

until recently. At the very most, researchers have sought certain similarities between this kind of theatrical creation and the so-called Polish minstrel comedies. But quite unexpectedly a few years ago, traces of familiarity with the *commedia dell'arte* have come to light in the writings of J. Brożek (the character of the cocky, but actually cowardly Captain Lęk—capitano Spavento). This was not a chance encounter. It is known from other sources that Brożek, an ardent admirer of the theater, who in his youth often organized school shows, during his stay in Italy collected texts of dramatic literature in print and manuscript, among them the *dramma comicum de sycophanto,* or slapstick comedy so prevalent in the so-called burgher dramas. This, then, would be an important indication of Italian influence brought back by the burgher intelligentsia in this field of art, and to this time considered to be native to Poland. This provides another link in the chain of the cultural influence of padua.

Finally, the stay in Padua was used for observation of political relations prevalent in the Venetian Republic, for understanding its government structure, the sources of its national power, economy and state of preparedness, the mechanism of its administration and the forms of its diplomatic operations. It was the favorite field of many future or actual Polish statesmen, into which they delved with gusto from the XVI century on. In the XVII century, there were undoubtedly a great many inveterate and unrealistic myths in these views on the Republic of St. Mark. Analogies were stubbornly made between the Venetian and Polish republican forms of government; the great range of civil liberty in Venice was stressed (for instance, W. Kochowski in *Liryki:* "Venice is laudable for its extensive freedoms"), although every-day observation demonstrated that it was not so. As of old, the myth of its world power was still believed.

The outer magnificence of the life of the upper classes worked on the imaginations of Polish observers—no wonder, after all, this was in the epoch of the baroque—the rich ceremonial of state occasions rivaling the oriental. A sharper eye might have noticed, through the outer coating of pomp and seemingly carefree life, negative features and phenomena. Stefan Pac, Prince Władysław's travelling companion, immediately took note of the Venetians' inquisitorial suspiciousness toward the highest state officials. "They are so careful there when they deal with the mighty," he said, "that no one from the senate or the leading nobility can speak with any foreigner without permission or get together with him." [16]

It was only at the beginning of the XVII century that a scholar and pupil of Galilei, Paweł Palczowski, presented a picture of the state of Venice, its political system, state administration, geographic and economic state, military strength and organization of defense, so necessary for the Polish reader (*Status Venetorum*, 1604). The little book of Palczowski, a great admirer of Venetian organization and institutions as "the expression of the highest wisdom and purposefulness," did not offer a thorough analysis of national life in the Republic of St. Mark. The task the author set himself was more modest—it was to supply public leaders and statesmen with necessary information about Venice, and in this popularizing sense it undoubtedly fulfilled its role, replacing the old, classical book of Contarini. The brochure is another document of the intellectual coexistence of Poland with Padua. Half a century later a new, anonymous guide to the state facilities of the Republic of St. Mark (*Della republica e magistrati di Venetia*, Venice, 1650) was published, probably written by an Italian, which was linked with the name of a frequent visitor to Padua, Jan Zamoyski.

V

Now let us examine our final conclusions regarding what role Padua played in Polish intellectual life in the XVII century, what values it brought to it, and what its position was in comparison to the preceding century.

The number of arrivals in this century was undoubtedly higher than in the preceding one, which was estimated—rather

---

[16] *Obraz dworów europejskich na początku XVII w.* (Picture of European Courts at the Beginning of the Seventeenth Century) *by Stefan Pac*, J. K. Plebanski, ed., Wrocław, 1854. The same thing was noticed earlier by S. Reszka, who was sent on a diplomatic mission by Zygmunt III to the Republic of St. Mark; see his letter to Zygmunt III, Venice, April 21, 1588, Wierzbowski, *Materiały do dziejów piśmiennictwa* (Materials for the History of Literature), Vol. I, p. 280.

optimistically—at 1,800 "scholars." [17] But the XVII century had to take second place to the earlier age with regard to the quality of the personalities who formed their thinking and matured intellectually under Paduan influence. Among the Paduans of the XVII century we do not meet such representative figures as Nicholas Copernicus or Józef Struś in science, Marcin Kromer and Reinhold Heidenstein in historiography, Klemens Janicius and Jan Kochanowski in poetry, Stanisław Orzechowski and Łukasz Górnicki in prose, Andrzej Dudycz and Piotr of Goniądz in the field of Church reform, Hieronim Ossoliński and Jan Zamoyski in the arena of public service. But the cultural situation—both throughout Europe and particularly in Poland—was now different. The Paduan center lost its intellectual supremacy in Western European culture, becoming only one of several focusing points of civilization, equal in rank. In Poland, the XVI century was a time of the greatest, many-faceted closeness with Western culture; the following century, on the other hand, became the stage for a struggle between two antithetic trends: the European and the Sarmatian, which brought cultural regression, self-engrossment and disinterest in the vital currents of European thought. In the struggle between these two forces, Padua became an important factor in maintaining Polish ties with the West, owing to its tradition, its nurturing and diffusion of secular and rationalistic thought, its modern stand.

Outstanding representatives of Polish writing, such as W. Potocki, W. Kochowski, J. Chr. Pasek, never ventured beyond their native backwater. But others, did come in contact with the cultural atmosphere of Padua, such as Piotr Kochanowski, the accomplished translator of Ariosto and Tasso (he was in Padua twice: in 1609 and 1617), Rafał Leszczyński, translator of Du Bartase and author of original poetry, Stanisław Serafin Jogodyński, admirer of Italian literature, the brothers Krzysztof and Łukasz Opaliński (1630), the historians: Stanisław Temberski (1641), Samuel Nakielski (1625), Paweł Potocki (1642), Samuel Kazimierz Kuszewicz (1643), political writers and journalists: Piotr Gorczyn (1607), Stanisław Krzysztanowic

---

[17] S. Windakiewicz, *Padwa*, p. 80, 93–99.

(1609), Paweł Palczowski (1602–1603), Andrzej Rysiński (1634), Jan Heidenstein (1634), Marek Jerzy Lemka (1635). Polish polyhistors of this century also found themselves under the influence of Paduan thought: Szymon Starowolski (1624) and Protestant Jan Jonston (1635), scholars of the stature of Jan Brożek and Stanisław Pudłowski, and future leaders of the state: Jakub Zadzik, Jakub Sobieski, Tomasz Zamoyski, Jerzy Ossoliński, outstanding leaders of Protestantism such as Samuel Przypkowski and Jerzy Niemirycz. Finally, most Polish physicians got their training in Padua.

Unexpectedly, the professorial staff of Cracow University contained a surprisingly large number of Paduans. Probably half of its more outstanding members had been in direct contact with the Paduan scientific movement. If this Polish university did not degenerate completely and showed flashes of modern thought and intellectual stature, this was undoubtedly in great measure the result of these contacts with the Paduan environment. Especially the medical faculty shows a purely Paduan provenience, since out of twenty-four professors amitted to it during the century, only two were educated locally, in Cracow, four held doctorates from Bologna, while the rest, i.e., 75 percent of the professors, received their medical education in the city of Antenor.

Similarly staffed with Paduans was the royal chancellery of Władysław IV, the king who was able to oppose the extremist pressure of the Catholic counter-Reformation, and thus saved Cracow University when it was threatened by Jesuit expansion. He tried to bring about a reconciliation among different denominations, and his court was a place of modern experiments in physics.

For all the reasons cited above, XVII century Padua deserves an honored place in the history of Polish culture, no lesser than the place it had secured in the Golden Age.

9

The Twilight of the Leaders: Julian Ursyn Niemcewicz

Wacław Berent

"There were two authorities in the country," says one of the most prominent men in the Kingdom of Poland, "the physical: Constantine at Belvedere Palace, and the moral: Niemcewicz in town."

The hero of the battle at Maciejowice, friend of Kościuszko and Washington, after his return from America was proclaimed chief poet—over the head of Woronicz and somewhat to his own surprise. Of course, in time he accepted this as tribute due to him. What is more surprising is the course of his rather short stay on the pedestal of society, as the highest expression of its spirit. Admirers of the poet lavished a rather lapidary description on him: The Poland-Man. As a matter of fact, this was a variation on Niemcewicz's own words about Dąbrowski. . . .

Amidst the ministers, councillors of state and generals of the two countries—at that time puffed up in their importance and decked out like peacocks—at assemblies there sounded a trembly titter unbearable to them; it came from a squat individual with a profuse bush of grey hair falling in curls. He was in the habit of accompanying his own conceits and quips with his squeaky laugh, himself the most amused at them. From his whole appearance, behavior and arrogance—the dignitaries guessed—it could be no other but the aging man of letters. He irritated these gentlemen all the more, since he was so highly regarded by the ladies in the salons, despite the fact that his ditties, copies of which circulated through town, even made fun of persons in the highest government positions. It was impossible to take offense at Niemcewicz's "fables," although their *ad personam* allusions were obvious to all, not excluding the Grand Duke.

Through his spies, Constantine had the most detailed reports on "every word and poem of Niemcewicz, which sometimes did not spare the Cesarevitch himself." Yielding to Warsaw customs in this matter, as in so many others, he also tried not to become offended, but did not always succeed: "Tell Niemcewicz that as he once sat in the Petersburg prison, he can find himself there again." But these were only brief outbursts of irritation. At one time, Catherine had wanted to force the author to rot in prison for similar libellous allegations in the form of fables. On the whole, the Tsarevitch felt himself above the secret allusions of the pamphlets that made the rounds of the city. In the end he ignored these literary scribbles, which he considered insignificant; he had more important papers on his desk. He was content with surrounding this man of letters with the most vigilant police surveillance.

This did not deter him, when he met Niemcewicz by chance at the Boguslawski Theatre, from taking him graciously by the arm and, strolling with him in the lobby, telling him of . . . the exalted virtues of his wife. The aura of the theater and the waft of femininity from the stage apparently put the Tsarevitch in such a mood; women are not the only ones who share sentimental confidences with poets.

Delving mockingly into the subject, the malicious flatterer began to sing the praises of the tact, gentleness and inexhaustible kindness of the Duchess of Łowicz, whom he had known since her girlhood. The husband failed to detect the thorn directed at himself in the bouquet of compliments for his wife, since it was offered by a one-time experienced man-of-the-world, as well as a theatrical author obviously carried away by his dramatic fervor. The Grand Duke finally embraced him and said: "You're right, she's an angel, not a woman!"

Niemcewicz presented himself at the Belvedere only once, as

president of the Royal Society (of the Friends of Learning), to protest the intended censorship of the speech he was to make at the ceremony marking the unveiling of a statue of Copernicus on Krakowskie Przedmieście Street. The petitioner was rather taken aback to see the draft of his speech on the Grand Duke's desk. It had found its way there by some miraculous means, and the Grand Duke was in the process of censoring it himself with a red pencil in his hand. The poet stiffened and spoke through clenched teeth:

"One way or another, the 'immaculate' Mr. Novosiltsov will watch over the whole ceremony."

The Grand Duke turned red at once and, banging his fist on the table, sprang up from his chair.

"What is this persiflage of yours supposed to mean? Vous n'aimez pas Monsieur Novosiltsov?" he flew up to him. "Don't you know that he's a statesman who has performed the greatest services for the Russian state? . . . I will tell the Tsar of your impudence."

Murmuring some French excuse, the president withdrew from nearly under the Grand Duke's fist. And his horror grew at the thought of the mess he had gotten himself and his institution into. Not long afterwards he was able to write in his Diary: "The Grand Duke regretted his outburst and ordered that I be told of it."

Without any interference from the Russian authorities or censorship, without even the ordinary ferreting by spies, the ceremony was an inspiration to all. The day was rainy—leaden; at the moment the statue was unveiled, the clouds broke and the golden glory of the sun fell on Copernicus. The year was 1830.

The organizers of the street festival, the scholars of the Royal Society, decided to celebrate with a banquet at the hotel on Tłómackie Przedmieście. Novosiltsov himself appeared at the banquet unexpectedly, undoubtedly on orders from the Tsarevitch, and proposed a toast . . . in honor of Niemcewicz.

"We cannot get into our heads Novosiltsov's participation in our Dutch-treat party," stormed one of the banqueters. The scholars apparently had not taken into consideration the fact that the Duchess of Łowicz, as a pole, was bound to succumb to the seduction of the words: chief poet—and even more so after her husband undoubtedly repeated to her the way that Niemcewicz had raved about her.

As a matter of fact, this man of letters was not completely indifferent for the Grand Duke either. He did wear the signet ring of Paul, given him by that Tsar when he freed him from the casemates of Petropavlovsk together with Kościuszko. For Constantine, who loathed the very mention of his grandmother Catherine, but did honor the memory of his father, this ring on the hand of Niemcewicz became a sort of inherited dictate of immunity for him.

This could only be confirmed by the attitude of the Tsars that followed toward Niemcewicz. Even earlier, Alexander I had taken a liking to the wit and courtliness of this European gentleman with extensive connections at the French and British courts, and in time also among the most outstanding American people. Even a later Tsar, Nicholas, deigned to greet him at the Palace with the stiff compliment: "I've known you for a long time—through your renown." This renown had reached the Russian court through the Russian poet Zhukovski, the tutor of Alexander II. The latter, who was only a young boy at the time, appeared in a Polish uniform at the coronation of Nicholas in Warsaw, and spoke Polish quite well. He insisted that no one but Mr. Ursyn-Niemcewicz had to take him to see the venerable poplars in Vilanov. . . .

The Muse of political satire must be the daughter of Chronos and one of the Danaides—to put it "classically"—since she is the daughter of time and censorship, both toiling to no avail.

The rapid pen of Niemcewicz supplied Warsaw with summary reprisals of malice against all guardians of authority at that time, and their satiric bite lay in the very unprintability of these leaflets. Seldom did he go so far in exposing such a monster of his time as in the poem about General Zajączek. This satire was rendered all the more piquant by the fact that, despite a long-standing antipathy toward the Viceroy, this ex-revolutionary and Jacobin, later enriched Napoleonic opportunist, and finally a servant of the Tsar, for some time was on close terms with him and his family.

This singular poet not only wrote libellous verses about the highest authorities in the country with impunity, but also slammed the doors at the seat of these same authorities. But who among the dignitaries of the time could be unmindful of his renown with the Tsars, the Grand Duke's indulgent attitude toward him, and the universal adoration showered on him by his countrymen?

In this sacrosanctity from all sides, be became—this capricious tease, bothersome to so many—a "holy cow" in Warsaw.

* * *

But this curious beatification at the height of literary popularity nevertheless wove a rather meager wreath for the poet. He was valued and revered mostly because . . . everyone liked him. Such is the logic of popularity.

As everyone knows, women are most susceptible to this logic, and they "spoiled him like mad."

Their bold advances often became extremely embarrassing as he grew older. It was difficult for him to explain to every lady on the settee that . . . "he already had one foot in the grave." Almost everyone who came in contact with him mentioned these sighs of senile coquetry.

If we want to understand the real man, first of all it is necessary to strip off the screen of pathos that descended over Niemcewicz in the history of literature. Supposedly, he was not only the personification of the best traits of the gentry of the time, but also "worthy of the traditions of his ancestors." His extended stay in America, the American wife he married there, finally the whole family of this widow—all this must have somewhat alienated him from his native customs. And his association with Washington and his people may have "denobilized" him in his thinking as well.

An eye witness, the young Słowacki, reliable if only because of the naiveté of his account, relates a story about him which illustrates that he strove to emulate the edifying customs of his ancestors:

"Niemcewicz, chatting with his guests, at the same time played with the two little daughters of his coachman, whom he held on his lap. They teased him in an extremely familiar fashion. 'You are just as stupid as I am,' parried the older one, obviously referring to an earlier allusion to her silliness. Amused to tears by this, Niemcewicz ordered the older girl to kiss him on the face. 'Who are you?' he finally asked. 'Your wife,' she replied."

This little barefoot girl, with her contrary banter and white-toothed smiles, was greatly familiar, to say the least, if that is how you want to put it. But the frolics of Niemcewicz himself, these ostentatious caresses with the daughter of his coachman, would have inspired horrified astonishment in every Polish country house. Niemcewicz's manners had gone far afield from the native canons.

The quoted story is one of the many that circulated about him then, including bawdy ones. The writing of memoirs at that time was remarkably gossipy, mostly through the participation of women. There are people today who are fond of looking at the past as if through a fragrant fan of old-fashioned beauty, behind which past events take on the semblance of an amusing minuet. That is one way of looking at it.

The only trouble is that the salons in the time of the Kingdom of Poland (formed in 1815 at the Congress of Vienna) were far from the rococo charms already long gone. Instead, a bureaucratic dryness and stiffness of "all of Warsaw" was dominant, that is, of all the higher bureaucracy, with the usual sprinkling of country squires in the offices, along with puffed-up would-be gentlemen and a few wise aristocrats. And these were the centers not only of Niemcewicz's literary, but also political fame—throughout the whole of Warsaw, which was soon to undergo a drastic change.

A theatrical air emanated from this dramatic author, especially during his public appearances. This was not because of any acquired pose, but through the sensitivity of the poet wandering through the Forum; he could not differentiate between the stage and this arena: people's hearts beat the same for him on both.

When, at the time of the Insurrection, at a joint session of both houses, there was a move to elect him senator, he defended himself as he could from this "violation," pleading poverty: "I have only a few acres of land, for which I pay 48 zlotys in taxes!"

This was not an oratorical reply, but a dramatic ploy: in contrast with the high tone of the wealthy gentlemen around him, he presented himself as a modest man with mundane worries. Since the response of the lawmakers was completely different than in the theater, since a hush descended over the gathering, he continued in this mournful tone: "The King of Saxony of revered memory (and the Duke of Warsaw), when he entrusted to me the position of secretary of the senate at the time I was 50 years old, wished it to serve as a place of rest for me. . . . But the burden of 74 years is bearing down on me, my mind is already weakened. . . . When peace comes with God's help, I will even give up this post of secretary I value so highly. And I will then step into the grave opened for me. . . ."

The speaker did not gauge accurately the way that this self-pity would sound in the cold halls of parliament.

"Niemcewicz," was the harsh answer, seeming to pull him down from the stage to the public arena, "you have always been obedient to the will of the people. We do not demand that you physically take your place [thus he was incidentally reproached for his Saxon sinecure], but we want you to bring honor and adornment to our senate."

The grateful candidate thanked them, moved to tears, claiming that this was the happiest day of his life, but continued to squirm out of the offer. They could not come to terms with him. Such was the instinctive reluctance of the old poet, standing over his open grave, to accept the "honors and decorations" of the politicians.

He preferred to be one of the hidden springs of the times he was living through, rather than their plummet or even "show ace." His *Memoirs* bear witness to this, concealing with considerable modesty his participation in great events. It is quite significant that it was said in parliamentary circles: "In the most difficult matters, Niemcewicz was consulted and the voting [in the Senate] went according to his advice."

This old man, claiming publicly that he was decrepit and dull of mind, was soon to take up a task that demanded acute alertness of his mental powers. He was entrusted with the mission of unofficial emissary of the insurrectional government to England, putting to use his knowledge of the language and extensive connection with the upper classes there. Czartoryski attests to the fact that he discharged his duties with ability and the greatest devotion. And if his diplomacy was not as modest as dictated by the tragic moments of the soon-to-expire Polish revolution, this was caused by a violent flow of his energy and temperament. He slammed the doors of British dignitaries, as he had recently done at the palace of the Viceroy; all that he refrained from doing was writing satires, although there was no shortage of material there either, judging by his letters from that time.

And when all public hopes were falling in ruins, and personal fortunes and destinies wavered, when he did not know how he would maintain himself before long, he would still get up at dawn to attend lectures, held early in London, in botany which he loved so well, or in chemistry which was "fashionable" at the time.

Such was the inexhaustible energy of the old man.

Extremely hard-working, and incessantly broadening his mind, he acquired a great deal of knowledge of the literary kind. His enterprising dilettantism, without a consistency of goals, contributed greatly to the decline of the Royal Society after Staszic had died.

After the death of Staszic, the candidacy of Niemcewicz, as the most popular man in Poland, was obvious. In a draft that has been preserved, the candidate expresses his thanks for . . . his unanimous election (because how else could it be!). In this draft, after the more oratorical phrases, there is a long series of periods for the anticipated interruption by applause. Surely, no actor learns his role from the point of view of such expectations.

During his term as president, technical skills took precedence over learning (at that time a difference was made between the two terms) through the ardent and extremely dedicated work of engineers and representatives of military science, which certainly was not due to any merit of Niemcewicz. Meanwhile, the department of literature that was close to his heart was bogged down in sluggishness owing to the inflation of unyielding pride all around. The confidence of these old men must have spread to the president as well, since in the regular, triennial report (the last before the Insurrection) he took the following position on romantic poetry:

"The excessively fierce struggle between the old and new school impels me to make *our* voices heard in this matter." This dignity, carried all the way to *pluralis majestaticus,* was rather belated. And it ill became the good-hearted image of the chief poet who, following another versifier, wanted to end by kindly and amicably advising all poets in Poland to ". . . join the virtues of the two schools, smoothing out faults." A most academic message.

The bustling activity of their senior often annoyed the other scholars and poets. He incessantly spun like a top, he had business with everyone, either on scraps of paper or whispered in the ear, not excluding ceremonial meetings attended by the public, when he should have presided with all the pomp at his command. Women and the public were delighted with exactly this mobility of the old man, and with his insouciance at the meetings, even in the presence of state dignitaries. But serious malicious wits made fun of him for this unruliness, and some of these epithets have been preserved in their memoirs.

In his popularity among women and the public there was also a little dose of contrariness. There is no shortage of prigs anywhere, but there are never enough lively people. The ladies and the public could not know that his apparent liveliness could be like the dying out of a candle. The fact that the spirit of the Polish Enlightenment had already smouldered down to nothing contributed more than anything to the moribund state of the Society after Staszic. Its last feeble flame was Niemcewicz: he no longer shone, but flared and dimmed.

The fruit of his own work (already in manuscript form) in the last years before the Insurrection was much the same.

We know that, as it often happens, he achieved fame through the popularity of his weakest works, while many of his more valuable writings (which were, above all, more telling of the times of the Kingdom of Poland) mouldered in manuscript caches of his native Skoki in Lithuania, in Warsaw, Cracow, Paris and, as it has been learned recently, America. Despite the fact that he was "deified" beyond measure by his countrymen, he was not an opportunist for literary fame; he had a truly lordly indifference to his own writings. He could not be persuaded to turn his pen evasively in keeping with the demands of censorship, as the Viceroy wished him to; during the time of his greatest fame he preferred to store his writings in a drawer. It is hard to find another man like that.

The most famous, and at the same time the weakest of his works published during his lifetime was *Śpiewy historyczne* (Historical Songs). Is it necessary to recall here again the influence of this "organ grinder's chant" on Mickiewicz, later on Sienkiewicz, and more recently on Żeromski? And each of them admitted wholeheartedly to the effect these Songs had on the sensibility of their newly awakened imaginations. These are childish things heard on a mother's knee, as Goethe was to say: "Vom Mütterlein hab' ich die Lust zum Fabulieren." This impulse for taking up the lute flowed to these Polish children from the frail lute of Niemcewicz. And from something more, from the aura of his personality. Mickiewicz was to say: "We got used to hearing of his exploits and adventures from our mothers."

What is our present criticism in comparison with that?

It is unavoidable to dwell here at length on his superhuman qualities, since they overshadowed his whole value as a writer in the eyes of his contemporaries, making him the idol of popularity, of the "nation" or, said another way: the favorite pet of the classes which then considered themselves the nation.

But the time has come at last to look at his solitary moments, at the whole gamut of his inner resources, then put down in writing those works of his that could not be published. Naturally, he did not expect that so many of his writings would not be published outside the Kingdom of Poland until several decades after his death, or that a number of them would be dispersed until the present time, as we have said, from Lithuania all the way to America.

But it is these lost writings that allow us to understand his later behavior until those dreadful days of 1830, when the idol of the salons, humanized by solitude, would reach for the moral leadership of the nation. Was it really so? It came to be.

Four years before the Insurrection, he finally took the measure of that salon-bureaucratic, political-gossipy mill of Warsaw life, in which, up to that time, he no longer just frittered away his time, but in which he pulverized himself into gossip about his person. He finally moved away from Warsaw to a previously purchased "residual property," as we would call it today: to a center of subdivided estates. He called this quiet hideaway Ursynów, after his cognomen. (Earlier, this residence near Warsaw had been called "Delight.")

It was a freshly vacated temple of other people's delights in ostentatious opulence; a castle which encumbered, rather than adorned, this peculiar poet's abode bore witness to the past splendors. Whether he wanted to or not, he had to put "what the pen earned" into the support of these walls. "Of what use to me are these boudoirs, these salons and plafonds, these columns and other people's coats-of-arms!" he grumbled when it was too late. "I would have been satisfied with a thatched-roof cottage."

He appeared there not so much as the wheelwright as a Quaker farmer: in a long linen duster down to his feet and a huge straw hat. Thus he toiled at planting rare trees and bushes, some of them brought from as far as Philadelphia. He also wore this outfit as he busied himself with the beehives—the duster, his hands and even face covered with trustworthy bees.

It was a picture symbolic of the times. Warsaw was in the process of changing into a teeming beehive, increasingly artisan and industrial. An independent class was growing, one that based its existence only on its own work and provident care.

In their Paris conversations, it might have puzzled Mickiewicz that the old Niemcewicz became attached to the Mazovian land, about which he said that "At times it depresses me, and then again enchants me."

Mickiewicz was not familiar with the sadness and fascination of this seemingly monotonous land, but so lilting from the music concealed in it, together with the charm of songs and colors so strangely specific. It would be immortalized by the lyres, lutes and paintbrushes of many generations—headed by Chopin. He was ahead of them all, if only by his sentiment, the old recluse of Ursynów, who even in front of Mickiewicz could be moved to tears thinking of these unforgettable sights. (Everything becomes more beautiful when encountered by the longing of poets.)

To the east of his hermitage, the old man had completely different sights: "the shining roofs" of Warsaw, during that time so feverishly rebuilt and adorned with new buildings for the future, as it was dreamed, capital of the united lands of all of Poland. Niemcewicz's old-man's pessimism did not share in these dreams. . . .

The second bard in exile, Juliusz Słowacki, knew well the "secluded spot" that the Lithuanian kinsman of Mickiewicz missed so much, since he longed for it.

"The lovely Ursynów of the old man, overgrown with wild trees, looks rather like a virgin forest than a garden. In a little meadow, Niemcewicz's only cow is grazing; she brings him an income of two zlotys a week."

This was the sober appraisal of the young romantic (at that time a treasury clerk) of the modest abode of the classicist who, enamored of its luxuriant nature and deeply familiar with it, learned through his inquiring mind, the origin of all these trees, whether from near or far, and their scientific names; these trees that the romantic thought to be wild. . . .

If someone wandered into Ursynów today, he would find neither the stumps nor even the roots of the one-time virginal oasis of these wild trees. Near the unattractive castle, in place of the old park, he would find a plowed potato field and, if he examined the furrows, he might discover a deep cavity in the earth, and in it the underpinning of the summerhouse where Słowacki mused so sadly during his stay there. His host had made him wait a long time; with the coquetry of an eighteenth-century man-of-the-world.

A chance companion of Słowacki's pilgrimage, and of his wait in the summerhouse at that time, "seeing me unusually wan and despondent [the young poet says about himself], asked me the reason. 'Happy,' I answered, 'is the man who can write like Niemcewicz, so sweetly and pleasantly, without being consumed by inner fires. Happy is the man who can take his ease in such a quiet little house [he pointed melancholically to the castle of someone's recent delight and perhaps debauchery, which had disgusted Niemcewicz from the first days he spent there]. He will take his ease here long after the grass grows over the graves of those younger than he.' "

As we know, this augury of envious melancholy failed to

come true. Słowacki lived eight years longer than Niemcewicz, who had to leave his Ursynów a year after the young poet's visit.

While at the beginning of the conversation Niemcewicz groused about Wilno poetry, after hearing an act of the young man's first drama *Mindowe*, "the old man suddenly turned toward me, frowning; I could see that he was concentrating hard. From that time, he looked me in the eye, as if trying to see through me."

"I am glad," he said at last, "that I see you before I die (he did not miss this opportunity to sigh about his imminent demise), that a poet appears in Poland with great talent, and that he will uphold the civil spirit of the people."

For him, this spirit was the crowning of all gifts of human nature. This was much more modest than the exalted patriotism of the young on the lofty Zion of exile. It was simply an inner dictate of nature that was much less complicated, still military from the times of Kościuszko and Dąbrowski. Changing such people into émigré Werthers, Hamlets, and Manfreds was an obvious impossibility. However, they could be rendered insensitive by their exile and over their heads an inferno of émigré squabbles.

It was not only the most recent national catastrophe that depressed Niemcewicz so much in exile.

Słowacki also had a hand in it, ridiculing the old bard in the drama *Kordian*.

Ursynów, confiscated by the Russian government at the same time as Niemcewicz was condemned to death *in absentia*, in time was bought by General Wincenty Krasiński, who wanted to settle his son Zygmunt in this secluded, poetic spot, which still held some traditional charm for Warsaw at the time.

But this young brilliant dandy was not at all impressed by this quasi patronage of the senescent poet's spirit, and by the idea of rubbing against the melancholy quarters of his one-time residence. He capriciously announced that he would not condescend to live in Ursynów, rebuilt for him by his father at tremendous expense. He preferred to put his unloved wife there. He himself extended his stay in Paris.

The alteration of the castle disfigured these walls all the more, with the already petrified classic Warsaw style which, finally, leaned—one could say—to the Paskevitch style, as can still be seen in more than one building in Warsaw and its surroundings today. In every period, the authorities leave their mark on the architecture of the country.

This was the last mark left on the prepartition Delight and Ursynów as it is today. It is useless to search for any trace of the old man's secluded spot. And would that the sneering mask of these walls today could remind us instead of some fragment of the life and work of the third bard, instead of the well-filled purse and the melancholy wife of Zygmunt Krasiński!

It was necessary to interpolate here a description of the later attitude of the Three Bards to their predecessor from the time of the Kingdom of Poland. It is only in this later light that one can see more clearly how many chords had Niemcewicz's frail lute, on which more talented hands would later play. Also, the great authority of this émigré triad springs from the moral heritage of the Ursynów hermit. None of the later great poets, including Mickiewicz, in their lifetime received even a fraction of the popular backing for moral leadership in Poland that would soon come to Niemcewicz. . . .

*   *   *

Piotr Wysocki, instructor of the Cadet School in Warsaw, made a pilgrimage to Ursynów, following in the footsteps of Słowacki, but for a completely different purpose, and with the stealthy stride of the conspirator, even though he was in military uniform. He did not drive up to the front of the house, but unexpectedly stepped in front of the old man during his evening stroll. This white figure in the somber thicket of the park might have seemed to the soldier a monk before the monastery walls. And truly, as before a monk, he soon leaned toward his ear with all the fervor of confession, and awaited absolution from him, one could say—in the name of Polish society. Niemcewicz in turn undoubtedly gazed deeply at the young man as well, in order to "see through him." It was not a gnawing ambition that was etched gloomily on this brow; the young man exuded a profound calm of determination.

Wysocki was able to tell his friends, "Niemcewicz was deeply touched to endorse our good intentions, kindling our will to further efforts. He only said, 'Now is not the time yet, but the right moment will come.' "

When the young man had disappeared into the falling darkness, as if sinking into his conspiratory underground once more, Niemcewicz dragged himself with heavy steps to a bench under a spreading linden tree. He saw in the east, over Warsaw, a cloud darker than the night, rent with short bolts of lightning, without thunder; it seemed that the ghosts of an approaching storm called to each other in this silence by secret signs. And he became fearful for Warsaw, for the whole country, for all its people. Soon a gnawing doubt came over him: perhaps this time again he should have checked this new folly.

In the days that followed, he felt not as a gardener, but as a worm in the field that could be crushed at any moment. A tempest was coming that would bring all human efforts to nothing; it would also wrench him away from his beloved Ursynów.

Every tool falls from his hands; his arms hang useless.

After a few weeks of this anguish, he was suddenly seized by a vision with such swarming scenes as sometimes come during a high fever. From this crowded vision there emerged the certainty that on that very evening everything had begun. Although night was approaching, he ordered the horses to be harnessed and rushed off to Warsaw. As he shook along in the bumpy carriage, tears ran down the old man's face under the autumn gale. In the excitement of the moment, he once more relived Maciejowice.

Just as he passed the city gates, he heard pell-mell shots in the distance. A loose band of soldiers going by his carriage shouted in his ear: "To arms!" He ordered the carriage to stop and scrambled down from the seat at this summons, but he neither received a rifle nor saw these soldiers again; they had rushed on. People hid in the gateways, or furtively ran alongside the walls.

A horse shied and suddenly rammed the carriage all the way to the wall. On the pavement, the body of a Polish general lay in a huge puddle of blood. Down Trebacka Street, with tremendous rumbling, sped a heavy army coach; its horses clearly out of control. In the square before the post office, no sight of battle or a clash of any kind; the sword of the fallen lay in its sheath.

Had he been dragged out of his carriage? . . . At first there must have been a conversation, or persuasion of some sort, since his saber was not in his hand; and then in a sudden quarrel—a bayonet in the heart. A similar sight on Senatorska Street. He had no strength left to look at it. He only heard these calls again: "To arms!" and someone's sputtered curses.

So this is how it started? he thought, thoroughly shaken—from our own? Was this for what he had ignited young hopes? . . .

There was only one thing that the man of letters did not realize. That this was the finally bagged game of his own satires and fables; that what the pen had begun, was ending in an outburst of revolution.

*　　*　　*

Throughout that sleepless night, he paced the rooms of his Warsaw apartment like a caged animal, pondering how he could bridle the vengeful frenzy of the hottest heads among the insurgents. (Soon someone who knew the most about such things was to say: "It is to him that Polish generals, considered Moscow adherents, to a great extent will owe their lives.") In the meantime, he had no need to seek out the young people in town; they visited him that night without delay as soon as they learned of his arrival. The next morning his apartment could no longer hold them all. But now, when he put a barrier of bitterness between himself and these young people, his old pessimism poured forth from his heart with unchecked fury:

"I told the truth to these madmen who lay siege to my house day and night. You did not consult me before you began this mad revolution, so now leave me in peace and tumble down the precipice!"

This was undoubtedly said in the proper tone and with equally desperate gestures. The dramatic author unnecessarily struck the chord of tragedy—too much of which was in evidence already.

Mochnacki diagnosed this belated change in his outlook by saying: "Only a traitor can talk like that!"

The old man lunged at the whipper-snapper, shouting: "Thomas, my scimitar!" so that the whole house could hear him. But the horror of the indignity he suffered made him reel;

he swayed, dropped to a chair and, to everyone's great consternation, broke out in loud sobs.

It was this moment of old-age weakness in the adored hero of Maciejowice that struck the most sensitive nerve of the sentimental popularity that was showered on him. The youth turned away from Mochnacki violently—all the youth, starting with the military.

There was also another reason for this. Shortly afterwards Mochnacki broke in on General Chłopicki, to accuse this most deserving of the living legionary leaders because he did not act rapidly enough. The insulted general, instead of simply reaching for his pistol or having the madman arrested, in his fury fell into an apoplectic seizure, got a stroke of some kind, and "nearly lost his life." In Chłopicki's apartment on Krakowskie Przedmieście, one day a green and black curtain was drawn in the window as a sign of someone's agony.

*   *   *

In the anarchy that followed, the arrival from Ursynów was among the first to recover and try to save the situation. And as he had done so many times in his life, he rubbed the eyes of the poet to awaken in himself a sense for the public interest. He realized that, since war with Russia was inevitable, only three guarantees of strength and order counted: the leader, the soldiers, and the people of the capital. He did not have long to wait for Chłopicki's miraculous recovery after his agony.

The bravest of the field commanders of the old Dąbrowski Legions, in his old age Chłopicki became petulant and irritated at everyone, not excluding his motherland ("She didn't even give me shoes," he was to say). Right from the beginning, he removed himself from Constantine's parade army, and wanted nothing to do with it. Completely idle, he fell prey to the vice of card playing then rampant among army men. This warrior, who smelled of gunpowder more than any of his contemporaries, late in life became a habitué of salons and a suitor of high-born ladies. One of the most enlightened generals of the time was to say of him: "He loafed a great deal, and never read any military books."

He approached the matter of the Insurrection from the professional point of view: "Give me one hundred thousand trained soldiers, and then we can talk." And since such a number was not available, he could not make up his mind to take over command, or rather unceasingly hesitated and pouted. Mochnacki's behavior and the effect his supposedly permanent injury had on his health, could not have served to encourage him. But he could not remain indifferent to the persuasions of Niemcewicz, his old friend and Kościuszko's adjutant. While he continued to grumble, bellow, and thunder, in the face of incantations on all that's holy, and finally the tears of the venerable old man, Achilles gave in.

At long last, Chłopicki decided to accept supreme command, together with dictatorship, and in the confusion of those days this was greeted as a guarantee that "the Fatherland would be saved."

Niemcewicz himself did not fully share this hope, ever oscillating between yesterday's delight with a person and tomorrow's disappointment—as writers do. When, under pressure from public opinion and his friends, he decided to join the Provisional Government, crowd demonstrations, this time joyous, broke out in the streets with endless cheers for the poet. People cheered themselves up by saying: "Since Niemcewicz is there, everything will go well."

Thus, this most unusual of all poets indirectly set up the supreme command and the dictatorship, and restored the people's confidence in the government; "There is no power without confidence," said Prince Czartoryski laconically. The poet created power. Illusory, would say anyone knowing the course of even the few weeks that followed. But this is also an illusion.

It was towards him that the most fervid gratitude of public opinion was directed, always more anxious for a fetish than a leader. After the cheering in the streets, the flower of the day's youth was to confirm the adulation for Niemcewicz as well. The students of all institutions of higher learning, already enlisted in the Academic Guard, and outraged at the still unpunished insolence of Mochnacki, sent the following public proclamation to Niemcewicz from their barracks, signed by all company commanders of this regiment:

"The terrible news horrified the academic youth, who nur-

tures the purest reverence and attachment for You, a monu-
ment of our old Polish fatherland, witness and participant in its
glorious and tragic history! The insolence of one hothead,
struck by the curses of his countrymen, will not succeed in
erasing from Your brow the sacred imprint of the blessings of
Washington and Kościuszko. . . . Our model and glory! . . .
The hope of our future! . . . (now the youth soared in its
exaltation) . . . Father of Our Country? (They did not hesitate
to shout.) We will never stop deploring the insult you suffered."

This virtual eruption of laments, the fountain of tears from
all sides, even in the first days of armed fervor, eloquently
attests to the fact that in the sentimentality of the people of that
time, the recent classicism expired once and for all.

Propelled to the head of his generation by his popularity,
"canonized on Mount Parnassus" by the idolatry of the youth
(as Mickiewicz was to tell him to his face), at the end he was
acclaimed in Warsaw as national hope for the future and father
of his country, this first leader of a hetmanless day.

Plato would not have called such a man the incarnation of the
spirit of the Republic. And would not have crowned his herm in
the Agora.

10

Mickiewicz at the Collège de France

Wacław Lednicki

On December 22, 1840, at two o'clock in the afternoon, the author of the epic *Pan Tadeusz* stood in the Collège de France. Before him was a brilliant audience, which included the Polish poet Niemcewicz, a veteran both of Polish culture and of the struggle for independence; Prince Adam Czartoryski, the leading figure among the Polish emigrés; Charles Montalembert, the great politician and champion of the Polish cause; Faucher, the playwright and journalist; Nicholas Turgenev, author of *La Russie et les Russes;* Salvandy, former Minister of Education; Jean-Jacques Ampère, son of the great physicist and himself professor of French literature at the Collège de France; a scattering of German, Dalmatian, Montenegrin, and Russian listeners; and a crowd of French and Polish auditors. The hall was packed.

"I am a foreigner," the lecturer began, "and must express myself in a language which has nothing in common with that which habitually serves as the organ of my thoughts. . . . I must make you know and judge monuments of literature and works of art. To make them known means to transmit the enthusiasm which has created them. . . . Even if we had the time, would the preparatory sciences assure us of the power to extract from any masterpiece the secret life which is hidden in it, which is the real mystery of art? Not in the least. To make this flame burst forth, one must speak the creative word, and it is impossible to speak this word without knowing all the secrets of a language. . . . I am used to all those difficulties . . . . If I should heed the whispers of my self-love, if I cared only for seemly literary dignity, I would surely renounce the dangerous honor of speaking from this chair . . . But very weighty considerations have obliged me to accept it. I am summoned to speak in behalf of the literature of nations with which my own nation is closely connected by its past and future, to speak at a time when the spoken word is a power, to speak in a city which—I may say as a foreigner—is the capital of the world. Thus nothing can restrain me. . . ."

Mickiewicz's first lecture was a huge success. Even Russians admitted that he was worth hearing. The Parisian newspapers were filled with enthusiastic reports and articles. The lecture was a great event, and the Quartier Latin was satisfied. The lectures which followed attracted great crowds, among them such famous personalities as George Sand, Michelet, Quinet, Chopin, and even Cousin himself. Quinet, Michelet, and Cousin wrote articles full of enthusiastic praise.

Mickiewicz did not read his lectures, but spoke extemporaneously, a method which conformed to his nature and, more important, to his principles. In this fashion he delivered a hundred and eighteen lectures in the course of four years. The stenographic reports take up a volume of more than a thousand pages, full of facts, quotations, dates, opinions, refutations, interpretations, rich in historical material, literary history, and grammatical analysis. All this material was presented within a plan for the comparative study of Slavic literatures. It was based not only on things Slavic, but on Greek, Latin, French, German, Italian and English literature, and it all led to general conclusions, to a philosophy of history and civilization, to a moral evaluation of human culture and, finally, to a religious synthesis. Thus was formed and evolved the first comparative history of Slavic literatures, history, and culture, the first study of its kind on such a scale.

But, in the last analysis, was this the real essential significance of Mickiewicz's course in the Collège de France? Assuredly not. But before I discuss this question we should understand how and why this chair of Slavic literatures and languages was established in the Collège de France. Let me anticipate on one point—this chair is now over a hundred years old. It did not perish when Mickiewicz resigned in 1845; the poet's first successor was Cyprien Robert, from 1846 to 1857; after him came a Pole, Aleksander Chodźko, a pure philologist, from 1857 to 1885; then Louis Leger, from 1885 to 1922; from 1924 to 1951, André Mazon, mostly interested in the Russian field. . . .

The creation of a new chair in the Collège de France, one of the oldest and most illustrious universities of Europe, was as difficult as the insertion of a new passage in a canonical text. At that time not even a chair of Germanic philology existed in the Collège de France. One of the deputies, M. Auguis, launched a fierce attack against the project in the Chamber of Deputies. He asked if there were any reasons for extending the hospitality of the Collège de France to languages which had no literary tradition—such was his opinion of Slavic literatures. He further stated that, if such projects were to be presented, it would be much more reasonable to create chairs for the French dialects and patois, such as the Limousin, the Gascon, and the Auvergnat, which he thought had much more literary interest than the Slavic languages. These he believed belonged in the School of Eastern Languages at Paris.

The argument advanced by Auguis was not unreasonable, but there was a political background to his speech. The Slavic chair was a problem of French foreign policy. At the time, Poland had sympathizers everywhere in France and England, but they were only in society. The government of Louis Philippe was obliged to act very prudently towards Nicholas I. The last struggle of certain French politicians with their government took place on the occasion of Nicholas's famous speech in Warsaw in 1835. To the municipality the Tsar had said: "You have, gentlemen, a choice between two eventualities: to persist in your illusions concerning an independent Poland, or to live quietly as loyal subjects under my rule. If you persist in your dreams of a separate nation, of an independent Poland, and of all chimeras of this kind, you will only draw great hardships upon yourselves. I have ordered a citadel to be constructed here, and I declare that on the slightest demonstration I will destroy the city—and it certainly will not be I who will restore it. . . ."

This speech provoked waves of indignation in France and England. In France, Montalembert, Bignon, Odilon Barrot, and Saint Marc Girardin, with the support of the press, attacked the French government in the *Chambre des Députés* for its lack of courage and energy. In the British House of Commons, some years before, a Scotch member, Cutler Ferguson, had related what had taken place in Poland: libraries seized, churches destroyed, schools closed, children separated from their parents, families deported to the Caucasus, and long convoys of exiled Poles walking barefoot in the Siberian snow. Two hundred thousand Poles underwent those cruelties—five thousand nobles were transferred from their native localities—children, who were held to be poor, vagabonds, or orphans, were sent in vans to military colonies. Westminster was in an uproar; Glasgow, Hull, Leeds, Sheffield, Manchester, and Birmingham all published addresses "To the brave men of Poland." But the government was silent, even in England.

The creation of Mickiewicz's chair showed France's generous comprehension and sympathy. But the government had to be discreet. Nicholas was not alone; there was Prussia with her Poles, and Austria and Turkey with their Slavs. During the discussion in the Parliament it came to light that Cousin intended to confer this teaching post upon Mickiewicz. Mickiewicz was a refugee, a refugee who had published in France the third part of his *Forefathers' Eve,* an anti-Russian pamphlet of terrible power, and his *Books of the Polish Nation and Polish Pilgrims,* a bible of Polish slavery and martyrdom. In the circumstances, Cousin's purpose obviously possessed real political significance. He had the courage to make his proposal because he felt the support of French society, but naturally his purpose did not conform to the views of Russia, Austria, and Prussia. The embassies were at work.

M. Auguis may have been a sort of fifth columnist of his day, since he made a characteristic maneuver in his speech when he remarked: "I know very well for whom the request is made; but

I say that it is not honorable for a nation to give a chair in a French institution to a foreigner, especially when this foreigner is a distinguished poet in his country, but who knows only one of these dialects. Then say openly that you wish to create a chair of the Polish language and that the Polish language will be taught." The point was clearly made, but it was not fair. Mickiewicz not only knew Polish as his native tongue, but also possessed a good command of Russian and was familiar with Czech. Besides, he was an excellent Latinist, and knew German and English well (he had translated Byron and Goethe). But Cousin was thoroughly prepared in his arguments. Far from being the tissue of errors and absurdities which Leger later called it, Cousin's speech was well organized. Though Leger alleged that the orator relegated Russian to second place, Cousin's exact words were: "Of all the Slavic dialects, the one most spoken after the Russian is the Polish." Furthermore, he referred to Nestor, *The Tale of Igor,* Peter the Great, the cultural role of Catherine, the Russian Academy, the university, the libraries, and the Russian translators of Homer.

Apart from Mickiewicz and a few Russian emigrés, no one then in Paris was better qualified to speak on Russian literature than Cousin, and he derived his information from Mickiewicz. He further gave a very satisfactory outline of Polish culture and literature. He spoke of the Serbs, the Croats, the Czechs, and others. The discussion in the Chambre des Pairs was certainly remarkable. Mickiewicz was appointed, and began his lectures.

The nomination of Mickiewicz produced an unfavorable reaction not only in official circles, in embassies and governments, but also in the foreign press.

Another complication lay in the fact that Mickiewicz's *Books of the Polish Nation and Polish Pilgrims* did not enjoy an odor of sanctity in Vatican and Catholic circles. As a friend of Montalembert, Lamennais, and Quinet, Mickiewicz represented the tendency towards the "Christianization" of the Church and of social and political institutions in general. The Vatican at the time of Gregory XVI had so far lost its dignity as to offer servile support to Nicholas I with an eye to the interests of the Church. Thus for some people Mickiewicz was not orthodox enough, while for others he was insufficiently democratic. The religious character of his later works and articles shocked some readers, while his good relations with Russians were reason for others to fight against him. But, as we can see now, he was definitely the right man for the post. The chair was not being created for a pedantic study of Church Slavic. Its purpose was to show the spiritual culture and the history of the civilization of the Slavic world. The accomplishment of this task required a man of great spirit and talent. And it was at the same time a kind of moral reparation for Poland, a recognition of her secular cultural tradition and a spiritual indemnity. A great Pole deserved that important post, and Poland had none greater than Mickiewicz.

The poet had undergone solid classical and philological instruction at the University of Wilno, then in full flower. Once graduated, he was appointed teacher in the high school of Kovno, where he taught Polish history and literature. In Moscow, during his exile, he worked intensively at history, literature, French, Italian, German, and English poetry, Greek and Latin poetry and prose. He also studied Serbian popular poetry and was considered by Pushkin to be the best authority in this field. After leaving Russia, he went to Prague, where he discussed many literary and historical problems with Hanka and Šafařík, and attended lectures on philosophy in Berlin. Since Bohemian history was so intimately bound to Polish history, Mickiewicz, who was well advanced in his historical studies, was able to obtain a good knowledge of Czech culture and history. And finally, before his appointment to the Collège de France, he was full professor of Latin literature at the academy of Lausanne, where he enjoyed brilliant success.

Mickiewicz was at that time a famous personality in France. Just a year before the debates on the Slavic chair, George Sand had published in the *Revue des deux Mondes* an article in which she placed him beside Goethe and Byron and compared him with Dante. She said that not since the plaints of the prophets of Zion had a voice risen so powerfully in song on a subject so vast as the collapse of a nation. He had friendly relations with Montalembert, who translated his *Books of the Polish Nation and Polish Pilgrims*. He exerted a great influence on Lamennais, he was connected with Quinet, Michelet, Ampère, Alfred de Vigny, Victor Hugo, Alfred de Musset, Chateaubriand, Nodier,

Armand Carrel, Ozanam, David d'Angers, and Delacroix, who painted his portrait. In Weimar Goethe had received him with great hospitality. He knew personally Uhland and Schlegel, and all great Russian personalities of the day. He had traveled in Germany, Switzerland, and France, and lived a long time in Rome. Of course, Mickiewicz was not a scholar in the precise sense of the word. But he was unquestionably a wise and experienced man of great personal culture, as well as a well-trained philologist.

As a Slavicist he had great difficulties to overcome. The first of these was the fact that Slavic studies were not as yet organized. They were, indeed, only in the nursery. Dobrovský, Durich, and Vuk Karadžić had assisted in its birth at the beginning of the nineteenth century. More important, it began to develop its legs before its head, that is, the study of language before literature, the comparative history and grammar of the Slavic languages before the comparative history of literatures.

If some modern Slavic scholars accuse Mickiewicz's course of not being sufficiently scientific in Slavonic comparative procedure, I may answer that we are still waiting for a course that would be satisfactory in this regard. Very little, if anything, had been done in this field before Mickiewicz, who was forced to make his way almost alone through the Slavic forest without any great help. In particular, in Paris in those days there were no books, no source materials, and no professional preparation in our present-day sense. The most important works for Mickiewicz were those of Nork, Šafařík, Kopitar, Jungmann, Surowiecki, Maciejowski, Lelewel, Naruszewicz, Woronicz, Niemcewicz, Staszic, and Brodziński for Poland and the Slavs in general, as well as Karamzin and some others for Russia.

I may quote on this occasion Professor A. Brückner: ". . . especially in Russian subjects, the poet [Mickiewicz] shows himself much better informed than the Westerners. What he said about Lomonosov, Derzhavin, and Pushkin was a novelty for Europe; how much had he heard from the original personages, such as Pushkin! Many times he was the first in Europe to quote names about whom information came only after 1925. . . . We must admire the knowledge of the poet, who could not rely on a more or less rich library; his acute judgment, which was never swayed by appearances . . . his clear views, which embraced literally the entire Slavic world. How small in comparison are those who accused him of under-estimating Polish culture! How many pertinent judgments he gives on Russian literature!".

But, of course, the peculiar difficulties of Mickiewicz's course were due not only to lack of sources and scientific preparation. There were other and perhaps more important elements: the poet's personality, his spiritual nature, his understanding of his task, and the nature of the atmosphere of the Collège de France, of France, and of Europe itself at that time.

Mickiewicz was a great poet, perhaps one of the greatest of that period in Europe. He was essentially a Romantic poet, inspired in mind and soul. In Russia he had aroused admiration and astonishment as an inspired improviser. His name was on everyone's lips. Pushkin never spoke of him without the epithet *svyše vdokhnovenny*—"inspired from on high"—*on s vysoty vziral na žizn'*. All Russian friends—Boratynsky, Prince Vyazemsky, Kireevsky, Aksakov, Pogodin, Shevyrev, even the famous philosopher Soloviev stressed this same trait. The same is true in France: George Sand, Michelet, Quinet, Hugo, Sarrazin, Schuré, even Renan; and, outside France, Cavour and Mazzini. They all emphasized the inspiration and fervor of his metaphysical and heroic poetry, which at the same time possessed such realistic plasticity.

In his *Ode to Youth* and other poems written in his younger days, Mickiewicz spoke of men "wise by fury, wise by exaltation" and about the "wisdom of the heart" opposed to the rationalism of the "glass of the savant." In *Forefathers' Eve* he presented, in his "Improvisation," a wonderful revelation of poetic inspiration.

In 1833 he published in Paris an article entitled "On Reasonable and Exalted Men." Here we have the same division as in Helvetius between *"les hommes sensés"* and *"les hommes passionnés."* Here he alleges that, in times when "ill and sophisticated minds allow themselves to discuss everything, human wisdom, expelled from books and conversation, hides in the last trench, in the hearts of feeling men . . ." He also demonstrated how, at the time of the first partition of Poland, there were men who, in the name of reason, advised ceding one part of the country in order to preserve the rest. We have seen today whither such calculations may lead.

The poet possessed a wonderful power of suggestion—I call it his genius of personality—of which his gift of improvisation was the most essential and genuine manifestation. It is with this personal prestige that he seduced and captured the hearts and imaginations of his Russian friends in Petersburg and Moscow. But he also possessed a great self-confidence and awareness of his dominating force. He had nothing of the Usurper, of the Pretender about him. He was a lord and knew it. What did he do after the insurrection in which he took no part? He wrote the Third Part of his *Forefathers' Eve,* in which he gives the story of the imprisonment of himself and his fellows at Wilno in 1823 and 1824. This story, in spite of the terrible consequences of the insurrection, became the poetic *summa* of Polish martyrdom. And what were the sufferings of young students of Wilno in comparison with the sufferings of Poland after 1830–31! But he possessed the magnificent power of making his conception valid.

Now let us see what Mickiewicz actually accomplished in the Collège de France. In the first place, his was a very personal course. It could not be otherwise for the objective and subjective reasons we have already noted. It was conceived very broadly, constructed around certain ideas deeply bound up with the personality of the professor. This course had its own method, with which Mickiewicz tried as best he could to initiate his audience into the Slavic world. It had a political purpose, but Mickiewicz made a tremendous effort to be as objective and impartial as possible in the circumstances which he confronted. His performance was uneven. Sometimes it was full of genius, perspicacity, brilliance, and originality, containing appreciations valuable even today. Sometimes it was less successful—too personal—and included errors and inaccuracies.

Kallenbach, the enthusiastic Polish monographer of Mickiewicz, has complained of the omission of certain facts. He notes the poet's tendency to give highly colored pictures, bold generalizations, great syntheses which are not always in accord with the true facts or with concrete historical data. Leger limited his criticism to the assertion that Mickiewicz's course constituted a very noisy enunciation of Polish Messianism and that he never knew anyone who had the patience to read the volumes it occupied. Mazon found the course rather *"une introduction au slavisme"* than to Slavic philology, and added that for the organization of "our studies" this course is useless. He took pleasure in stating that the successors of Mickiewicz, Robert and Chodźko, introduced the study of texts and locked themselves up in grammar and linguistics.

Finally Pogodin, the Russian admirer of Mickiewicz, author of a Russian monograph on the life and works of the poet, indulges in recriminations in behalf of Russia. He is displeased with the Pole's lack of objectivity, with his ingorance of the development of Russian romantic literature, remarking that his lectures on Russian history simply followed Karamzin. He quotes Šafařík's opinion that there will be little profit for learning from Mickiewicz's lectures.

I shall not attempt any polemic against Leger; he said that he never knew anyone who read the *Slavic Literature* of Mickiewicz. This seems to me a matter of exaggerated egotism, a generalization from his own opinion. Kallenbach's reservations are concrete. But was it so important that Mickiewicz did omit those few facts? I should like to see a modern Slavist who could give a general and absolutely thorough general Slavic course. Perhaps a Czech, for Slavic philology is their great love. But at the time of Mickiewicz, even Šafařík's *Slavic Language and Literature* was a very modest book.

Nor did Mazon, one of the successors of Mickiewicz's chair, convince me. Mickiewicz presented the morphology of historical ideas, the syntax of great cultural events. The problems of Slavic linguistics, dynamic as they are, could not be a suitable frame for his Slavic studies. He made certain efforts in the field of grammar and etymology, but his etymological conceptions were unfortunately strongly influenced by his mysticism. They cannot be defended against scientific criticism. Mazon at least is right, but in a sense which he does not seem to approve himself, when he remarks: "But great as this action was, it was more a question of Slavism than of Slavistics, and actually Mickiewicz was not thinking of an introduction to the study of the Slavs which he wrote then, but one of the most singular chapters of Slavic ideology on the summit of romanticism."

My old friend Professor Pogodin, a tested friend of Poland, has been with regard to Mickiewicz's lectures a victim of his own great knowledge, and, I fear, of his lack of a sense of psychology. It is the more astonishing that Professor Pogodin himself in the same book, a few pages above, evinces a very keen understanding of Mickiewicz's personality. It is true that Mickiewicz did not discuss the development of Russian romanticism; his knowledge of Russian literature, as treated in the course, ended with Pushkin in 1829–31. The reason for this is simple: a lack of sources, absence of books and information, in spite of what he received from certain Russian friends—Turgenev, Mme. Circourt, Baron Eckstein, Mukhanov, and Prince Vyazemsky.

Even Polish literature he finished with the *Undivine Comedy,* written in 1833. How did he describe the development of Russian literature? I have no space here to quote his wonderful characterizations of Derzhavin, Zhukovsky, Batyushkov, and Pushkin himself, with keen psychological insight and all sort of personal details. He analyzed "The Prophet," *Boris Godunov, Evgeny Onegin,* and many other works. Even today the finest and most honest explanation of Pushkin's complicated relations with Nicholas and the Decembrists is that of Mickiewicz. Professor Pogodin complains that Mickiewicz is not sufficiently enthusiastic in his appreciation of Lomonosov, but this is a matter of subjective opinion. Mickiewicz spoke of *The Tale of Igor,* to which he devoted two most penetrating lectures, of Nestor, and even about Drakula and Shemyaka, of Kantemir in great detail, of Lomonosov, Dmitriev, Karamzin, Fonvizin, Vyazemsky, Russian Byronism, and the intellectual atmosphere in Russia at the beginning of the nineteenth century. All is told carefully and seriously, with traces of authentic personal knowledge of Russia and its important personalities. He presented certain noteworthy pages, certain splendid characterizations of historical figures, such as Ivan the Terrible, Boris Godunov, Peter the Great and Catherine. He recounted in precise detail the overthrow of thrones, the murder of Paul, the Decembrist revolt. This material could not be taken from Karamzin, whose history closed with the beginning of the seventeenth century.

Is it unnatural that Mickiewicz attacked Russia, her policy, the Russian autocracy? Scarcely ten years had passed since the Polish insurrection, and persecution still raged in Poland. Even in these circumstances, so trying for Mickiewicz as a Slavist at the Collège de France, he tried to achieve the utmost objectivity in his exposition of Russia itself. It was a miracle of elegance and high humanity. His hearers were amazed by his generous efforts to sacrifice his national feelings on the altar of his scholarly mission. We have a witness of these struggles, moral struggles for moral dignity, in Michelet himself: "Just to think of it makes me tremble. The Russians who were there were astounded and cast their eyes to the ground. The Polish auditors presented a faithful image of pain and misery. Exiled, banished, condemned old men, broken by age, living ruins of former times and battles; poor old women in the garb of the masses, yesterday Princesses—today women laborers; everything lost—rank, wealth, blood, life. Their husbands and children buried on the field of battle, in the fields of Siberia! . . . The sight of them pierced the heart. What strength was necessary, what enormous sacrifices and what heartbreak, to speak to them like this, to tear from the forgetting and the forgiving, to deprive them of everything left to them and their last treasure, hatred."

Russians wrote letters to the Professor protesting against his Russophobia; he speaks of them in his lectures . . . Poles also protested, and maintained he was less Polish than Slavic and Russophile, that he gave too much attention to Russian literature. But Mickiewicz knew very well what he was doing, and the divergences of his critics prove him to have been right.

His course was essentially comparative. He compared the Slavs in their geography, languages, history, culture, religion, and literatures. Furthermore, he constantly compared Slavic phenomena with facts pertaining to Western European, Byzantine, and classic civilization. This made the Slavic world, exotic as it was in certain aspects, unintelligible in Paris. For example, he compared the Polish annalists and historians, such as Gallus, Kadłubek, and Długosz, not only with Nestor and the other Russian annalists and annals, but also with Philippe de Commines, Livy, and Machiavelli. He spoke about the great influence of Czech culture in Poland. His analysis of the psychology of the tyranny of Ivan the Terrible is based on a broad comparison with Nero, Tiberius, Caligula, Louis XI, Cromwell, and Robespierre. He makes a striking sketch of the character of Peter the Great, calling him a Russian *"communard,"* as did Pushkin, who compared Peter with Robespierre. Skarga is compared with Bossuet and Masillon, and a fine analysis is provided of the structure and style of Polish and French sermons. Rej is compared with Montaigne and Rabelais. Kochanowski with Ronsard, Tasso, and Ariosto, juxtapositions which have become classic and which originated with Mickiewicz.

The same may be said of his lectures on Czech history and literature, and on the culture and the literature of the Balkans. For example, he compared the Serbian epics with Homer . . . He compared Pushkin, Byron, and Goethe. He gave a sketch of Slavic Byronism, delivered lectures on Polish philosophy, and spoke about the German philosophers, Kant, Schelling, Fichte, and Hegel. He even discussed Emerson. He demonstrated with irony how, according to Hegel's system, the "historical God" is Prussian. He spoke extensively about the Baroness Krüdener, Joseph de Maistre, and the Russian Martinists. How enthusiastic is his picture of the "Russian Renaissance"—the beginning of the reign of Alexander I!—He gave a striking account of Ivan the Terrible's flirtation with England, a brilliant exposition of Romanticism and Byronism in Europe and in the Slavic countries, a picture of the sixteenth century, the Polish Golden Age, and spoke of Slavic antiquities in Rome.

Mickiewicz presented the history of Slavic nations in close connection with European history. Sometimes his characterizations are superbly perspicacious, as for example the few lines about Machiavelli in which he alludes to his conception of unifying Italy as based only on certain ancient memories without any connection with actual problems, on a utopia of his own making. Especially eloquent is the comparison of the Russian soldiers with the Scythian slave or the poor slave forced to be a hangman despite himself. And yet there was no anger in these symbolic juxtapositions.

Parallel to the comparative aspect of his course runs its historical structure. In spite of certain mistakes and errors, he grounded his literary material firmly on a historical basis. He established certain historical ideas, certain cultural conceptions and literary characterizations which have become classic, and have maintained their value to the present day. For example, his was the keen observation that the subtle aristocratic Greek and Latin traditions of Polish Humanism weakened the Jagellonian system, developing in Poland an overrefined spirituality and idealism in notions of individual freedom. He gave a highly colored picture of Pasek and his diary, a document of Polish life of the seventeenth century. He was not afraid to advance a dramatic description of the Polish eighteenth century, while, on the other hand, he presented an original history of Peter the Great, stressing the purely materialistic Europeanization of Russia. He asserts that Peter led Europe to Russia in order afterwards to lead Russia against Europe. His classic comparison of Ivan the Terrible and his age with Sigismund August and Batory and their age is completely original and arresting even now.

Of course the most essential and appealing part of his exposition was his conception of the historical and cultural, the ideological and moral duality of Russia and Poland. The ruling idea of Russian history is power, autocracy, despotism, the organization of the Empire. The ruling idea of Poland is freedom based on moral grounds, on the recognition of the dignity of individuals and nations. The Russian Tsar was a master. The elected Polish king was a sovereign servant and protector of the law. And Mickiewicz shows how the Russian idea had subordinated every part of Russian life, religion, social and political life, and even literature.

On another occasion he speaks of the absorption of the human personality by the state, of the contempt for public opinion, of material power as the most essential factor in the Russian government. An enemy of the Russian autocracy but not of the Russian people, Mickiewicz was conscious that the dismemberment of Poland brought the Russian state geographically closer to Europe, but at the same time removed the Russian nation from the moral unity of European civilization.

At that time the conception of the *moral* unity of Europe was not a fiction, and Mickiewicz was always an ardent defender of this idea. He stated the paradox that on one side we see the

Polish aristocrats fighting for freedom and liberty wherever this fight goes on, and on the other side the illegitimate power Russia everywhere defending the principles of "legitimism" in order to subordinate human freedom and liberty.

Many times in his course Mickiewicz sought to find a solution for the "eternal Russo-Polish Thebaid." He hoped for the spiritual transfiguration of the Russian state and Russian life, and he had the courage to appeal to that transfiguration and to a peace between the two greatest Slavic nations. He was the enemy of Russian autocracy and Russian slavery, but not of the Russian nation.

In his appeal for peace and understanding he was a priest and a prophet. He preached until the end of his scientific career: and his mission is partly expressed in his last lecture:

"I do not speak well in French. I learned this language only by use . . . I express myself with difficulty: my common conversation is often interrupted: I am not able to find the necessary word—and even, in this language, the most difficult of all that I know, in a language at which I never worked—I was obliged to speak to an audience of the Collège de France! But I had to speak about my nation and about my religion; I could not pay attention to these obstacles, I could not be busy polishing my sentences and choosing my words. I am a Christian: I remember that in the Gospel it was expressly forbidden to one who has to proclaim great truths to arrange previously in his mind what he has to tell. . . . I lacked every assistance used by everyone on such occasions. I had no Slavic library at hand, I had no Slavonic scholars whose advice I could ask—and I even was in need of books and advice. But everyday I said to myself—if I, a Pole, lacking means of influence over the French audience, lacking prestige, popularity and the gift to amaze, I who never spoke in a language of passion and never made any allusion to actuality, never courting any opinion, on the contrary—fighting against everybody—if I am able to find a union with my audience, if it recognizes me as their organ, it will be a sign, it will be a living proof that the nation to which I belong and which is in the same situation as I, is your brother in spirit, and will be able some day to awaken your national sympathy, develop it, and conserve it."

This was his last lecture in May, 1844. Two events which took place in Paris just before the beginning of his course eventually exercised a peculiar influence on him and led him far from his professorial task. On December 15, 1840, the ashes of Napoleon arrived in Paris. The same day saw Andrew Towiański arriving from Wilno on his small Lithuanian horse, with the sole aim of being present at the ceremony. After two days Towiański returned homeward, but in a year he was again in Paris. Soon Mickiewicz found himself under his influence. Towiański's mysticism, developed in Rome, and his romantic cult of Napoleon as a man of Destiny, prepared in the poet the way for his mystic doctrine. He began in his course to teach this doctrine and to preach the cult of the Great Emperor. It was under the reign of Louis Philippe.

He also taught love and respect for the suffering masses. He showed the revolutionary truth that the real creative power of human comprehension and love, the factor of international understanding, is to be found in the hearts of the common people. He showed how the faith and prayer of the Polish common people stopped Russian officers and soldiers whom Polish guns could not stop. . . .

Mickiewicz finally had to abandon his course. What is more, he devoted himself to new humane and religious enterprises. He had sacrificed poetry for his chair; now he sacrificed his chair for his Polish Legion.

11

Catholicism and Christian Democracy in Poland

Adam Żółtowski

The outbreak of the French Revolution (1789) marked the beginning of a new period in most countries of Europe, and Poland had reasons of her own for remembering approximately the same date as the opening of a new unhappy chapter in her history. The 3rd of May, 1791, witnessed the triumphant enactment of a new Constitution, an event which crowned long endeavors for political and social reform; in 1795, the three despotic neighbors of Poland, always opposed to this country's regeneration, finally partitioned her territory among them.

The impact of Catholicism on what can be called the Polish *ancien régime* was very pronounced. The period of the Reformation had passed almost without leaving a scar. The Church's position was unchallenged, her influence very far reaching, her wealth imposing. She could be considered as strongly welded with the old order of things, while the new order would be the work of secular forces. And yet the Constitution of 1791 was by no means anti-religious. It proclaimed tolerance for all creeds, but declared "the Holy Roman Catholic faith with all its rights" as the "prevalent national religion." This was at least partly due to the fact that the clergy had by no means been opposed to the reformist currents. If any one man had, before the middle of the century, done much to inaugurate the campaign in favor of educational and political improvement it was Stanislas Konarski (1700–1773), the provincial of the Order of the Piarists and author of a memorable work entitled *Effective Counsels.*

Thus the nation on finding itself deprived of its liberty and torn into three parts, at least was not at the same time alienated from its faith. On the contrary it is safe to state that through the Partitions a new bond was forged between the nation and the Church, and the Poles were taught to cherish Catholicism as the one great tradition and inheritance of the past which political calamities were not able to destroy. Such a way of thinking avowedly had its dangers, but it was a safeguard against secularism gaining complete mastery as it had, since the French Revolution, largely penetrated the atmosphere of Europe. It had its repercussion also in Poland, for in the days of the "Duchy of Warsaw" (1807–15) and of the "Congress Kingdom" (1815–31) religious concerns were not in the forefront and many leading personalities were known to be indifferent or even adverse to religion. Yet we have conclusive evidence that this trend had not been instilled into the depth of the nation's soul.

The works of Adam Mickiewicz, the greatest and most popular poet in Poland (1798–1855), who began to write at this very time, show the dominant position that Catholicism occupied in the mind of this man of genius. His great epic *Pan Tadeusz* begins with an invocation of the Blessed Virgin which is more than a literary ornament, as it is immediately followed by an allusion to the poet's miraculous recovery in childhood from a mortal illness. The true hero of the poem is no other than a penitent assassin who becomes a Bernardine friar and is seeking to expiate his sin. In another masterpiece of Mickiewicz, *Dziady* (Forefathers), two priests are among the important characters. One of them is evidently a Uniate, as he has lost his wife, and receives the hero in his house, where he is living with his children. This detail, introduced by the author as something entirely natural, also shows how completely the Church Union was merged in the life of Poland's eastern provinces. The other priest, Father Peter, plays a more momentous part in the drama. It is he who through his prayers saves the hero from the sin of blasphemy and of revolt against the decrees of Providence. Mickiewicz inaugurated romanticism in Poland, a literary current which in the whole of Europe marked the end of eighteenth century rationalistic "enlightenment" and a general tendency to return to religious belief.

In the period which followed the ill-fated insurrectionary war of 1830–31, the influence of religion was very powerful. Three attitudes towards belief can be distinguished among the representative personalities of the time. A traditionalist and mainly conservative attitude prevailed in the country, as is natural at a time when a nation feels that its religion is attacked and desires to defend it as one of the cherished treasures, inherited from the past. And at this time precisely, hostile measures against the Church were taken both in the new Prussian and Russian provinces of Poland. In Prussia the "secularization" of most of the convents was enforced, accompanied by confiscation of their property. In the east, Nicholas I carried out more sweeping measures. In 1839, the Uniate Church was suppressed at one stroke, and in 1841 the Latin Church was deprived of all its still very extensive estates. Not only did the Church thus become the pensioner of the Russian Government, but its traditional and concrete influence on social conditions in the countryside met with a sudden end. Soon a conflict also broke out with the Prussian Government over mixed marriages, which led to the imprisonment of Archbishop Martin Dunin, an event bound to make a deep impression on the country at large.

The activity of one of Poland's most renowned preachers Fr. Charles Antoniewicz, S.J., began about the same time. In 1846 he faced a social problem under specially dramatic circumstances. In February of that year the peasantry of western Galicia, at the instigation of the Austrian authorities, turned against an incipient Polish insurrectionary movement, represented to them as hostile to their emancipation, and carried out a massacre of the landed gentry in which about 2000 persons perished. Fr. Antoniewicz undertook a truly missionary tour of the most troubled districts and obtained astonishing results. Yet Poland in those days was not free to produce any bold initiative or new idea in its homeland, controlled as it was by despotic and suspicious governments. It is abroad, among the refugee communities that the most important developments took place. Here about 1840, a strong religious revival occurred. A significant step was taken in Rome to provide for the needs of the Polish Church and to face the new problems of the nation; a group of former Army officers, among which Peter Semenenko, Jerome Kajsiewicz and Alexander Jelowicki were the best known, founded a religious order known as the Resurrectionists.

The difficulties with which the Resurrectionists had to cope were a function of the general European situation. Political reaction was in its heyday at this time and the three monarchies which had partitioned Poland, with rare unanimity stood guard over the existing order. At the same time, however, those revolutionary trends, which had been driven underground since Napoleon's rise to power, had by no means become extinct. As the years elapsed, they bestirred themselves with ever greater energy. The July revolution of 1830 gave them their first encouragement, that of 1848 was their achievement, the Paris Commune of 1870–71 their repercussion. They were political in the first place, pursuing the overthrow of absolutism and the establishment of national independence and unity, as was in the case of the Italian *Carbonari*. Even there, however, social upheaval was by no means suppressed. In France the movement carried a heavy charge of social theories, mostly descended from the doctrines of the communist Babeuf and aiming at the destruction not only of absolutism but of the existing order of society, a venture considered as the necessary condition for any possible progress. The manifold varieties of revolutionary programs were also united in their hostility to the Church, which during the pontificate of Gregory XVI opposed them with justified determination, but did not proceed to develop any views or decisions of its own on the most urgent problems of the times. The Church in those years could have appeared to many as one of the elements of the established order which had thrown in its lot entirely with the forces of the past.

The position of the Poles was especially paradoxical; on one hand the past stood for everything they had lost and was their chief mainstay; on the other hand, the existing order was their country's doom, and its defenders their implacable enemies. It was understandable that many patriots believed in the cause of revolution and Poland's cause to be one and the same, and a universal upheaval their unique opportunity. This was on the whole the attitude of the left or "democratic" wing of the great body of political refugees from Poland after 1831, with the historian Lelewel, and a talented publicist, Maurycy Mochnacki, at their head. The chief social problem of the time in Poland was the position of the peasants who, with the exception of the now Prussian provinces, were still under an antiquated system of serfdom. The democratic party cherished the most sanguine hopes in connection with its plan of raising the peasant question in the whole country in a revolutionary fashion and at whatever cost.

This attitude of impatient endeavor found its expression also in the religious field. Many men who had endorsed the revolutionary program naturally became alienated from the Church and soon repeated the anti-religious slogans which they had learned in their new environment. But radicals were not always prone to irreligion. Some of them had a deep feeling for the traditions of their country. For that very reason they revolted against "the official Church's" apparent indifference to the crimes perpetrated upon Poland. These ideas and reactions present in many minds were to crystalize through the agency of a personality capable of giving them forceful utterance. Andrew Towianski, a country gentleman from Lithuania, who arrived in Paris in 1841, soon convinced many Polish refugees there that he was the bearer of a religious message of great importance. He formed a "circle" for the service of the "cause of God" and gained an extraordinary ascendancy over those who came under his influence. He is and probably will always remain a mysterious and controversial historical figure. The three bulky volumes filled with his interviews and conversations, mostly with men of some importance, make poor reading, although they are alluded to as *Symposia*. The ideas are propounded in a monotonous form and have the tendency to become vague and obscure. And yet the extraordinary attraction exercised by this man over many of his contemporaries including many non-Poles is unquestionable.

The Church authorities naturally were soon keeping a vigi-

lant eye on this movement. Certain theses attributed to Towianski were condemned, and the Resurrectionists opposed it
wherever it cropped up. Yet Towianski personally did not seem
to have incurred ecclesiastical rigors. In spite of the deep impression produced by him on many, his influence would have
remained necessarily limited, had it not been for the fact that
Mickiewicz, by this time at the height of celebrity, was among
the first victims of the "master's" extraordinary gift for gaining
power over human minds. The poet had entered upon the
second phase of his life, when his genius appeared to succumb
under the burden of public and private misfortune and to burn
itself out in a spasmodic struggle against destiny. But Mickiewicz was in a position in which he could effectively propagate
ideas, as he was called to a chair of Slavonic literature at the
Collège de France in Paris, where the teaching is given not only
to students but to the general public as well.

Mickiewicz in his much commented lectures developed his
views on "Messianism." This word had first been applied to a
philosophy attempting to lay down the laws of future human
progress by the Polish philosopher Hoene-Wronski. One definition given by Mickiewicz was the following: "The best developed soul is chosen as an instrument of the Godhead. That is
the principal dogma of *Messianism.*" The poet thought he had
discovered a chosen soul of this sort in no other than Towianski.
He also cherished and expounded broader views. All Slavonic
nations appeared to him as gifted with the prerequisites of a
higher spirituality and were on the point of developing it for
the benefit of the entire human race. Yet the actual birthplace
of the new spirit was in one Slavonic nation only—the one
which had suffered the most, which was closest to Europe and
which had served Europe most faithfully. And this was no other
than the Polish nation. The faith in such a historical mission of
the nation was to be known as "Polish Messianism" and was the
core of the teaching of Mickiewicz at this time. The founding of
a religious, political and social unity among all the nations was
the goal. Not only tyranny, but materialism and soulless routine
in all its many forms, were the chief obstacles to its attainment.
The poet at times bitterly denounced the "official Church" for
neglecting the great traditions of Christianity and failing to

impart to the European body those heroic and inspired impulses of which it stood in such dire need.

The attitude of Mickiewicz and his occasional outbursts were deprecated and criticized by many, yet he was never personally the object of any ecclesiastical censures. His lectures with those of two other professors, Quinet and Michelet, were suspended by the French Government on purely secular grounds. The restraint observed by the Church authorities proved beneficial. Three years later when Pius IX showed understanding and good-will towards the Italian national aspirations, conceded a certain liberty of the press, convened a consultive assembly in the Papal States and appointed a civil government. He was acclaimed with enthusiasm by the Poles who saw in these decisions the expression of the coveted unity of political and religious aspirations. In the spring of 1848 Mickiewicz, who was in Rome, made his submission to the Church and received absolution.

This act of humility did not bring peace to the poet's vehement and tormented spirit. Having failed to carry the Pope with him on a crusade of the free peoples against tyranny, he led a small body of men known as the "Polish Legion" from Rome to Milan where it was absorbed in the Piedmontese armies. Though the direct movement inspired by "Polish Messianism" ended in frustration, it had stirred up other intellectual forces, and powerful minds were already seeking for more correct solutions of the problems brought up in the "messianistic circles."

At the present time, when throughout a great part of the globe Karl Marx is quoted as a paramount authority, it seems doubly desirable to remember what some contemporaries of his, with no meaner talent and the very highest philosophical culture, thought of the future of the human race. In the same year 1848 in which Marx issued the *Communist Manifesto,* August Cieszkowski anonymously published a volume entitled *Our Father,* which contained his version of the philosophy of history. The author's approach to the great questions of the time was neither traditionalistic nor revolutionary. He was vividly aware that the world was nearing a great crisis, that an entire epoch of human history had come to a close and a new age was beginning, that the inevitable transition to a new order of things could bring into the world felicity or untold woe, that in order to accomplish it safely humanity must abide by the teaching of Christ, and make His Gospel its guide. Endeavors and undertakings in the social and political sphere, if divorced from religion, would always end in disappointment. For holy ends, holy means must be devised, as unholy means necessarily lead to catastrophe. As for revolution, it was sterile and never to be conceived as essential to the attainment of social and political ends. The paramount role and dignity of freedom were among Cieszkowski's conceptions on which he most eloquently commented. He argued that religious standards applied to the affairs of the world were not only desirable but alone adequate; that the social question was basically a religious one and the entire history of mankind amounted to the unfolding of a religious theme, the relation between humanity and God.

After the middle of the century, the atmosphere of Europe began to change rapidly. The great expectations of 1848 faded, positivism raised its head, utilitarianism set the tone, and in Poland the unfortunate insurrection of 1863 sounded the knell of romanticism, the protagonists of which had by this time passed away. But it was of great significance for the future that in Poland faith had left its lasting imprint on the highest sphere of artistic and intellectual achievement. Although events once more forced Catholic thought back to a mainly traditionalist and defensive position, yet its continuity was never broken. It was partly secured by individuals such as Stanislas Kozmian, who was Krasinski's schoolfellow and his intimate friend, and who after 1831, spent twelve years in England, largely devoted to political activities. His brother Fr. Jan Kozmian was founder of the periodical *Przegląd Poznański* (Poznań Review) and the inspirer of a Catholic group in Prussian Poland headed by General Desiderius Chłapowski who introduced new methods in agriculture, originated a popular press and vocational education of the small farmers. In that province which, since 1840 had been under a relatively liberal government, some other ventures of social character brought excellent results. One of them was the Society of Educational Assistance founded by Karol Marcinkowski. The society collected funds and distributed them among needy youths exclusively in the form of repayable scholarships. In a century of stable currency the scheme proved a great success. The clergy were among the chief beneficiaries and in due course among the most active supporters of an institution which in part compensated the Church for the loss of her ancient affluence.

Since 1848, after 17 years of complete absence of parliamentary institutions on Polish soil, the Poles under Prussian sovereignty were called upon to elect representatives to the Prussian Diet. Here the clergy immediately occupied a conspicuous place. Among the first to be elected was Fr. John Chrysostomus Janiszewski, later to be bishop coadjutor of Gniezno. He sat not only in the Prussian Diet, but also in the German National Assembly of 1848–9 at Frankfurt where he voiced the protest of the Poles against the plan of including the Polish provinces of Prussia in a German Empire. He was also a member of the Polish League, convened in 1849 on the initiative of Cieszkowski, as a sort of National Council of Poland, but soon suppressed by the Prussian authorities. Bishop Janiszewski was a brilliant preacher and gained special renown by his funeral orations which often had a political background.

Another priest, Fr. Alexius Prusinowski was also for many years a deputy to the Prussian Diet where in 1852 he, in collaboration with Cieszkowski, raised the demand for the establishment of a University of Poznań, and proved that the estates and funds which had served public education before the Partitions and had been confiscated by Prussia, amply justified such a demand. He also devoted much labor to the editorship of several popular periodicals, thus contributing to the gradual rise of general culture in the Polish provinces of Prussia.

Even before the insurrection of 1863, another event symbolized the change of the times. Prince Adam Czartoryski died in 1861 at the age of 91, after having been for many years responsible for most Polish endeavors in the international field. In his youth Czartoryski had known eighteenth century aloofness from religion. By the time he became the most influential Polish political leader, he had no doubts about the need of religion for the survival of the nation. By this time it had become a subject of constant Polish concern that the Holy See be adequately informed of conditions in Polish lands and duly prepared to counter the diplomatic maneuvers of the Partitioning Powers, especially of Russia. Czartoryski pursued even bolder aims. In order to oppose Russian penetration of the Balkans he endeavored to bring about the Union with Rome of the National Churches there, especially in Bulgaria. As early as 1827 he had written a book entitled *Essai sur la diplomatie* in which he put forward the idea that the world could not exist without peace and that peace could only be based on a league among the nations and the restoration to them of their full rights. Just before he died he wrote an aphorism which expressed his deep and mature views: "Catholicism should not be founded on the love of country, but patriotism on the love of God."

After the insurrection of 1863, a peaceful development of Catholic thought was impossible, as far as the Polish provinces under Russia were concerned. A storm broke out over the Church. The newly appointed archbishop of Warsaw, Mgr. Felinski, was deported; the same fate was reserved for the bishop of Plock, Mgr. Popiel, and the bishop of Sejny, Mgr. Lubienski, who died on the way into exile. The deportations of the bishops of Wilno, of Samogitia and of Luck were soon to follow. The imprisonment of priests, the closing of churches, and dispersion of religious communities were the order of the day. The power of the "Catholic College," a government department for Church affairs, was extended to the point of placing all relations of the Church with the Holy See under its direct control. Two dioceses, those of Podlasie and of Luck, were suppressed by a unilateral decision of the Russian Government. The most cruel attack was directed against Catholicism by the violent abolition of the Uniate Church within the boundaries of the Congress Kingdom where it had still been allowed. The only conclusion that could be drawn from these loathsome events was that in Poland, for better or for worse, the destinies of Church and nation were interlocked. The courageous language used by Pius IX in his famous allocution of April 24, 1864, and in his Encyclical of July 30 of the same year showed that the Church was still, as of old, a mainstay of freedom.

These developments were far from having spent themselves
when a conflict between Church and State broke out in another
quarter. The origin of the so-called "Kulturkampf" in Prussia
was Bismarck's desire to subdue the Catholic Church to a similar control by the State authorities as that exercised in relation
to the Protestant Churches. By a series of laws enacted in May
1873, the education of the clergy, appointments to ecclesiastical
positions and benefices, ecclesiastical jurisdiction and certain
other activities were made dependent on the secular power.
When opposition against this interference with the life of the
Church proved determined and unanimous, all payments from
the Treasury for religious needs were stopped and almost all
the religious orders expelled.

The purpose pursued by Bismarck in relation to the Church
was in fact very similar to the aims of the Russian administration, yet his action was limited by a Constitution while the possibilities of his opponents were correspondingly increased. The
Church in the Polish provinces suffered considerable losses,
probably most of all through the expulsion of the religious
orders. On the other hand the Catholic community was con-
solidated by the struggle, the position of the clergy raised and
many desirable developments prepared for the future. The
Archbishop of Gniezno and Poznań, Mgr. Miecislas
Ledóchowski, who was imprisoned for his unyielding attitude,
gained immense popularity and universal veneration which
reached its peak when, on March 15, 1875, he received the
Cardinal's purple while in jail at Ostrowo. The Polish people
resolutely ranged themselves on the side of the Church; the
Polish Party in the Prussian Diet stood beside the Catholic
Centre in the forefront of the parliamentary battle and a
number of ecclesiastical members such as Mgr. Florian Sta-
blewski (later to be Archbishop of Gniezno), took rank among
the political leaders of the nation.

Again, circumstances were not favorable for theoretical investigation, but practical solutions and developments in a
Catholic spirit made visible headway. The Catholic press was
one of the greatest needs in such a crisis and found a talented
promoter in the person of Fr. Kantecki, editor of *Kuryer Poznański*. Popular periodicals and publications multiplied rapidly.

The need for defense of the Church braced men in all fields of social activity and the final capitulation of Bismarck's government, even if only gradual and partial, heartened the Poles in their struggle for their nationality.

When political liberty was attained by the Poles in Galicia, in 1867, a group of men headed by Joseph Szujski, Count Stanislas Tarnowski (both university professors) and Paul Popiel formed a conservative party with the ideas of countering the irresponsible dealings of politicians who might have plunged the country into new disaster. If this program, after a time, proved wanting in some respects, its authors nevertheless did not use Catholicism as only a pawn in the political game, but truly believed that without religion, the world would relapse into barbarism. As scholars they perceived that historically Catholicism had been one of the elements of Poland's greatness, and they gave expression to that belief in their teachings at the University of Cracow. It was a priest, the Resurrectionist Fr. Valerian Kalinka whose influential book, a picture of Austrian rule in Galicia, revealed its many shortcomings. His confrere, Fr. Stefan Pawlicki, a classical scholar and historian of philosophy, advocated the application of philosophical thought to social problems. The Jesuit Fr. Jan Badeni dedicated himself to the study of social conditions and having become the Provincial of his order, directed its efforts to the social sphere, giving every encouragement to Catholic workers' organizations and to a popular press.

At Lwow where another conservative group had its center, Albert Dzieduszycki taught philosophy and aesthetics in the University, but he was equally well known in Vienna as a leader of the Polish party in the *Reichsrat* and a man of fascinating personality. He lectured and wrote on numerous subjects with great versatility, but in his last works he pointed out, with astonishing perspicacity, the perils threatening modern society and recommended "integral Christianity" as the only true remedy.

Rerum Novarum, described by Cieszkowski on his deathbed as a document of great significance, thus found Poland deprived of many possibilities by the fact of its dismemberment, but not unprepared for its reception. Especially in western Poland where social and economic conditions were the most favorable, the decades following the issue of this famous encyclical witnessed a most active initiative in social organization. Workers' Unions, smallholders associations, popular reading rooms and parish assembly halls sprang up everywhere. A cooperative model organization for savings and credit acquired great importance and a high reputation. Some priests deserved well of this branch of social service. An entirely original undertaking was the founding, on a social basis, of a banking institution, *Bank Ziemski,* to help peasants acquire land. It proved a complete success. The atmosphere peculiar to western Poland at this time was a result of the unrelenting oppression the Poles were suffering at the hands of the Prussian State. This produced the fundamental solidarity among them which is so precious an asset in social development.

The same conditions did not exist in Galicia which, till approximately the turn of the century, still labored under the consequences of past neglect. Yet the possibilities offered by political freedom were put to good use. The personality of Hedvige Zamoyska will long be remembered. When expelled from Prussia, she transferred her school of domestic economy to Zakopane in Galicia. Here she continued for years to inculcate into her numerous pupils principles of Catholic piety and the great traditions of Polish public spirit of which she was the living personification. Near her school stood a house of the Third Order of St. Francis founded by Brother Albert (in his worldly life Adam Chmielowski, a painter of good standing), who devoted his life to the service of the poor and renewed the most severe traditions of the mendicant orders. Mother Marcelline Darowska, the foundress in 1863 of the order of the Immaculate Conception, belonged to the same generation as the preceding two, and her aim was to give the young generation a firm basis of religious education to prepare it for social duties. The four large educational houses which she established in her lifetime, later to be followed by many others, largely contributed to Galicia's position of preponderance in education, which it enjoyed up to 1914. A significant fact in those years was also the creation (in 1914) of a chair of Christian Social Sciences in the University of Cracow.

The developments and reactions in the Polish provinces of Russia were necessarily inhibited by the rigid political system to which they were subjected. The Church was actually placed in such a position that the most it could achieve was to endure. And when the revolutionary movement of 1905–6 set in, the rapidity and violence of events seemed to be unfavorable to mature and fruitful progress. Yet in the Congress Kingdom a campaign against the Tsarist Government schools and in favor of free education was brought to a favorable issue. Free schools sprang up everywhere, in which the teaching was in Polish. Religious education gained much by the change. Mother Darowska established a house at Szymanow near Warsaw, and Fr. Jan Gralewski founded a well-known boarding school for boys. Such individual achievements were characteristic of these times of transition.

The restoration of the Polish State after the First World War brought back to the entire Polish people opportunities missing for more than a century. This great change was nowhere more distinctly to be felt than in Church affairs. On large territories where the Church for nearly a century had barely been tolerated every initiative could now be realized, if only the necessary means could be found. For the intellectual needs of the Church the Catholic University of Lublin was founded and maintained from private funds, while four State universities had theological faculties. In addition there were thirteen Institutes of Religious Culture in various parts of Poland. Monastic life could again flourish freely and some new establishments attained great importance. The Catholic press attained a circulation greatly in excess of pre-war times. However, the center of Catholic thought was undoubtedly the University of Lublin of which the Dominican Fr. Hyacinthe Woroniecki was one of the founders. Besides being a philosopher and theologian he studied many contemporary problems such as that of nationalism. Here Fr. Anthony Szymański lectured and wrote on social problems and Fr. Stefan Wyszyński, at the present time Primate of Poland, devoted much attention to social needs and developments. A pleiad of students not only propounded the theories concerning social questions current among Catholics in industrial countries, but took up the rural and

agricultural aspects of these questions which were of paramount importance for Poland. Some sociological books of
a high intellectual level were produced. In Wilno Fr. Alexander
Wójcicki became the historian of the working class in Poland,
while in Cracow Fr. Jan Piwowarczyk, a publicist of considerable talent, belied the suggestion of Catholic subservience to the
propertied classes, at the same time stressing the divergence of
Catholicism and socialism. At Poznań there existed a Catholic
School of Social Science with a strong substratum of sociology.
On the whole these schools of Catholic social thought were
decidedly reformist, distributionist and progressive. Some of
their followers advocated social transformation with so much
insistence that they were accused of neglecting stability and
economic exigencies. In any case this intellectual movement
had not said its final word when the catastrophe of the Second
World War cut it short and withered many promising prospects. Cardinal Hlond formed the Social Council of the Primate
of Poland, established to prepare opinions and pronounce-
ments on current social questions. The Cardinal himself had
not waited for this important body to be convened before he
addressed his people as a teacher. Of his personal letters none
was more important than that of 23 April 1932, on *Christian
Principles of Political Life*. Having to deal with a government
inclined to exaggerate the role and powers of the State, the
Primate reminded his flock that the individual and the family
had inalienable rights, that the liberty of the Church and its
teaching could claim unqualified respect, that the Church never
could be used as a means to any ends foreign to her and that
Catholics in public life could not under any pretence betray
their principles.

These exhortations did not fall on deaf ears. The vigorous
religious revival among the youth of Poland was a striking fact
and this religious current made its way into political circles as
well. There were the Christian Democrats who advocated the
direct application of papal doctrines in social life. There were
political groups which considered that Christian principles
should necessarily figure in a political program. There were
individual politicians who stood for the age-old Catholic traditions of the country. Among these Mgr. Joseph Teodorowicz,

Armenian Uniate Archbishop of Lwow, was the most conspicuous figure.

There were also political schools whose ideas were unconnected with religious thought. The influential National-Democratic party was a case in point. Founded in the age of positivism, it still bore that mark. It was therefore no mean event when Mr. Roman Dmowski, the actual leader of the party, in a much-remarked essay, *Church, Nation and State,* declared that in his opinion good patriots owed unreserved allegiance to the Catholic Church. Dmowski was accused of want of sincerity and of making the Church an object of party maneuver, but the impression produced, especially on the younger generation, was profound and the consequences far-reaching. The ageing statesman personally showed how much he was in earnest.

At the present time any outline of Polish political thought would be incomplete without mention of a personage who by universal consent is considered as one of the most forceful figures ever produced by the Church in Poland. In one of his Paris lectures Mickiewicz said: "A nation is educated in religion, in politics and in morals by great examples alone." That remark would best seem to explain the ascendancy of the late Cardinal Sapieha over his countrymen. He was venerated and beloved not for what he thought, said or wrote, but for his inexhaustible charity, for his courage that never faltered and for his determined stand for the dignity of man, of his country and of the Church. His life is in itself a page of political thought that will guide and educate many generations.

12

Polish Illegal Publications Under Russian Rule

Józef Piłsudski

INTRODUCTION

Someone once called the Poles a nation of conspirators and revolutionaries. He was referring to the period prior to the Rising of 1863, which culminated in that epic struggle. I doubt, however, whether that description was ever more accurate in the past—except, of course, for the brief periods of armed combat and of immediate preparation for it—than it is today, at any rate in the part of the country under Russian domination. The revolutionary movement, clandestine organizations, and circles have now proliferated there to such an extent and have found such wide acceptance that probably the major part of the Polish community in that area is linked to them in one way or another.

Some are wholly absorbed by revolutionary life and become professional conspirators; others are partly involved, modifying to some extent their private, nonrevolutionary life; others yet are involved indirectly, through the former, as sporadic participants in revolutionary actions, or as people with ties of family, love, friendship, or simple acquaintance with the revolutionaries. Finally, the repercussions of the struggle waged by the freedom forces against the tyranny of the Russian government reach every member of the public. They do so through underground publications, strikes, demonstrations, arrests, and police searches, which are the daily news fare of Poles under Russian rule and a subject for constant comment.

Despite the broad scope of the revolutionary movement and its intrusion even into the private lives of countless people, its nature is not widely known. This is due mainly to the fact that people are familiar only with the outward manifestations of the movement, which obviously reveal little of their deeply and deliberately concealed authors. The inevitable secrecy under which the revolutionaries must operate does not help to make them known. Finally, the overwhelming majority of those now active in the movement wield the plough and the trowel rather than the pen, and therefore it is difficult to expect their revolutionary life to find a reflection in literature.

Consequently most evaluations of the revolutionary movement in Poland are characterized by exaggeration in one direction or another. Some build up a myth of the allegedly vast extent and power of the movement, while others underestimate it as a mere extravagance of youth, without appreciating the tremendous effort of the moving spirits and organizers of the revolutionary machine.

As a member of a revolutionary party, acquainted with many of its representatives and as an occasional participant in its activities, I have collected abundant observations and data, which I tried to collate for my own use, so as to get an accurate picture of the situation in Poland.

I divided my work into three parts. The first, presented here, deals with the aspect of revolutionary life concerned with the development and distribution of clandestine publications. The second part will be devoted to revolutionary organizational work and agitation, and the third to the effects of the revolutionary activity and the resulting social change.

SOME HISTORY

Bibula means in revolutionary slang any illegal publication [1] which does not bear the imprint of the Russian censorship

---

[1] Initially "blotting-paper" or "tissue paper," from the Latin "bibulus," fond of drinking; illegal publishers used paper of inferior quality.

office. The output of such publications is steadily growing and they reach an increasingly wide circle of readers. This is acknowledged by the government. Prince Imeretynski stated in his well-known memorandum that illegal books are to be found even in peasants' cottages and that they contribute to anti-government attitudes among rural populations. One should not assume, however, that all illegal publications in Russia are revolutionary in character. The Russian government is so restrictive in its control of social life that there is nowadays hardly a political party that does not publish illegally, by-passing the censorship. Even supporters of collaboration with Russia, basically opposed to illegal activities, published some books abroad and then smuggled them into the country, just like revolutionaries, to distribute them secretly. There exists ecclesiastic, patriotic, socialist, even collaborationist *bibula*. We find among these publications works of the highest artistic merit, such as those of Wyspiański or Zych, and patriotic-clerical scribblings; we find heavy historical volumes and the pamphlets of various parties; even simple prayer books, periodicals, appeals, pictures, newsletters, and so on. All this material somehow is carried accross the border and penetrates wherever people can read Polish, filling the needs of an ever growing class.

Before illegal literature won its present popularity, it went through many stages of development; its beginnings were very modest and timid. I recall vividly my first contact with *bibula* in my childhood in a small country manor in Lithuania some ten years after the Rising of 1863. The memory of the rule of Muraviev "the hangman" was still so fresh that people trembled at the sight of a Russian uniform and paled when they heard the bell heralding the approach of one of the representatives of Muscovite power. My mother used to take out from a hiding place known only to herself some small books, which she read to us children, making us learn some passages by heart. They were the works of the great national poets of Poland. The secrecy, mother's emotion—shared by her youthful audience—and the prompt change of scene effected whenever a stranger accidentally intruded upon our family conspiracy, all left an idelible impression in my mind. These books, together with a few others—the historical songs of Niemcewicz and some pre-insurrection pamphlets—were the only uncensored literature available at the time. They were the remnants saved from the cataclysm of the Rising, religiously preserved like relics, sometimes hastily destroyed through fear whenever real or imaginary danger threatened, but without any wider influence beyond that of the family circle.

The illegal literature was preserved in those days by the stubborn guardians of the national and revolutionary fires, quenched with the blood of the heroes of 1863 and barely flickering. These were like candles on graves, casting a pale and fitful light on the haggard faces of the survivors of the disaster. But fresh grass sprouts on graves, with a new life rising from the ashes, eager for sunshine and freedom. There was a greening in Poland, then one vast graveyard; a new life sprang up and a new movement, breaching the posture of prayerful reverence for the past and opening a new era of clandestine literature. It was the socialist movement.

Socialist publications began to appear sporadically between 1875 and 1876. Their readership was naturally very limited at first, but the enthusiasm of the supporters of the socialist idea and its appeal to the working classes won the publications a wide acceptance precisely in circles which had previously little acquaintance even with censored books. Socialist *bibula* were for a long time the only kind available to the Polish community terrorized in the aftermath of the insurrection of 1863. Gradually, however, the fear and the apathy it had induced wore off, especially when the struggle waged by the socialists had demonstrated that defiance of the barbaric tsarist rule was not impossible. In the eighties, the socialist books and pamphlets were augmented by other illegal publications—foreign editions of Polish classics, historical books, or pamphlets and leaflets commenting on the current situation in Poland under Russian rule.

While the circulation and the volume of these publications increased steadily, their growth faced serious obstacles. They were twofold. First, there was at that time no organization capable of setting up a system of distribution which could serve at least those who were steady readers of that type of literature. The clandestine publications were produced sporadically, at irregular intervals, and distributed haphazardly, so that there was never any assurance that they would reach their public.

The revolutionary organizations where ephemeral and their technical facilities dependent on luck; as a result, *bibula* sometimes were plentiful, but then months might go by without any new supply. No wonder that *bibula* were for most people something extraordinary, brought to the country as if by a miracle, something that one could appreciate, but hardly expect.

Aside from this external obstacle, there were also inner ones. People were simply afraid of the illegal activity of which the clandestine publications were a manifestation. The mere possession of an illegal book promoted its owner, in the eyes of his acquaintances, to the rank of revolutionary activist, while the fear of reprisals and the childish belief in the omniscience and omnipotence of the tsarist police were still so widespread that people generally shunned illegal books. They had to be persuaded to accept and read them, reassured that they would not be in any great danger. Some viewed the possession of an uncensored book as heroism, others as folly, some as a crime, and a few as a means of indoctrination, but hardly any regarded clandestine literature as a necessity to overcome the conditions imposed on Poland by tsarist rule.

In such circumstances the activity of the Polish Socialist Party, known by its initials as P.P.S., opened a new era for illegal publications. It was the first of the revolutionary organizations in post-insurrectionary Poland which existed continuously over a decade, and which developed such technical efficiency that its publishing and distributing activity has never been seriously interrupted. The party publications smuggled in from abroad were at first received with some suspicion. Soon, however, the volume of these publications increased, and the party started publishing in Poland itself its organ, *Robotnik* (The Worker), even while the gendarmes tried to track down the party's printing plant. In the meantime the distribution acquired a certain regularity and the publications began to reach all readers, both in Warsaw and in the provinces, with the result that the public—both the workers and the intelligentsia—accepted them as a permanent feature of their lives.

The success of the P.P.S. made a tremendous impression throughout the Russian empire. Soon suggestions were made to import from abroad various publications. By 1900 there was hardly any revolutionary organization in the whole of Russia, however small, that had not made such proposals to the P.P.S. People came from St. Petersburg, Moscow, Samara, as delegates of various circles, asking us to bring in illegal publications or printing equipment. I recall an amusing interview I had in London in 1897 with one of such delegates.

An earnest looking gentleman, slightly greying, turned up from somewhere in deepest Russia and appealed for my help in establishing contact with the P.P.S.; he had brought with him suitable introductions.

"What business do you have with the P.P.S.?" I asked.

"Well, it's a very complicated business. You see, we have formed in Russia a society for abolishing censorship."

"Censorship?" I cried in amazement. "But, dear sir, wouldn't it be simpler to start with overthrowing the tsar who instituted that censorship?"

"You don't quite understand me. The tsar is one thing and the censorship another. Let others take care of him and we will deal with the censors."

Then he began telling me at considerable length how censorship is one of the most deplorable institutions. I could not but agree, while asking him to explain how he proposed to abolish it and what exactly was the P.P.S. supposed to do about it.

My visitor then proceeded to demonstrate to me with great eloquence that all the revolutionary parties have an interest in the abolition of censorship. He convinced me.

Finally he came to the point of presenting his plan. It consisted in bringing into Russia and distributing such a vast quantity of illegal publications of every kind and variety that the censorship would become futile because of its ineffectiveness.

I was getting more and more impressed by the scale of the task which the association was willing to undertake, so I asked him again what was the role assigned to the P.P.S. in his plan of action. "It's very simple," exclaimed the serious gentleman. "We will deliver to the P.P.S. the necessary publications at any point in Europe, and the P.P.S. will give them back to us at a point of their own choice in Russia."

So it appeared that the colossal plan for the abolition of censorship depended upon the transport capability of the P.P.S.; I

was quite moved by the confidence the naïve delegate had in
our potential, but I tried to explain to him that the P.P.S. had
somewhat different objectives than combatting censorship and
that it could hardly promise to concentrate on that task alone.
The delegate went back, disgusted by the "intolerance of the
P.P.S."

In Poland, where people don't have such "big souls," we did
not have any organizations for the abolition of censorship, but
many individuals and circles based their publishing plans on
the ability of the P.P.S. to smuggle their books into the country.
The printing and distributing activity of the P.P.S. brought
some rays of Western light into the grim jailhouse and by doing
so emboldened people. Illicit literature was no longer anything
unusual, people became accustomed to it, so that after a while it
became possible to introduce a new policy among the recipients
by selling at least some part of the supply. The periodicals
published by the party even had regular subscribers.

The example of the P.P.S. was soon followed by other underground organizations in Poland—the Jewish socialist "Bund"
and the National Democratic party, active among other seg-
ments of the population than those reached by the P.P.S., so
that the number of people familiar with illegal activities and
uncensored publications was steadily growing.

Aside from the party publications, other books were also imported, mainly history and serious fiction, both proscribed in
Russia if they dealt with problems vital for the Poles, such as
that of the conquest of Poland by the Russians. That latter type
of publication reached even the most timid, most collaborationist minded among the Poles. Besides, the collaborationists themselves, if they wanted their views to be
known, had to use the medium of illegal publishing. The first
publication of that type to gain some popularity was Leliwa's
Polish-Russian Relations. The well-known memorandum of
Prince Imeretynski, purloined and published by the P.P.S., acquainted even reactionary minded people with *bibula*. The book
was distributed in thousands of copies and was probably read
by most educated Poles.

The volume of the illegal literature in circulation is hard to
determine with any accuracy. I can only rely on figures pub-

lished in the report of the Central Committee of the P.P.S. for
the period up to 1900. The report states that 99,872 copies of
various publications were distributed in 1899. Other parties did
not publish similar reports, but knowledgeable persons believe
that the total circulation of literature of other than P.P.S. origin
is at least the same. By doubling the P.P.S. figure and making
allowance for the fact that, since 1899, all the parties intensified
their activity, we may conclude that approximately 250,000 to
300,000 copies of clandestine publications are distributed an-
nually in Poland under Russian occupation. I am not familiar
with the corresponding figures for legal, censored publications,
but it is clear in any case that the illegal literature constitutes a
substantial proportion of all the reading matter available in
Poland under Russian domination.

It readily will be seen that the presence of such a vast volume
of illegal publications must have exerted a significant influence
upon the attitude of the public toward all illegal activities and
particularly toward the uncensored books themselves. An illegal book, because it is common, is no longer the object of awe,
nor does it inspire fear of reprisals, but it undermines the government's authority and respect for its power. The term *bibula*
itself, familiarly jocular, implies that such books are widely circulated; they lost the aura of mystery which surrounded them
in the past.

The change in this respect is so striking that it cannot fail to
be observed by anyone who is in a position to compare the
present situation with that of a former period. I have met recently a comrade who had been arrested before 1893 (the year
the P.P.S. activity started) and returned to work after ten years.
When I asked him what impressed him most after his return,
he replied without hesitation that he had been amazed by the
current wide dissemination of illegal literature. "We had to beg
people to take our books," he said, "plant them, slip them into
their pockets. Now I see people asking for *bibula,* demanding it
and buying for cash. Hah, there may even be some hot deals
and profitable speculation in such books." Actually some of the
illegal publications were so popular that one could make money
on them. For example the *Collected Poems,* published in London,
were in such demand among Warsaw workers that the first

batch of five hundred copies was sold within a month and soon the black market price for the small booklet reached 25 kopecks. The term "paying *bibula*" was given to those books which showed a profit.

Even the peasants are acquiring the habit of reading illegal books. I could quote innumerable facts to prove it, but I will mention only two examples. The peasants in a village on the Vistula had been receiving regularly National Democratic publications, as well as occasional copies of Socialist ones. When the *bibula* stopped coming for some reason, the farmers decided to look for them at the source. They collected some funds and sent a delegate charged with finding contacts; he was instructed to look not only for the National Democrats, but also for Socialists. I don't know the details of the odyssey of the village delegate, by horse cart and on foot, but he finally met a P.P.S. man some twenty miles from his village and, having accomplished his mission, returned home.

Another incident occurred in deep Russia, in army barracks. It is well known that Polish draftees do not serve in Poland. The government sends them to Russia or to the eastern regions of the empire, where half the soldiers of some regiments are Polish. It seems that some local students became acquainted with the Polish soldiers in that Russian city and they soon supplied them with a lot of *bibula*. When the news reached Warsaw, they sent there one of the more experienced comrades to deal with the problem. He pointed out to the enthusiastic activists the danger involved in the mass distribution of illegal publications among soldiers and told them to withdraw such literature from the barracks.

When the decision was communicated to the soldiers—and they were mostly peasant youths, straight from the plough— they held a meeting and replied to the agitators as follows: "We cannot get hold of such books by ourselves. If you don't give them to us, we will not have any. But please forgive us if we keep the ones we have got. We want them as our own."

The vast amount of illegal literature circulating in Poland constitutes a new phenomenon under tsarist rule, while the habit of reading it developed among working people in the cities and villages seems to realize the dream of Mickiewicz, himself author of books proscribed in his time, who wanted his works to "find their way under thatched roofs." It is a phenomenon which could not escape the notice of the government. I have already referred to the fact that Prince Imeretynski not only admitted that the peasants read forbidden books, but regarded it as ground for certain improvements in education and a counterpropaganda by the government. The impact of that tsarist cultural offensive proved minimal, or even nil, but it is clear that the government yielded to the influence of *bibula* and retreated to some extent.

Its retreat did not take the form anticipated by the delegate of a Russian association who had visited me in London—censorship was not abolished—but there is no denying a change in the official attitude toward readers of prohibited books. When illegal publications were scarce and their "demoralizing" influence small, the government viewed everyone in possession of such literature as a revolutionary and the discovery of party publications in a home was considered as prima facie evidence of membership in a revolutionary organization. Now, however, when *bibula* is widely circulated, when even people wholly innocent of any political involvement own and read illegal publications, it would be impossible to indict anyone for something that only recently was subject to severe penalties.

First, some *bibula* was recognized as being partially legal, such as the foreign editions of our classics, more recent poetry and fiction published abroad, and, of course, the publications of the collaborationists. Gendarmes searching a home often would not even report the presence of such literature and simply put the book back on the shelf, muttering *"nu, eto pustiaki"* (these are trifles). Or if they did take it, they would not file charges. A gendarme confiscated, in the course of a search in one of my friends' house, two volumes of Limanowski's *Social Movements in the XVIII-th and XIX-th Centuries*. After the case was disposed of, my friend went to the gendarme and asked for the return of the books. The gendarme smiled and handed the books back, advising him to keep them in some other apartment than his own. "You see, at your place, since you are a suspect, the books are some kind of evidence, but elsewhere they would be the normal thing. Everyone reads such stuff, I've read a part of the book myself and it was interesting." I was told a similar story by Lieutenant Colonel Gnoinski. After he had arrested me at the printing shop, I asked him to let me have in my cell the works of Slowacki found at my place. "It's nothing, I realize that one can find this sort of thing in the home of every educated Pole. We don't file charges for it, but I can't let you have it in the cell, because it is, after all, an uncensored publication."

The official concessions were not confined to the category which I described as semilegal *bibula*. In view of the wide circulation of the party and revolutionary publications, they were also included in the softening of the attitude toward illegal literature. The gendarmes realize that the readers of party literature were so numerous (in Warsaw at any rate) and that it was so readily available that it would not be practical to make a case of every copy of a party periodical or pamphlet. Captain Konisski, who interrogated me in Warsaw, said that he doubted whether there was in that city a single working man who had never seen "your *Courier*," as he jocularly described the *Robotnik*. It is true that persons found in possession of such publications are arrested or at least summoned for questioning, but in most cases there is no penalty, or (I know several such cases) a minimal one—two weeks' arrest. Only fresh copies or those in larger quantities attract the attention of the gendarmes, in the absence of other incriminating evidence, as they would suggest the suspect's closer connection with revolutionary organizations.

We observe the retreat of the tsarist government under the pressure of a tidal wave of *bibula,* which compelled it to grant some extension of human rights. This is one of the many examples of the relative flexibility of the Russian system. Since it is based not on law, but on the arbitrary authority of officials, the tsarist government has to accept the natural consequence of that situation—the inconsistency of governmental rulings and frequent exceptions to the established laws and regulations. Since every official shares to some extent in the tsar's autocracy, he carries on his personal policy and, being influenced by his environment far more than the central government is, he is more inclined to compromise and overlook all kinds of infractions.

That was what happened with the attitude of the gendarmes toward illegal publications in Poland.

The laws and regulations of the central administration had not undergone any revision, but their enforcers tacitly accepted a certain class of offences and began to ignore them, to avoid a lot of effort and trouble. The illegal publication remains prohibited under the law, but it has been legitimized to some extent de facto.

It is to be noted, however, that such a legitimization, being without legal force, is neither permanent nor universal. The law, rusty through lack of use, can nevertheless be brought back at any moment and used to punish the offender. In the provinces, especially in rural areas, where the administration and the gendarmes are less busy, the possession of illegal printed matter can still bring harsh penalties. I am convinced, however, that the continuous growth of the popularity of *bibula* in Poland will eventually make it tolerated even in the most remote parts of the country.

Illegal literature is therefore not only in demand by a large proportion of the Polish reading public, but it is also a force with which the powerful tsarist government has to reckon. That is why it may be important to determine who wields that force and who fills that demand. The figures I mentioned give a partial answer to these questions. The great bulk of *bibula* is produced and distributed by the party organizations of the P.P.S. and the National Democrats. The publications of other organizations are not significant in volume, it seems that only those of the Jewish Bund are distributed in some quantity. The nonparty publications, which account for a lesser part of the illegal literature available in the country, are delivered to the reading public either through the efforts of the same parties, or smuggled across the border individually in the pockets of travelers.

The greater number of party compared to nonparty publications is not coincidental. For the general reading public the illegal publications are desirable; they make enjoyable reading, and some people are even willing to take risks for their sake, but they are hardly a necessity. This is not the case with political organizations, which exist through their membership and constantly have to endeavor to enlarge it, as well as fill the gaps left by governmental persecution. Obviously, this can best be achieved when the organization exerts a widespread influence and its views are propagated amongst the greatest possible number of people. Otherwise, in view of the inevitable erosion of the ranks of a party, it would risk losing strength and the capacity to grow.

The only means by which political organizations in tsarist Russia can influence public opinion is the printed word. All others, such as associations, meetings and other oral communication, are very limited in scope under Russian conditions and can be relied upon only to reach a small number of people. The book has therefore to be substituted for the agitator and speaker, to be relied upon to pave the way for the organizer and to assure him of a favorable reception. The book, incidentally, makes a particularly good political activist under tsarist conditions.

The book does not leave traces, as does a human agent: it operates in silence, can be destroyed at any time, remains silent during interrogations, does not attract as much suspicion or draw as heavy penalties as a man. In many cases *bibula* is simply the only weapon available to a party. When an organization is young and still small, without cadres of people capable of carrying on personal propaganda, at time of increased police vigilance, or whenever a particularly concentrated thrust is needed, the *bibula* in the form of pamphlets, copies of a periodical, or a special flyer, is quite indispensable. Let us also bear in mind that, when illegal literature becomes for many people a real need, those filling that need gain influence; furthermore, for people not closely associated with the party, its *bibula* is the only evidence of the party's existence. Altogether the importance of such publications for revolutionary organizations under the tsarist regime is exactly similar to that of blood in a living organism.

I heard the same analogy, though expressed in other words, from one of the leading activists of the P.P.S. in a provincial town. Passing through that city, I called on him to get a report for the *Robotnik* and a certain sum of money for the party. I was annoyed when he gave me only half the amount I had expected and asked him the reason. "Well, comrade, we haven't had any *bibula* for some time. Tell them in Warsaw to send us some." "Ah, so you sell here so many books?" I said, thinking that the shortage of funds was due to lack of saleable merchandise.

My friend laughed and produced a small book with his accounts. "Look here! We get very little for the *bibula*. Most of the money is used for agitation among new recruits, who are not overeager to pay. But without *bibula* we could not collect much among our own comrades. We are only alive when they are coming. We are asleep, comrade, the *bibula* wakes us up."

A political organization functioning under tsarist rule needs publications as a body needs blood; without them it suffers anemia, debility, and slowly dies, unable to exert a wide influence.

Under such conditions, the first and foremost task of every illegal organization is to supply its members with *bibula,* placing in their hands this indispensable weapon. In the house of slavery that Russia is, this is not an easy assignment and it absorbs a large proportion of every organization's efforts.

The illegal publications have to be produced. They are divided into domestic and foreign, the latter predominant in volume, since it is obviously easier to publish abroad than under the watchful eye of the tsar's police. But foreign publications have to overcome the serious obstacles set by the borders of Russia, jealously guarded by the government as a barrier against such imports. That is why every revolutionary organization has to establish channels for bringing its literature from abroad and distributing it secretly in the country.

The *bibula* has to brave countless hazards and obstacles, first of all in crossing the border zone.

RISKS AND SUBTERFUGES

Most of the border, except for the Dąbrowa industrial district and Kalisz, is an agricultural area, cut off from the rest of the country by Russia's deliberate policy of not building railroads which could assist an invasion. Consequently it is not easy to find a comrade who could undertake these duties, especially as

all the localities near the border are under a particularly strin-
gent police supervision. Planting someone specially for that
purpose is also difficult, as there are in these small towns that
are out of the way few opportunities for some legitimate occupation which could serve as cover for an agent.

Only after overcoming these initial obstacles, which may take
months unless some lucky coincidence happens to come along,
can one get down to business. One has to give the comrade
selected for the job a chance to look around and reconnoitre his
field of operation. If he is a smart fellow, he will soon notice
many chances for doing some good work: a channel for getting
bibula across the frontier, an opportunity for getting it out of
the border zone, people who can give some assistance, know-
ingly or otherwise, and so on. After a time a pattern develops,
permitting a regularity in the use of various recurrent situa-
tions.

Comrade X was one of the most accomplished transport ex-
perts. He took a job in some small factory near the border
especially for the purpose of organizing the transfer of illegal
publications. He had a peculiar gift for winning the confidence
and loyalty of people. Within a short time he learned everything about the border zone. He knew the network of relation-
ships between local people and managed time and again to
secure a collaborator in a hazardous enterprise—not an easy
task in a backwater. When he selected someone for this role, he
would first win him over with various services and favors, binding him to himself by the warmth of his friendship, which was
partly sincere, as he grew to like his people genuinely. He proceeded slowly and artfully, without showing all his cards at
once, so that when the "victim," as he used to call his collaborators, realized that he or she was a small cog in some
transportation machine, it was too late to back out—each was
already enmeshed in an intricate net and generally stayed in it.

He found a use for everyone. One person helped him, quite
unwittingly, in building up his reputation among the green
ones, another served as cover for a transport crossing the border, a third took some *bibula* to the nearest city in the guise of a
present, another yet passed on to him some official secrets, and
so on. His mind was constantly at work devising means for

improving the efficiency of his operation and covering it against the curious eyes not only of the green brigade, the police, and the gendarmes, but also the small town gossips.

His most comical "victim" was a fat saloon keeper across the border, who served as intermediary in receiving *bibula* from foreign sources. At first, captivated by some small present, he was asked to order some merchandise in his own name—not books, of course, but ordinary contraband goods. He agreed readily, as such requests were common in the border zone. Later, *bibula* started arriving in the parcels, made to look as if they contained products associated with the city of their origin.

The packages multiplied in number, but the saloon keeper handled them willingly, as our comrade had helped him in the meantime in some business with the Russian customs men, using the contacts he had established with them. Despite the steady flow of parcels, the fat publican suspected nothing, seeing our comrade always genial and smiling, ever ready to help him with his business on the Russian side.

Finally, however, the fat man's face turned longer and sadder as he discovered that the merchandise he had been handling was *bibula*. He had heard about the revolutionary movement in Russia, as well as about the cruel persecutions and tortures—somewhat exaggerated in the telling—suffered by the enemies of the "established political and social order" under the tsar. Terrified, he bitterly reproached our comrade for endangering him in such a way and refused any further cooperation.

Our man wanted to maintain the relationship, for the tavern provided an excellent cover, and the large number of parcels did not attract undue attention, as their recipient was known to be active in business. The man's excessive fear of reprisals served as a means of keeping his collaboration.

Comrade X also knew how to cope with the situation. He told the tavern keeper that their "friendship" was common knowledge in the town, and that if he refused to help, the traffic would have to be organized through other channels, less secure. It would then be discovered and the relations between the two "friends" would be given a new meaning by the Russian gendarmes. Then, the tavern keeper would be in real danger.

After long hassling the unfortunate "victim" yielded, especially as our comrade's arguments were supported by the gift of a fine watch. He only asked that the shipments be less frequent. Every month or so thereafter the unhappy saloon keeper tried to work his way out of the trap and every time he failed. He lived in constant fear, particularly whenever a shipment of *bibula* was at hand; he trembled every time a green or some other Russian official entered his bar, or when there was some agitation at the border. To calm down his "friend," our comrade had to comply with all kinds of silly stratagems with which he hoped to protect both of them. He was only allowed to call at the tavern at certain hours; he had to change frequently the packing of the *bibula,* to build a special closet with double walls for hiding it, and so on.

One of the things the tavern keeper was particularly concerned about was that our comrade should never be seen in his private apartment. This gave rise one day to an amusing scene. After taking a million precautions, pulling down curtains, pushing our friend into a corner every time someone passed by the windows, the German finally permitted him to peek into the closet where a fresh shipment of *bibula* was hidden. Unfortunately, just as our comrade was sorting out the books and packing them in a way suitable for taking them across the border, and while the saloon keeper was running all over the room from one window to another, steps were heard at the door and the handle squeaked. Our comrade hardly knew what had hit him—the huge German pushed him to the floor and threw a sheet over him, at the same time closing the cupboard containing the books.

It seems that the tavern keeper's sister-in-law was looking for him for some reason. The involuntary revolutionist, scared stiff, could not understand for some time what she wanted and made desperate efforts to shield the corner of the room where our comrade was lying, with one foot sticking from under the sheet. Finally, realizing the futility of his efforts, since his sister-in-law could not help staring at the revealing foot, he grabbed the bewildered woman and threw her out of the room. The incident drove the tavern keeper to despair, especially as my friend berated him for behavior which was more likely than anything else to compromise him. The German then devised a weird curtain screening the part of the room in which the closet with the illegal books was hidden. Our comrade was pushed behind the curtain as soon as he entered and he could then manage his *bibula* in the dark.

After two years of such torment the man could stand it no more and left his tavern. He moved to a quieter part of the country, far from the frontier, but in the meantime he had rendered vast services to the enemies of the tsar.

Among our comrade's other "victims," more aware of her role in this case, was the wife of one of the customs officials.

Mrs. Z belonged to a Polish family of German origin and was employed at one time as governess in the home of a rich Russian dignitary. She had married a relative of her employer, who happened to be a customs man. Mr. Z, when our comrade made his acquaintance, was a human wreck, worn out by disease and a dissolute life in his youth. He might have been intelligent once, but by then he was little more than a carcass of a man, with only the ability to digest and move about sluggishly. He was kept in office because of the backing of a relative, a high official in St. Petersburg, who wanted to give him a chance to earn a pension. The couple had a teenage daughter, in a girls' school in Warsaw.

Mrs. Z, bound to a man only half alive and separated from the daughter she loved, was lonely among the crude, mostly drunken Russian officials who surrounded her. Comrade X made her acquaintance accidentally. He was leaving for Warsaw on the business of the factory employing him and he agreed to deliver to their daughter in Warsaw a small present from Mr. and Mrs. Z. When he came back with a letter from the girl, a social relationship developed, which he carefully cultivated with a view to future prospects.

He started by telling Mrs. Z that a friend in Warsaw had asked him to deliver a few uncensored books and that, since they might be easily noticed in his bachelor apartment, he would appreciate it if she stored them in the meantime. When Mrs. Z agreed, he brought some volumes of Polish poetry and history, specially selected for that purpose. The idea was to familiarize the "victim" with illegal literature and gauge her reactions. Mrs. Z not only stored the books, but also read them.

As he had done with the tavern keeper, Comrade X steadily increased the number of books he left with Mrs. Z, and began to bring in books that were more and more provocative. Mrs. Z observed all this, but it did not deter her. As a result, our comrade finally told her of his membership in an antitsarist organization and asked her to help him occasionally in his work.

Her friendship with Comrade X and involvement with illegal activities filled a void in the life of Mrs. Z, who may have sympathized with a young man idealistically risking so much. She made her apartment and her services available to him, which was a major contribution to the revolutionary cause. The Z's lived in a large building housing the families of several officials; it was therefore strictly out of bounds for the green brigade. Mrs. Z, through her husband, provided a perfect cover for clandestine transports of *bibula*.

AGENTS ARE BORN

Only those with a talent for that kind of operation can achieve significant results and protect the *bibula* already in the country from seizure by the greens or the gendarmes. A pamphlet left inadvertently on a table, a wrongly chosen time of departure, failure to observe any change in the surveillance of the frontier by the greens, insufficient perceptiveness in sizing up the personal characteristics of all the people involved in the enterprise—every small error may attract unwelcome attention and result in the arrest of the agent and the seizure of the material.

If we bear in mind that the conditions of such an agent's life are particularly onerous, that the border area is for the most part a rural or small town cultural desert, rife with gossip and poor in educational or social facilities, we realize how difficult is the task of the comrades who assume such duties. They have to exert constant vigilance and never miss the smallest trifle which might have serious consequences; incessant playacting and lying are their principal occupations and they are lonely, without congenial company or entertainment.

No wonder that such work soon exhausts people and wears out their nerves. I believe that good transport agents are born, not made. They have to have a thorough knowledge of the border conditions in general and a minute knowledge of the local situation, iron nerves, and coolness in the face of ever present, though sometimes invisible danger, as well as a special ability, a peculiar gift for blending with the surroundings and deliberately keeping a finger on the weak, but nevertheless complex pulse of the frontier community. Such people are obviously not easy to find, the more so as natural born smugglers are usually natives of the border area and, as I noted before, this is with a few exceptions one of the country's backwaters, least susceptible to revolutionary infiltration. The hardest task facing the transport agent is the organization of regular shipments of *bibula* already smuggled into the country to its destination in the various provinces. If it was only a matter of getting the printed matter across the frontier and hiding it for some time in a safe place, the inflow of *bibula* from free countries to Poland would be several times greater than it is. But one does not import illigal literature for storage in the border zone. It has to be delivered to the ultimate consumers.

I will not deal here with the problems faced by the men entrusted with that task . . . I must mention, however, the relationship between the transport agents and the party, which is a major obstacle in the accomplishment of that mission. The transport agent himself and his assistants are tied to their place of residence. In order to protect their cover, they cannot move about freely and their infrequent trips do not provide adequate opportunities for moving the books inland. Other persons have therefore to come to collect the accumulated *bibula*. This inevitably attracts some attention and may arouse suspicions of smuggling activities. In those cases where a fortunate coincidence provides a convincing cover for frequent visits by strangers, the operation may continue for a long time. Mostly, however, that is not the case and there is an inevitable erosion, both through the exhaustion of the transport agent and through his excessive exposure to suspicion.

That is why the hunt for new outposts, new holes in the wall of China, goes on relentlessly; hence even poorly organized and unsafe transfer points are sometimes used. Thus we occasionally experience a shortage of *bibula,* at any rate, at certain times and places. A well organized frontier transfer point is the elusive goal which we pursue constantly, and it remains one of the main concerns and endeavors of the party.

13

The Working Class in Poland

Feliks Gross

I. THE SOCIAL ORIGIN OF THE POLISH WORKERS *

Background

The French economist, Francis Delaisi, once drew a line dividing Europe into two worlds, the Europe of the steam-horse and the Europe of the draught-horse. This line runs through the heart of Poland from Gdańsk to Cracow, and in tracing it, Delaisi took into account not only statistics, but also social and economic realities. Naturally, the division is not as clear-cut in actual fact as it is in theory. Besides this, the frontier area between the two parts is one where the two systems interpenetrate; it extends for some distance and cannot be fixed by a line. Yet in its general implications Delaisi's idea was valid. Both sociologically and economically, Poland was a land of transitions.

Poland has always been the tragic crossroads of Europe. Not the will of her people but history has imposed upon the Poles a destiny full of suffering and heroic struggles. Because Poland is on the road to the East—to Russia, the Balkans, Turkey—she has been swept by great wars and conflagrations more frequently than other European countries. The Swedes, the

---

* This section was written in 1944, published in 1945.

French and the Germans have passed over her territory and Tartars, Turks and Russians have invaded her. The dogs of war have always trampled the great crossroads of civilization.

The country had no sooner recovered from one war and laid the foundations for a new life than another invasion turned villages and cities into shambles. This was one of the main historical reasons for the poverty of Poland, despite her natural riches. It has also had an important influence on the psychology and customs of the people, who from generation to generation have lived with the memory and under the threat of tragic conflagrations, forever engaged in the effort to reconstruct their country.

Another important factor in shaping Poland's destiny was her century and a half of captivity. From 1772 to 1918, Poland was partitioned among Russia, Austria and Germany, all of whom subordinated the economic and industrial development of their Polish possessions to their own economic interests. The Polish state that arose after 150 years of captivity was thus composed of three heterogeneous parts, and the economic life of each of these parts had been integrated into that of a different usurping power. In addition, the population had developed differently as a result of various political and cultural factors. The integration of the new Poland was therefore a difficult task. Although between 1918 and 1939 this integration proceeded vigorously and the differences caused by the partition rapidly diminished, they left their mark on the economic structure of Poland.

Finally, geographical causes, particularly the distribution of Poland's natural wealth, lay at the root of her division. The main coal and iron deposits are in the southwest, the Cracow region, the Dąbrowa Basin and Silesia. In the southeast there was oil. Poland's heavy industry, her mines and foundries, were situated also in the southwest, near her coal deposits. These regions are so industrialized that the landscape sometimes gives the impression of an uninterrupted manufacturing and urban terrain. In Silesia, the train moves through an endless chain of towns, factories and mines, as typical of this country as the many-colored cultivated fields are typical of the eastern regions. Western Poland, the Poznań region, was dominated by industries connected with agriculture. The textile industry was concentrated in the northwest, around Łódź; there were also two big textile centers in Bielsko (southern Silesia) and Bialystok, east of the Vistula. During the second half of the nineteenth century, Warsaw became an important center (food, chemical and dry-goods industries). But the densest concentration of industry followed the line of the Vistula. During the last years preceding World War II, a great industrial center, the so-called COP (Central Industrial Region) was created for strategic reasons in the triangle formed by the San and Vistula rivers, and as a result the industrial population moved eastward.

The structure of Poland's population must be therefore considered in the light of her regional differences. The industrial workers were concentrated in the west. As we move eastward, the percentage of agricultural population became higher, and in the eastern provinces agriculture was prevalent.

The Old Stock: Miners, Founders, Masons

It is generally believed that the Polish working class has only recently appeared on the scene, and that it is still bound to the village by tradition and family ties, rather than to the factory. This opinion is in part correct. To a considerable extent the Polish working class is still a young class; its members come from the country and are often still connected with it. Yet there are trades, types of production and regions in which the Polish working class is a socially old element, that is to say, has been for many generations associated with a given industry or mine.

The industrial revolution compelled many artisans to abandon their workshops and to earn a living in the factories; many handicrafts ceased to exist altogether, as for instance the craft of the armorer when the technique of warfare changed, and mail-coats and shields became useless. Similarly, the needlers disappeared when the manufacture of needles was taken over by the capitalist machine producers. As the crafts disappeared, the traditions and customs of the artisans also disappeared; only remnants of them survived in the factories, which constituted an entirely new environment.

The situation was, however, different in the mines, e.g., the salt mines. Here the industrial revolution took place in the same locality, in the same workshop. The miner continued to do the same work in the same shaft, nor was the technique of mining fundamentally altered, as it was in the production of manufactured goods. In the mines, the industrial revolution merely brought about the replacement of the hand elevator by the mechanical elevator and the hand pump by the steam pump. Horses and wagons were used in the mines until very recently; the automatic drill is a comparatively modern invention (second half of the nineteenth century), and the technique of using it was learned by the same miners who had used the more old-fashioned tools. Thus, in certain districts, the miner continued his connection with his old workshop not only functionally, but also organically.

Polish mining began long ago: the first salt mines of Wieliczka and Bochnia near Cracow can be traced back a thousand years. In the Middle Ages and afterwards the Polish salt miners were organized in so-called "gwarectwa," which had a certain legal resemblance to the corporative crafts. The miners were thus freemen, and their social and cultural status was high. The founders were also free. A poem by Walenty Rozdzienski, a Polish founder from Upper Silesia, entitled *Officina Ferraria, or The Foundry and Workshop with Smithies of the Noble Iron Craft,* written in Polish and published in Cracow in 1612, gives a striking picture of the conditions prevailing in the foundries at that time:

We live in shabby houses, and little
Do we care for splendid buildings and
Luxurious beds. The walls are made of
Peat thatch; we sleep on dry leaves,
The prey of fleas and flies.
So do not ask in this foundry
For the comforts people covet in the
World outside . . .
We enjoy the freedom we inherited
From our ancestors, and though poor,
We love one another.

Freedom is our sole delight, the sole reward
Of our misery, not treasures, not money!
Since the Cyclops' time we have never been
Slaves to any tyrant. Free to come
And go as we please, after one year
In one place we can move to another. . . .

This is only a short excerpt from this poem which is an interesting historical document. Freedom was the fundamental privilege of the miners' and founders' crafts. In seventeenth century Poland, Rozdzienski emphasizes its value when the peasants were serfs, bound to the soil. This freedom, like the trades themselves, was hereditary, handed down from father to son.

The same poem contains other interesting details. Its author depicts the Silesian mines, where people like himself, Polish miners and also foreigners worked, and relates the legends which Rozdzienski himself accepted at their face value. Similar survivals of miners' culture and folklore are to be found in the old Wieliczka mines, where, in addition to legends, we find plastic art—carvings in blocks of salt. This branch of popular sculpture developed in the Wieliczka mines in the course of long centuries.

In the second half of the nineteenth century, when Polish mining as an industry began to develop particularly in that part of Poland occupied by Austria, that is, the Cracow Basin, Polish miners were often brought from Wieliczka or Silesia to the coal mines. These miners trained the local unskilled laborers in their trade, and acted as foremen or guides, who brought to this region not only their professional skill, but also their traditions, customs, organizing abilities and legends. Thus the legends about kindly spirits and treasure-keepers who haunt the mines of Upper Silesia—legends which Rozdzienski quotes—were retold to the author by aged miners in the relatively modern coal shafts of the Cracow Basin.

The mines and foundries were, then, the early breeding ground of a working group conscious of its own interest, which succeeded in bringing certain elements of its old handicraft into modern industry. Despite the industrial revolution, these groups passed with all their cultural capital into the new productive system and were integrated into the new social order.

We find examples of similar cultural inheritance and links between the old artisan elements and the modern workers wherever the technical transformation that took place during the industrial revolution left undisturbed the continuity of the trade. This was not true of the production of manufactured goods, in which the technical changes were so considerable that the handicraft organizations and the handicrafts themselves disintegrated as a result.

Continuity was preserved in the carpenter's and even more in the mason's trades. Bricklaying came to Poland with Gothic architecture in the thirteenth century and became widespread in the fourteenth, and from that time until the introduction of concrete the technique of building did not change. As a result, the masons have retained much of their traditional culture, and to this very day Polish masons mark the completion of the rough construction up to the roof by an age-old celebration, the so-called *wiecha* (bush). The mason's trade, too, has often been hereditary for many centuries.

Another survival of the past are the *Flisaks*. These are boatmen on the Vistula, who for centuries have transported various goods, lumber and later, chiefly coal, in their barges called *galars*. The *galar* is a wide flat-bottomed boat, a kind of large raft with a railing, in the center of which there is a tiny house with just room for two persons to sleep. There the *Flisaks* rest at night. The *galars* float down the river with the current; they are tugged up again by steamers—in olden times they were pulled by horses or were sold at the river's mouth. Until this day the *galars* sail along the Vistula just as they did a hundred or five hundred years ago, and with them some of the traditions, customs and organizations of the *Flisaks* have remained. Just as they have done for centuries, they still stop today at the inn in Niepolomice near Cracow or land at the bottom of the steps of the splendid castle of Wawel.

Another calling which has not changed in the course of centuries is that of the sand-digger, who today pulls sand from the bottom of the Vistula with the help of a bucket attached to a pole, just as his ancestors did centuries ago. All these crafts are old; they have been practiced for hundreds of years in the same districts of the cities, in the same villages and the same families. Here, the worker's social origin is as ancient as his tradition.

I hope my readers will forgive me if I briefly interrupt this investigation of the facts and laws of social development to evoke the sunny days I spent on the Vistula with the modern heirs of these archaic trades. I recall the Polish *Flisaks*, masons and miners with the greatest pleasure and their memory moves me as does the sound of the *Marseillaise* since the fall of Paris. They are open-hearted, gay, witty and original, with a peculiar sense of their professional dignity, inherited from their fathers. This originality manifests itself especially in their speech, that characteristic speech of the suburbs and the old trades which has borrowed many terms from foreign languages but has also preserved numberless old Polish expressions elsewhere forgotten. They have also preserved the old customs of the towns and in Cracow it was chiefly the masons who represented the popular tradition cultivated in that city for centuries. Yet these same masons were also the radical, progressive element in the trade unions and supplied the Polish Socialist Party with many recruits from the suburbs. They knew how to combine tradition with progress, and the same can be said of the other crafts. At the inns situated near the banks of the Vistula in the old quarter of Cracow one used to hear dialogues which made one think that Lucian was talking with these men over a glass of beer.

Industrial Revolution and Capitalism

These traditional and hereditary crafts, however, constitute only a small fraction of the Polish working class as a whole; we have devoted so much space to them because their social background is as typical as it is little known. In general, when we speak of the workers we mean first of all the industrial workers, the factory workers, the children of the industrial revolution. As a great social class, dynamic and conscious of its unity, they did not appear in the Congress Kingdom until the 1870's when modern industry became widespread.

The industrial revolution in Poland took place later than in Western Europe. Its first harbingers appeared only after 1815, that is, after the Congress of Vienna, which definitely partitioned Poland among Austria, Prussia and Russia; out of Cracow and its surroundings the Free City of Cracow was created. The territory under Russian occupation, the so-called Congress Kingdom, was granted a certain measure of independence, and had its own army, treasury, and administration under the crown of the Tsar, who also held the title of King of Poland.

Many Poles then determined that their country must be saved from abject misery, and realized that the Polish Kingdom must be developed economically in order to better resist Russian influence. The leader of this trend was Ksawery Lubecki, a highly talented statesman who held the post of Finance Minister in the government of the Kingdom. He was the real creator of Polish industry and trade.

Lubecki formulated the principles of his economic policy in this way: "Poland must have everything that is needed to secure her independence, otherwise she will lose everything. She needs three things: (1) schools, that is, enlightenment and education; (2) industry and trade, that is, prosperity and wealth, and (3) armament works." He gathered around him talented and energetic assistants who shared his ideas. The Minister's gaze was fixed on distant lands—on the vast expanses of Russia and far-away fabulous China, and in this boundless and completely unknown market he saw an immense opportunity for Polish industry.

Polish textile centers were created. Villages were transformed into small towns within a few years, and after several decades these towns were pulsating industrial centers. In 1824, nine years after the creation of the Congress Kingdom, the exports of Polish cloth to China amounted to 2,207,000 Polish zlotys.

In 1820, Lodz, now the Polish Manchester and one of the biggest textile centers on the European continent, had 767 inhabitants, and when questioned as to the occupation of his townsmen, the burgomaster of Lodz replied with one word: agriculture. In 1821, this town was granted the rights of a manufacturing city. In an official record dated 1825 we read the following: "This is a small town with wooden houses. Two years ago it was designated as suitable for various factories. Its location is very favorable for this purpose. At present there are 31 drapers with 59 workshops, 27 master-weavers of cotton with 46 workshops, and 5 linen manufacturing masters. Many buildings are under construction for manufacturing enterprises." Fifteen years later, in 1840, the population of Lodz had risen to 15,000, and it was more than 600,000 before the Second World War.

New cities sprang up and grew like mushrooms after rain— not only textile centers, but also mining towns. After 1815, workshops and manufacturers developed. The first steam engines reached the Congress Kingdom between 1820 and 1830; they continued arriving in the 1830's, but it was not until 1850 that industry based on steam engines began to develop rapidly. In 1848, the important Warsaw-Vienna railroad was built, connecting the Congress Kingdom with the West and facilitating the importation of machines and equipment.

Industry developed in spite of various obstacles and changing political conditions. In 1830, the Polish nation took up arms for its freedom and independence. The insurrection was crushed, and the few freedoms guaranteed by the Congress of Vienna were largely wiped out. The creation of the conditions necessary for industrial development grew more difficult; but the pioneering efforts of a handful of talented men had not been in vain, and industry continued to grow at an accelerated rate.

All over Europe labor conditions were bad. They were also bad in Poland which was moreover impoverished by the constant invasions it had suffered. The rate of exploitation during the industrial revolution in England was tremendous—for on it was based the primitive accumulation of capital. This was true also of Poland. The working day was not established by law, and lasted for at least twelve hours, usually more than that. On Saturdays and the days before holidays and market days, work in most crafts lasted until late at night and even until the following morning in order to complete orders or get merchandise ready for sale at the fairs. Printing shops and sugar factories as a rule did not observe Sundays and holidays. Elements of the old noblemen-peasants' relationship which originated in serfdom were often carried over into industry, and influenced the employer-employee relationship.

In Upper Silesia, the territory under German occupation, industry also grew rapidly: the management was German and the labor Polish. Conditions of work were very hard, sometimes monstrously so. Rudolf Virchow, the scholar and liberal who visited Silesia in 1848, has left a striking description of the misery and starvation prevailing in that province, and Hugo Solger, author of a monograph on Upper Silesia published in 1860, mentions the general use of the whip in the mines belonging to the Prussian coal barons. According to him, the working day in the pits was twelve hours long. Industry also developed in Galicia, which was under Austrian occupation.

Big Industry: The Positivists

After crushing the insurrection of 1830, the Tsarist government oppressed the Poles more than ever. Polish universities were closed, the prisons were overcrowded. The Russian authorities attempted to pacify the country by imposing such penalties as confiscation of property, deportation to Siberia and the gallows. In 1863 a new insurrection broke out, in which many workers took part. The oppression after this insurrection was ruthlessly carried out: young people were forcibly drafted into the army and sent to distant countries; there were mass executions and deportations to Siberia. After going through the Napoleonic wars and suffering defeats in two great popular insurrections, the vital forces of the country were exhausted. But out of this political situation new political and economic currents were born: "organic work" and positivism. "Building the foundations," the development of economic life, the enrichment of the country and the raising of its cultural level were the basic principles of this new trend. The elimination of the customs border between the Congress Kingdom and Russia opened up the possibility of a large new market, and the positivists wanted to make use of it for the economic development of the country. Poland had lost much blood—now, the positivists declared, she must gather new strength and equal the great economic and cultural progress of the other nations.

In the development of Polish capitalism, 1870 marked a turning point. Before 1850, weaving mills had been the dominant element in the new industrial economy; after 1850, machines became increasingly frequent, and from 1870 heavy industry began to develop on a really big scale. The positivist movement won public opinion for the cause of industrial development. The emancipation of the peasants in 1864 had enlarged the domestic market and created new reserves of labor power. Big banks and corporations such as the Warsaw Coal Mining Society came into being. Prior to 1870 Polish industry was in a transitional stage; after that date, big enterprises were created and large-scale capitalist industry financed by foreign capital began to develop. One of the economic historians of that period correctly states that the industry of the Kingdom of Poland was created by Western-European capital and native labor to serve eastern markets. Now once more, just as after 1815, new cities and new factories sprang up and thousands of new workers appeared on the scene. During the second half of the 1870's a small village became transformed into the big industrial town of Sosnowiec, which by 1939 had a population of 130,000 and was an important machine-building, chemical, textile, and especially mining center. Other small villages underwent a similar transformation.

The New Stock: Industrial Workers

Simultaneously with the growth of industry there grew up a new social group—the class of industrial workers. This was no longer a submissive and passive class like the fresh unenlightened peasant element of the 1830's: it was a young, politically active class, which grew rapidly. Thus, in Russian Poland, in 1870, 1 out of every 95 inhabitants was a worker; in 1882, 1 out of every 62; in 1897, 1 out of every 38; in 1910, 1 out of every 30.[1] From that time on, Polish history was not only the history of the people's struggle for liberation and national independence, but also the history of its struggle for social justice.

Whence came the Polish industrial workers? In certain crafts and mines, the continuity with the preceding historical period was unbroken. But this was not true of the new industries; in these the workers were recruited from three social groups.

[1] Stanisław Koszutski, *The Economic Development of the Kingdom of Poland*, Warsaw, 1905; and Alexander Woycicki, *History of the Industrial Workers in Poland*, Warsaw, 1929 (in Polish).

First of all, there were the landless peasants. The Polish peasants were given land in 1864 only in that part of Poland which was under Russian occupation. In theory, although not in practice, serfdom had been abolished much earlier—in 1807 in the Duchy of Warsaw,[2] when the Napoleonic eagles brought to the peasants seeming freedom. In accordance with the old laws, they had been attached to the soil which they were forbidden to leave without their lord's permission; they were forced to perform labor service, in return for the right to the land. The edict of 1807 issued after the occupation of Warsaw by French and Polish troops proclaimed "equality before the law." Legally this meant the abolition of serfdom; but in fact the peasants who remained on the land had to perform labor service as before. Moreover, the new laws gave the landlord the right of "notification," that is to say, the right to remove the peasant from the land he had always tilled. No land was then actually given the peasants. But this legal emancipation made possible the movement of the peasants into industry after 1815 when it began to develop in the Congress Kingdom, for they could legally leave their landlords. In 1864 peasants in the Kingdom were granted freedom, but even then there remained a mass of peasants who were landless or had only very little land, and from these peasants most of the workers were recruited. After 1864, there began a mass migration to the cities. The new soldiers of industry moved from place to place and the natural population increase, one of the highest in Europe, further multiplied the industrial reserve army. There were enough hands for industry both at home and abroad, for at that time began the great emigration overseas. Only the big landlords complained of a shortage of labor.

---

[2] The revolution of 1848 was a decisive moment in the history of the emancipation of the Polish peasants under Prussian and Austrian rule. In Prussia emancipation began in 1807; the laws of 1850 completed the long process of abolition of serfdom. But while the legal process was completed in 1850, in reality the change was much more gradual, and reached an end only by 1875.

The revolution of 1848 in Vienna marked the abolition of serfdom in the Austrian-occupied part of Poland. The law for emancipation was enacted in 1849.

In the Russian-occupied part of Poland this historical step was taken in 1864. This was also an act of political strategy in order to steal the thunder from certain groups that advanced the slogan of emancipation during the insurrection of 1863.

The second source of labor power was the disintegrating handicrafts, which, as everywhere else in Europe, could not compete with the factories. Thus hand weaving had to give way to machine weaving. Between 1870 and 1880, the period of the growth of capitalism in the Congress Kingdom, several thousand small handicraft textile enterprises closed down and the impoverished artisans increased the ranks of the workers.

The third source of the new industrial proletariat was immigration. In 1816 privileges that had been granted to foreign workers at an earlier date were confirmed, and several new rights were given to industrial immigrants. After 1820 thousands of Germans, Czechs, and other foreign nationals streamed into the Congress Kingdom, and rapidly became assimilated into the Polish environment and merged with the native population.

Industrial labor was increased by other elements also but because these had no mass character, they were of no fundamental importance. Thus, after 1831 and 1864 many small noblemen's estates were confiscated in reprisal for their owners' participation in the insurrections; their families were left without any means of subsistence, and some of the rebels went to work in the factories.

In the latter part of nineteenth century a salaried, industrial working class was already well established in Poland. In the eighteenth-century industry, forced labor in various forms was not uncommon in Europe (see Andrew Ure's studies on England, K. Hinze on Prussia and Nina Assorodobraj on Poland). However vagrant and "underclass" people participated only in a marginal sense in the formation of the Polish working class (for a different view see Assorodobraj).

Sailors

Certain industrial groups, which in other countries are very old socially and have a long tradition, were formed in Poland almost before our eyes: the sailors and longshoremen.

In the 18th and 19th centuries, Poland had no sea tradition. In the 17th century this tradition had existed although then it was not an important one. Thus the Polish marine was born in 1923 without traditions, and, like industry in Lodz or Zyrardow, developed rapidly. In 1923 the decision was taken to build a port in Gdynia, at that time a village of about 1,000 inhabitants. I myself once saw its miserable fishermen's huts. Eight years later, at the time of the 1931 census, the population of Gdynia was above 38,000, and shortly before the war this town had a population of about 120,000, and was one of the most important seaports on the Baltic, with a net registered tonnage of entrances higher than that of Danzig, Stockholm, Leningrad, Helsinki or Koenigsberg; it was the home port for more than seventy Polish ships. A new mass of workers was formed—dockers, transport workers, sailors. Today the crews of the Polish ships which sail the seven seas consist mainly of men born far from any seacoast. When the news of the establishment of a Polish port spread through Poland, young workers from all over the country began to stream to Gdynia; miners' sons from Sosnowiec and Dabrowa, mountaineers from Podhale, natives of Warsaw and Cracow. They brought their own organizational traditions with them which they at once introduced into the new Polish port. A strong trade union of transport workers was formed in Gdynia, embracing sailors and port workers. In this province of Pomorze the workers' organizations had formerly been particularly weak, but Gdynia was absolutely different from the old petty bourgeois Pomorze towns; here, the workers' unions and the Polish Socialist Party had a predominant influence. The procedures followed at the meetings and the manner in which these were conducted were reminiscent of the industrial and mining centers of southwestern Poland, the Dabrova Basin or the Cracow industrial region. Within fifteen years, a varied crowd of newcomers had been transformed into a compact, unified occupational group of Polish transport workers, sailors, and longshoremen, a new and dynamic group. The Polish sailors, although they had no tradition, learned their trade and created their organizations in a short time.

Partitions and Social History

The liberation of the peasants was accomplished by different methods and at different times in each of the three occupied parts of Poland; there was not one social reform of the Polish peasantry, but three different reforms, and as a result, three different developments. Furthermore, Poland did not go through one homogeneous industrial revolution and an identical process of the rise of capitalism. The Prussian part shared the history of German industrialization (especially Silesia). The Austrian part was influenced—and handicapped—by the Austrian developments; moreover in some fields, like coal and oil mining, it has an industrial history of its own.

Thus the Poles failed to go through an identical economic and social process in the most crucial periods of modern history, the period of national "awakening," the emancipation of the peasantry, the industrial revolution and the rise of capitalism. This fact had serious social and economic repercussions. The young Polish state organized in 1918 faced a hard task to combine three different territories and form a new pattern, an integrated social and economic system. Despite the difficulties, however, much was accomplished. The labor movement (particularly in the former Austrian and Russian parts of Poland), the trade unions, the Socialist movement, the educational organizations for workers and adults have made their contribution to this process of unification.

II. SOCIAL STRATIFICATION AND POLITICAL MOVEMENTS

Among the gray mass of people we encounter every day, certain individuals stand out. They are perhaps no better or worse than the others, and it is often difficult to put one's finger on the exact characteristic that distinguishes them from their fellows; all one can say is that they are different, that somehow they compel our attention, and in every circumstance assert their individuality. A painter often notices this individuality at first glance and says that such and such a person has an "interesting" face, one worth painting—although this face is not necessarily beautiful.

The same is true of social groups or classes. Some of these have no "individuality" of their own, are colorless and uninteresting, while others are picturesque, and full of character, although not necessarily superior in any respect. They simply have specific, irreducible features. Needless to say, the "individuality" of a group is not a hereditary or innate characteristic—it is the product of history and culture.

The Polish proletariat belongs to these distinctive groups. In the colorful amalgamation which constitutes the European working class, the Polish workers have a color of their own, not as brilliant as that of some of the great western workers' movements, but quite distinctive and interesting in its own way.

Karl Marx and the Polish Workers

There are various reasons for this phenomenon. In the first place, Poland's social structure had features peculiar to itself. Poland is an industrialized peasant country, and thus it is different from the classical homeland of the industrial proletariat, England, where class divisions were doubtless more clearly marked than in many other countries. There are no peasants in England, while neither in France nor in Germany do the peasants play the same political and economic role as in Poland. Even in Czechoslovakia their influence is less strong and the country's industrial character is more marked. Poland falls somewhere between Czechoslovakia, which is more industrialized and yet retains a peasant character, and countries like Bulgaria or Yugoslavia, which are fundamentally peasant countries. Thus the orthodox Marxist division into two classes which was adequate for the conditions prevailing in England, is inadequate when applied to Poland, unless we limit ourselves to industrial and agricultural laborers, for it does not apply to the large masses of the peasantry, nor to the numerous persons engaged in home industries, the small artisans and workers employed in minor industries.

In the small processing industries and handicrafts, there is no rigid class division; the employer is a "capitalist" one day and a "hired laborer" the next. The journeymen in such industries after a certain period usually become "masters" or employers, because in Poland only a small capital was required to found a workshop.

The relation of the *chalupnik,* that is, person engaged in home industry, to his "employer" is different from the relation of the salaried worker to the capitalist. The *chalupnik* works with his own tools and in his own home, and in appearance is entirely independent; his "employer" merely supplies him with raw material and sells his products. He is only a producer, not a hired laborer, and he has no "employer" in the ordinary sense of the word. And yet the homeworker, as well as the worker in the small industries, belongs to the most exploited and most poverty-stricken groups.

Similarly, the small peasant who owns two or even five acres of land is neither a capitalist nor a hired laborer, although socially and economically he was worse off than a Silesian foundry worker, who belonged to one of the best paid groups in Poland.

Any realistic analysis of the social structure of Poland must resort to the auxiliary term, social stratum. Here we will use this term to mean a group with a common social tradition, and well defined cultural, economic and occupational features. In social struggles individuals belonging to the same social stratum display solidarity.

Social Strata of Poland

In Poland, in addition to the proletariat—the peasants, landowners, the bourgeoisie, the intelligentsia, constitute such strata. Before passing to our main subject, the workers, it may be useful briefly to survey the other strata.

There is no doubt that the Polish peasants are a group apart, with their own tradition (serfdom and the struggle for land), and distinct cultural and economic characteristics. The peasants have similar needs, and whether poor or well-to-do, their expenditures have, so to speak, a similar purpose. Unlike the intellectual, the peasants did not spend their surplus money on travel, or improved housing conditions, but chiefly on the enlargement and improvement of their farms. Their ways of satisfying their needs are also different, and their amusements are unlike those of the cities, although the city is strongly influencing the village. The peasantry has its own art, music, customs and even a distinctive language. Finally, in all social, political and economic struggles, the peasants display unmistakable solidarity—a solidarity that is a result of a long historical development.

Just as peasants cannot be identified with workers, so the landowners in Poland could not be identified with the bourgeoisie. The landowners were not only an economic group possessing land, but also a cultural group, having their own social traditions and customs. To be a *ziemianin* or landowner, it was not enough to own a large acreage; one had to be born a *ziemianin,* and have a real or imaginary noble origin. A member of the city middle class who bought land did not by any means belong to the *ziemiaństwo,* and was not necessarily received in its circles on an equal basis.

The largest urban group is the proletariat, but as mentioned above, this includes not only industrial wage earners, but also—and these are the most numerous—the homeworkers, small artisans, workers in small industries, and even hawkers and peddlers. However, from the political point of view, not all the groups within the proletariat have equal importance, and the dynamic element is the class of wage laborers; especially the industrial workers—just as in every other country in the world. But in Poland, in addition to the industrial workers and miners—the building trades workers, the masons and the bricklayers are distinguished by special dynamism and activity.

The unemployed constitute a special category. I have in mind only the registered unemployed from among the industrial workers, whose number amounted to 440,000 in the 1930's, an imposing figure. I exclude the rural unemployed which will not be treated here. The social and political importance of this group is enormous. There is a profound difference between the employed and unemployed worker. In the system of social relations, the conflict between the wage laborer and his employer is an important element. It is between these two adversaries that the struggle for improved conditions, higher wages and a shorter working day is waged. The unemployed are not in conflict with the employer, but with the state; they struggle over the wages for public works, for relief, and other forms of social assistance that have never been adequate anywhere. This is a fundamental conflict with a system that deprives the unemployed of an opportunity for regular work, and thus a change in the system of government is of fundamental importance for them, and they long for it even when it is against the interests of the working class as a whole and their own. Such was the case of those unemployed in Weimar Germany who went over to Hitler.

As for the middle class, it is important to note that in Poland it never played the same active political role as in England and other Western European countries. In the first place, the Polish middle class is numerically small—a very "thin" stratum. Throughout her history Poland has lacked a strongly developed merchant class, nor did the Polish bourgeoisie go through a period of revolutionary social action such as did the French and English middle classes. The English middle class grew strong in its struggle against the king for personal and economic freedom, and by the end of 1688 it succeeded in restricting the king's rights. Similarly, the French *tiers état* played a great part in the history of French social struggles, contributed actively to the overthrow of absolutism, the liberation of the French people from feudal fetters, and the development of French democracy and parliamentary government. In the fields of trade and industry, too, the Western European middle classes displayed great energy. The merchants of the past centuries combined an enterprising spirit with ruthless profit-seeking; they accepted every risk, did not hesitate to travel to remote and unknown countries, founded companies and cities overseas, and crossed stormy seas in frail boats seeking trade, wealth and adventure. Marco Polo is typical of the thirteenth-century merchant. And when the period of the industrial revolution came, the middle classes showed great inventiveness and spirit of enterprise.

The Polish bourgeoisie lacks all these traditions of struggle against absolutism or bold sea-faring activity. In Poland, the struggle for the restriction of the royal power was waged by the magnates and the nobility, and until the period of the partitions Poland was as "gentry democracy" with an elected king. Nor did the Polish middle class contribute to the development of Polish parliamentary institutions—the Diet was a noblemen's representative body. Moreover, before the partitions Poland lacked an adequate coastline and merchant fleet, and therefore the sea did not play the same part in Polish economic history that it played in England or France. The Polish merchant did not seek distant markets nor sail in far-off seas—this was done much later by a few romantic intellectuals, like Joseph Conrad and Strzelecki. Finally, when machines and technological progress reached Poland, the country was exhausted by its insurrections against the foreign invaders, and lacked a numerous well-to-do bourgeoisie capable of developing the necessary initiative. There was none of that personal freedom and security, to which the English merchants and industrialists owe so much. Industry in the Congress Kingdom was built after 1815 by the initiative of the State, by the gifted Lubecki and his government, and only in the '40's and '70's of the nineteenth century did the large-scale capitalist appears in Poland, at which time industries grew at a rapid tempo, and foreign capital came in, often in a form unprofitable for Poland, during the inter-war period.

But even the Polish middle class failed to wield any great influence in the country, and remained a relatively insignificant stratum. Politically, its members leaned toward the clerical and nationalist parties.

It was different with the Polish intelligentsia, which played a far greater political role than the bourgeoisie. No adequate social analysis of pre-war Poland is possible without taking into account white collar workers, professional classes and the intellectuals. But before taking up this question with regard to Poland, a few general remarks on the intelligentsia are necessary.

The Intelligentsia

Neither in the United States nor in England has this stratum had the importance it has had on the European continent, especially in its eastern regions. More than that, this stratum does not exist in the Anglo-Saxon countries as a separate entity: the "professional class" and the "managerial class" are completely integrated with the upper or middle class. In Eastern Europe the situation is different: the intelligentsia comprises the extensive group of all people who work intellectually and not physically, from the lowest civil servant through the liberal professions (lawyers, physicians, engineers), to the "authentic" intellectuals, that is to say, the scientists, artists and writers. All these categories belong to the same group; they display economic, social and cultural similarities.

Economically, the intelligentsia had an average standard of living higher than that of the proletariat. Individual intellectuals may be capitalists, or hired employees, they may belong to different classes, yet because they belong to the same stratum they display common features, which, because of their intimate relation to culture, are difficult to define in a rigorous manner. In one instance, however, it can be done: the nature of their expenditures. The intelligentsia, for example, in general spends more on housing than workers do, a comparison of course which has meaning only if the incomes are equal. This is only a detail, but it is characteristic. A high salaried worker did not usually spend the same amount of money on his flat as did the intellectual in the same wage bracket. A highly skilled worker, even if he earned 500 zlotys, did not rent three or four rooms as did the man of the intelligentsia in the same wage bracket. He was satisfied with his two rooms, saving the rest of his money, usually in order to buy a small house with a garden.

In a sociological analysis of the intelligentsia the most important element is its social functions.

The countries of continental Europe had numerous bureaucracies. Outside the cities the administrative system was based not so much on self-government as on a centralized bureaucracy with appointed civil servants. The relationship of these civil servants to the State is different from that of the hired worker to the employer, for as Marx justly says, the essence of the relationship between capital and labor is power. But the civil servant who is hired by the State acquires power and disposes of it; in a country based on a bureaucratic system he is the ruler. Thus, in a bureaucratic system, government is an attribute of the intelligentsia, although the legislature may retain ultimate control.

The professional intellectuals are also scientists, professors, and teachers. They monopolize science and knowledge, grant diplomas, and the right to practice professions, and as teachers also transmit knowledge and human experience, or as physicians, lawyers or engineers, they apply it. Journalism, radio, information in the widest sense of the word, are also intellectual professions—thus the intelligentsia also influences public opinion.

Government, science (which also affects control of social mobility), public opinion—these three essential social functions were thus concentrated in the hands of the intelligentsia. The orthodox socialists often forget about one important social group, quite definite in continental Europe (contrary to the U.S.A. and Great Britain), which cannot be placed either in the capitalist or in the employee group: the army—especially the officers. In Europe this is a factor in itself. The demobilized soldiers and officers have formed the bulk of the fascist movement in Europe, and subjectively did not care at all for the capitalists. During the war they had risked their lives, and the non-commissioned officers and officers had power, while after demobilization they went to their civil professions, lost their splendor and often had to face quite a hard and unjust economic position. Fascism was for many of them a chance to get back into power, and gave them many illusions.

The officers' corps especially, and the army generally, is a social group in continental Europe with great power and influence, which had played an important role in such countries as Germany and France. The officers' corps was linked with the intelligentsia by family and friendship, as well as by education.

The intelligentsia appeared as a separate stratum in continental Europe toward the beginning of the nineteenth century. Earlier, in the seventeenth or eighteenth centuries, the professions which today are represented by the intelligentsia were part of the middle class or the nobility. The nobility, the magnates, and the court monopolized government power; science and the liberal professions belonged to middle class categories. After the overthrow of feudalism, and the French Revolution, modern administration arose in Europe, and with it the number of civil servants especially trained for the job of government began to grow. The introduction of compulsory education led to the creation of a large number of teachers. There was an increasing need of engineers, and the development of trade and industry was accompanied by a growing number of lawyers. Even new schools and universities trained an ever-increasing number of professional intellectuals.

By the end of the nineteenth century the development of this stratum was more and more noticeable. Karl Kautsky called attention to the fact that between 1882 and 1885 the number of workers in Germany grew by 62% while the "new middle class" grew by 118.9%.[3] This tendency has continued and the number of intelligentsia has constantly grown.

In Europe, the dynamic and numerous stratum of intelligentsia played a prominent political role. Controlling the political as well as the economic and educational apparatus, it was a decisive factor in shaping the ideology of several countries.

The Polish Intelligentsia: A Ruling Group

In contrast with the colorless and passive Polish bourgeoisie, the Polish intelligentsia was an active, dynamic and numerous group at the turn of the century. Under the Tsarist occupation, the oppression of national minorities barred the way to a professional career, and after 1831 there was not even a Polish university in Congress Poland. This fact contributed to the radicalization of the Polish intellectuals. Many of them went abroad to study or to find work. There were many Polish students at all the European universities, and Polish scientists and scholars vied successfully with those of other countries.

The influence of the intelligentsia in Poland was strong in all the political parties: the socialist (PPS), the peasant party (*Wyzwolenie,* the radical fraction of the peasant movement), the nationalists (ND), the conservative nationalists (Right). Before the war of 1914, the Polish intelligentsia largely followed radical and progressive slogans, and especially under the Russian occupation played the part of a political leaven. Quite many were closely connected with the underground socialist movement. They also ardently supported and enlisted in the nuclei of the future Polish army, formed under the Austrian occupation as riflemen's battalions and, later, Legions; from these Legions the higher officers of the armies of independent Poland were later recruited. The Polish colonels of 1918 and the 1920's

---

[3] Karl Kautsky: *Bernstein und das Sozial demokratische Programm*, Stuttgart, 1889.

and generals of the new Polish State were different from the high-ranking officers of other armies; they were for the most part ex-students of philosophy, law or medicine, and after 1926, when Jozef Pilsudski rallied his former comrades from the days of the anti-Tsarist struggles and the Legions, he succeeded in winning over a large portion of the Polish intelligentsia, formerly a progressive and radical element.

During the 1930's in independent Poland, only an insignificant group of intellectuals joined the socialist camp, and those who joined the peasant camp were even less numerous. A large fraction of students formed the backbone of Rightist, sometimes even fascist-like organizations, and the professional intelligentsia, too, largely followed nationalist slogans. During the same period a democratic opposition began to form among the moderate university professors and members of the liberal professions in Warsaw, Wilno, Cracow and Lwów, and especially among teachers. Also a peasant intelligentsia began slowly to emerge, professional intellectuals who came from the village, and maintained contact with it despite their urban occupations, and vigorously defended its interests. Although small, this group was influential. But, to be clear, in this period a large majority of the Polish "educated classes" followed Pilsudski or the nationalist camp, while only a minority joined the socialist, peasant and workers' camps.

The Polish intelligentsia as a whole controlled the bureaucratic state apparatus; and a not inconsiderable part of Polish economic life was controlled by the State.

The military officers also formed a large and most influential group in Poland. The expenses for the army in the State budget were large, as was its power. In the 1920's the officers were devoted followers of Marshal Pilsudski, and the majority held progressive and democratic traditions; many of them were socialists and populists. In the 1930's many from the old guard retired, while others abandoned their old ideals. The younger element was imbued with a quite different spirit. The officers became more and more conscious of the army's power; and simultaneously, a closed officers' corps with a feeling of *esprit de corps* and with faith in "uniform's honor" was replacing the old democratic setup. Marshal Rydz-Śmigły, a one-time socialist, now became a symbol of these tendencies which were so different from the old democratic traditions.

Piłsudski, Rydz-Śmigły, and their partisans controlled the army, and that gave them the power over the State. Piłsudski's regime was a regime of intelligentsia, basing its power on the army and opposed by the Peasants' Party, the Polish Socialist Party and the Unions.

Social Forces

According to the census of 1931, the total population of Poland was 32.1 millions. The number of "white collar" workers, employed and unemployed, was 664,500, including 17,000 engaged in agriculture. If we add to this figure about 78,000 members of the liberal professions (lawyers, physicians, engineers, etc.), we shall obtain a total of about 743,000 people. According to the same census, there were in Poland 4,217,000 workers active in their trades: 1,468,000 in agriculture, fishing, forestry, and gardening; the rest, 2,749,000, in other occupations—industry, mining, transportation, trade, etc., 633,900 workers were occupied in big or medium industries; in 1939 the number of such workers reached 886,000. Finally, in 1939 there were 313,000 unemployed workers; their number was growing in time of the crisis and during the first quarter of 1937 reached 470,000.[4]

All salaried workers of Poland (agricultural, industrial, trade, commerce, mining, etc.) were about six times as many. Roughly, the workers employed in urban settlements were about four times as many, but the industrial workers in large and medium-sized industries (mining, foundry, manufacturing, electric power plants and water industries) alone averaged about 800,000 and the intelligentsia about 700,000 so they were nearly even. In urban communities the intelligentsia even numerically formed a considerable force.

---

[4] The figures are taken from *Mały Rocznik Statystyczny* (Concise Statistical Yearbook), 1939, Warsaw, 1939, except the figure of liberal professions which is taken from *Annuaire des Statistiques Du Travail, 1941, Bureau International du Travail*, Montreal, 1942. There is a slight discrepancy between the ILO figures and the figures of the Polish Statistical Office, probably caused by the fact of omitting or including of some wage earning groups.

The middle class was not very large, but still conservative or rightist in its majority. Thus the intelligentsia, students, and the middle class in its large majority formed the political base of the government. This group, in terms of sheer numbers, was quite significant, to say nothing about its influence in government, business, industry, journalism and radio.

The overwhelming majority of workers, and a small group of intelligentsia mostly in liberal professions, was to be found in the opposition and democratic camps in the cities. Not all the workers were in the socialist and even progressive camp. There were workers of Rightist tendencies. There was also an influential Catholic (Christian-democratic) Labor movement, especially in Silesia and western Poland. But still the socialist movement gave a general imprint to the Polish labor movement, as was the case in Russia before the revolution.

Socialist Ideology and Polish Reality

The social structure also influenced the ideology of the working class movement. When an independent Poland was created, about 75 percent of its population lived in the villages, and in the nineteenth century, this percentage had been even higher. Thus the working class movement had first of all to adjust itself to the peasant population. The presence of a large stratum of intelligentsia was another political reality. In its fight for political and social emancipation, in its everyday struggles against the employer for the improvement of the economic condition of the workers, the working class movement could not disregard these two important social strata. The peasants, emancipated from serfdom in the middle of the nineteenth century, were slowly maturing and taking a part in political life, and were the natural allies of the workers; the socialist movement thus was extended to the countryside. In the part of Poland formerly occupied by Austria, it gained considerable influence. An agricultural program adjusted to Polish reality rather than to dogmatic requirements was necessary. In independent Poland, the radical faction of the peasant movement always cooperated closely with the socialists. After 1930, in the struggle for the democratic reconstruction of Poland, the unified peasants' movement worked closely with the working class movement.

The Polish Socialist Party accepted the same premises as the peasant party in its agricultural program. For the only democratic solution of the Polish agrarian problem was the creation of small independent homesteads and co-operatives. The Polish peasant was adverse to collectivization of land, a fact which influenced the Polish socialist program.

The intelligentsia of independent Poland failed to create the vigorous progressive-democratic movement which was so vitally needed, and there was no progressive democratic party capable of rallying the intellectuals. Only a few years before World War II the Democratic Club, and later, the Democratic Party, were born and began slowly to organize the educated classes. The Polish working class movement did not follow the path of Machajski, whose theories, incidentally, were not very much known in Poland. On the contrary, Polish socialism probably recognized the need of extending its activity among the educated classes earlier than other European socialist movements. In the 1930's this need was taken for granted by many leaders of the P.P.S. (Polish Socialist Party) and influenced the party program.

Poland's international situation also strongly influenced the ideology of Polish socialism. Years of subjection to foreign rule and oppression taulht every Pole to value national freedom and independence. But even after independence was achieved, Poland was not secure. Her proximity to powerful and dynamic nations, and the absence of an adequate international system of collective security, influenced her internal policies. After Hitler's accession to power, foreign intervention in Poland became a real threat, and the domestic policy of the Polish Socialist Party had to take this threat into account, for violent internal struggles might have only prompted a new partition of the country. Thus, the working class and peasant movements were limited in their choice of tactics in the struggle for the reconstruction of Polish democracy by their sense of responsibility for the independence of the Republic.

Likewise, in the international arena, the Polish socialists sought solutions that would reconcile the national independence with institutions of an international community. They supported all forms of international cooperation based on the equal rights of great and small nations. They supported the League of Nations and collective security. After 1933, the Polish working class and peasant movements took a pro-French attitude and opposed the bilateral pacts.

The character of the Polish socialist movement, its dynamism and its combination of parliamentarianism and revolutionary dynamics, were shaped by many years of struggles. The 150 years of Polish captivity, the iniquitous partitions, weighed heavily on all spheres of Polish life, including the development of the working class movement. This development followed different paths in the parts occupied, respectively by Hrussia, Austria and Russia. Under Prussian occupation, the socialist movement lacked the dynamism and importance it gained in the other two parts of the country. The causes for this are various and are beyond the scope of the present inquiry.

In the provinces occupied by Austria the Polish socialist movement developed under constitutional conditions; the Polish socialists (PPSD) participated in the elections to municipal bodies and parliamentary institutions, they organized powerful unions, as well as educational, cooperative and health insurance societies. Thus, all the forms of modern labor movement were represented here. In the Vienna parliament, the representatives of the Polish Socialist Party soon gained prestige and influence among all the progressive and democratic groups. Party committees organized in towns and villages constantly supported the political activity of the movement. Thus at the turn of the century in Galicia a modern and excellently organized working class movement dedicated to democracy made its appearance.

The conditions in the territory occupied by Russia, the so-called Congress Kingdom, were completely different. Here, ruthless oppression and lack of political freedom drove Poland's political life underground. The working class movement was compelled to follow the same path as that of Russia itself— illegal struggle. Thus, while in Galicia the Polish socialists followed Western European constitutionalism and parliamentarianism, in Russian Poland they chose the path of revolution. Later, the socialist party of independent Poland became a synthesis of these two currents.

Insurrectionism in Polish Socialism

Polish socialism under Russian occupation was not divorced from tradition; its ideology and tactics were strongly influenced by its heroic past of the three tragic insurrections. Polish socialism was born before the modern Polish working class appeared; its ideas were adopted by the insurrectionists who emigrated after 1831, but socialism as a working class movement appeared in Poland only in the 1880's, and from the beginning, despite its international character, was full of "insurrectional traditions." Up to this day insurrectionism has remained the original and characteristic feature of Polish socialism.

The Poles participated in nearly every nineteenth century European struggle for freedom. They never forgot the insurrectional tradition, and introduced their own ideas and insurrectional tactics into foreign countries.

The personality and actions of Ignacy Hryniewiecki, a Pole active in the Russian socialist movement who made a terroristic attempt on the life of Tsar Alexander II, is an excellent illustration of this. Hryniewiecki came from the small Polish nobility of the Grodno region, and as a student at the Technological Institute in St. Petersburg he came into contact with the Russian revolutionary youth, although he also belonged to illegal Polish groups. Reproached by his colleagues for devoting so much energy to the Russian cause instead of giving all his strength to the cause of Poland, he replied: "When you take to the woods, I will be there, but now when you are not doing anything, I will work for the cause of Russian freedom." This incident, characteristically enough, was mentioned in the *Przedświt* (Dawn), a Polish socialist periodical published in Geneva, in its issue of 1883, which contained an obituary notice about Hryniewiecki. His words are typical of the revolutionary tradition of the Polish socialist movement. "To take to the woods," is an old insurrectional phrase which means to join a revolutionary detachment hiding in the forest, fighting with inferior arms from ambush, and displaying all the courage that is required in a hopeless and heroic struggle.

For many Poles, the socialist movement in Russian-occupied Poland meant "taking to the woods," and the working class movement itself was another form of insurrectional activity. This was the attitude of people of the type of Józef Piłsudski, who came from the Polish Socialist Party.

From the insurrectional point of view, the struggle for independence is ideologically an integral part of the Polish socialist movement. Former participants in the insurrection often joined the first socialist groups. Thus the *Proletariat,* the first socialist organization formed in Poland, despite its strongly pronounced international character, never forgot the insurrectional tradition; this is evidenced, for instance, in an article entitled "1861–1881," published in its underground organ on the occasion of a clash with the Russian army (1861 refers to the date of the January insurrection in Poland).

Later, the historical development of the socialist ideology in Congress Poland is marked by a split, for the two opposing currents differed in their attitude toward the question of an independent Poland. One faction, grouped around the Polish Socialist Party, considered the struggle for independence the most fundamental problem. The other, grouped around the Social Democracy of the Kingdom of Poland and Lithuania (SDKPL), struggled only for the realization of social postulates, did not desire the separation of Poland from Russia, and conceived of Poland only as a member of a gigantic international organism. The fact that the problem of independence could split the Polish socialist movement is a proof of its significance. The great leaders of international socialism supported the independence of Poland: Marx, Engels, Liebknecht. And although the Polish Social Democracy joined the Comintern after World War I and became the Polish Communist Party, Lenin declared himself in favor of the classical thesis of Polish socialism, that is, in favor of Polish independence.

The insurrectional tradition also left its mark on the initial organizations of the socialist movement as well as on the technique of the underground struggle. For instance, in May 1878, when a handful of students, workers and intellectuals founded in Warsaw the first nucleus of the future Polish Socialist Party, they took for their model the decimal organization of the 1863 insurrection. The larger unit, the section, was in 1863 called the "district," and this name (in Polish, *dzielnica*) has persisted to this day in the Warsaw workers' movement. But this is only a detail. The insurrectional character of the struggle is clear also in its militant action. While the Russian socialists confined themselves to attacks on individuals, that is, to terrorist attempts, the Polish socialists developed actions that sometimes assumed the character of guerrilla-warfare. Such was the attack on a train near Rogow, which was prepared and planned in a strictly military fashion. The demonstration in Grzybow Square in 1904 was in many aspects reminiscent of the demonstrations of 1861–1863, commonly called the January insurrection. Finally, the leadership of the Polish socialists sought a military form of organization. After the 1906 congress, they refused to become merely "a gang of public street cleaners constantly engaged in sweeping up Tsarist mud."

While individual terrorism was the chief method of the Russian revolutionists, the O.B., the Fighting Organization of the Polish Socialist Party, conceived its task differently. The organization strove to prepare the greatest possible number of organizers of the future insurrection, the imminent armed struggle. This tendency, after the defeat of the 1905 revolution, led to the formation in Austrian-occupied Poland of the paramilitary organization, *Strzelec* (The Rifleman), and later to the Legions, destined to fight for Polish independence.

The action itself had a character of its own, marked by boldness and dynamism. Famous was the escape from Pawiak prison in Warsaw, where ten political prisoners were being held awaiting sentence, some of them threatened with execution. One morning a group of policemen commanded by an officer came to the prison and presented an order for the immediate transfer of the prisoners. Far outside Warsaw, the prisoners learned that their escort consisted of disguised members of the Polish Socialist Party.

Small wonder that so much heroism and romanticism strongly influenced public feeling. Polish writers of that time, like Zeromski and Brzozowski, devoted their talents to the cause of the Polish socielism.

I am not emphasizing the insurrectional features of the Polish working class movement because I believe they are the most essential, but because they give this movement, whose ideology and international action were based on socialism, a special character.

The Polish Socialist Party justified its tactical, strategic and ideological "insurrectionism" by pointing to its social importance. Thus in the program of 1907 written by Feliks Perl, we read that real, complete democratization is impossible under conditions of subjection to a foreign country, for such subjection "hampers normal social development, harms the interests of national culture and exposes the country and the people to intensified exploitation and oppression on the part of the foreign invaders. Only in a free and independent country can the working class develop freely, manifest all its strength, fully carry out the democratization of government institutions and the objectives of socialism. For that reason, the PPS, while aiming at a democratic republic, combines this goal with independence, and struggles for an Independent Democratic Republic."

Insurrectionism is not the only characteristic feature of the Polish working class movement; it is distinguished from previous insurrectional movements in many other fundamental respects. First of all, the Polish socialist movement was not conspiratorial, not based on an isolated group of conspirators or partisans, but on mass support, and it aroused mass sympathy. Although lacking (in Russian-occupied Poland) trade union apparatus, the PPS was able to organize mass strikes and bring thousands of workers into the streets. Both in the leadership and the rank and file of this movement, the workers played a fundamental part, and this is the essential difference between the socialist movement and the old insurrectionary movements. Kościuszko's insurrection (contemporaneous with the French Revolution) mobilized the peasants, and in Warsaw it was even led by a simple artisan, the cobbler Kiliński; nevertheless, it was basically a national people's uprising. But despite the Połaniec Manifesto, which treated the peasants in a friendly and democratic spirit, this insurrection did not solve the agrarian problem by the total abolition of serfdom. The insurrection of 1831 was a military one and perhaps for that reason had greater chances for victory than any other insurrection, but again was unable to solve the agrarian problem in a radical way. The

Cracow uprising of 1846, although even socialist in its ideology, was purely local. The insurrection of 1863, despite the best intentions of its leaders, did not succeed in fully tackling the social problems of the country, especially the agrarian problem. The Polish socialist movement was the first insurrectional movement in Poland that connected the problem of social justice with that of national independence, and succeeded in drawing in the masses of the people.

The Polish working class movement was also the first political movement based on permanently organized mass movement controlled by its leadership and controlling this leadership. While in Russian-occupied Poland only a "vanguard" was organized, and the masses of the workers merely responded by action to the party appeals, under the Austrian occupation where the movement was imbued with organizational discipline, and was bbased on strong trade unions, there was a permanently organized influential political party of dues paying members.

After 1918 and the creation of an independent Poland consisting of territories previously occupied by three empires, there arose a great legal working class party—the PPS (Polish Socialist Party)—and powerful trade unions controlled by it. This party combined the daring of the party active under former Russian occupation, with the ability to carry on parliamentary work to initiate social insurance and advance working class legislation, which the Polish socialists had acquired under Austrian occupation. As a result, the PPS, while displaying great organizational versatility and ability for constructive work, did not lose its special militancy and spirit of sacrifice.

The Polish working class thus had great organizational capacities. In the course of several decades the socialist (PPS) and trade union movements had educated an army of local leaders, a kind of party of "noncoms." Found in every little town, every factory, these "noncoms" formed the nucleus of the organization, and were workers loyal to the flag of the party. During periods of persecutions they lost their jobs and filled the prisons, but returned to their posts. They also organized various local committees, distributed literature, posted placards, spoke at meetings, lent their apartments for party gatherings, and carried on agitation in the villages. These humble militants built the movement with their faith and self-denial, demanding little for themselves.

Influence of the Polish Socialist Party spread beyond the movement itself. It manifested itself in municipalities, social insurance organizations, labor courts, village arbitration committees, educational organizations, co-operatives, etc. Nor did the party remain silent on any important governmental questions. The working class movement also succeeded in protecting itself from political corruption. The Polish Socialist Party remained and still remains the center of the Polish working-class movement, and has never yielded to the communists or other competitors, who in their attempt to gain mass influence combatted the Socialists. The splits caused with the help of the government in 1930 did not succeed in breaking the PPS, and although membership in the trade unions decreased somewhat, and several former leaders, loyal to Piłsudski rather than to the party, left, most of the workers remained.

The Polish Socialist Party was never an orthodox Marxist one. First of all, a party consists of individuals and groups. A general program supplies a sense of direction, but, in a free and democratic movement many political orientations may flourish. There was of course a Marxist theoretical influence. However, the official party program did not accept a Marxist theory of state. Dedicated to democracy and political liberties, the party leadership as a rule rejected dictatorship, and advocated a democratic, parliamentary republic. Humanistic, ethical tendencies of socialism appeared early (Limanowski, later Posner). In the agrarian question, co-operatives and small landholdings were suggested as an answer. In consequence, the party advocated a radical land reform.

There were of course ideological differences between groups; there were of course the Marxists, and on the other hand pragmatists, concerned with every day problems, as well as humanists (Ethical Socialists). But even the Marxian elements in Polish socialism had a special character. Many socialist writers sought their own paths, among them Stanislaw Brzozowski, an independent thinker who greatly influenced the Polish youth during the first decade of the century. Similarly,

Abramowski, the theoretician of the co-operative movement, and Krzywicki, show many original features. Long talmudic discussions about the interpretation of the master's words were not carried on in Poland, and orthodox Marxism, alien to Marx himself, and more akin to religion than to science, did not gain many partisans in Poland. The beginnings of World War I mark the decline of old Marxian ideology in the Polish Socialist movement. The reality of totalitarian states, the brutality of exploitation and forced labor, cruel persecutions, shifted the emphasis to ethical issues and humanism. At the end of the war, humanistic, non-Marxian socialism began to displace orthodox Marxist creed both in Poland and among Poles abroad. This development was, however, interrupted by the extension of the political sphere of the Soviet Union.

Let us still return to the "intelligentsia," a social stratum which played such a significant role in Polish life. Social scientists took up the problem of the intelligentsia at the end of the nineteenth century. Karl Kautsky tried to fit it into the orthodox class division, assigning part of it to the bourgeoisie and part of it to the proletariat. Valuable work was done also by Robert Michels, and Max Nomad raised this problem in America. In the 1930's the Belgian sociologist, Henry de Man, and the Czech sociologist, Arnold Blaha, attempted to define the functions of the intelligentsia. Lewis Corey outlined a constructive solution of the problem of co-operation of the intelligentsia—the "managerial class"—with the workers, within the framework of an organized economic democracy.

In Polish socialist theory this problem appeared early in the writings of Wacław Machajski. He developed a radical and rather negative interpretation of this problem, and advanced an anti-intelligentsia class theory. Criticizing the socialist trends of his time, he asserted that the new emerging middle class was the intelligentsia, which mo..opolized education and exploited its privileged position in order to obtain higher pay through the indirect exploitation of the proletariat. Machajski considered the intelligentsia to be a separate class bound by its interests to the capitalists and opposed to the proletariat.

A far more sophisticated view of the same problem was advanced by Machajski's personal friend, Max Nomad, the author of *Apostles of Revolution, Aspects of Revolution,* and other works. Nomad, who settled in New York, became a naturalized American, and wrote widely in English, advanced a sociological theory of competition and struggle between the "out" and "in" elites in practically all advanced societies.

14

Recollections of the Camp at Sachsenhausen (1939–1940)

Stanisław Pigoń

1. THE KINSMAN

. . . Our block manager assigned to the group of professors his "platoon leader," a long-time prisoner named Zeische, who was to serve as our custodian, keeper, and helper. This prisoner, tall and slim, with an engaging, intelligent face was—as we soon found out—a Berlin attorney. He had been sent to the camp right after the outbreak of the war. A friendly man of good will, he became our first Virgil over the infernal territory. He initiated us in the camp's mysteries and way of life, in its snares and dangers, indicating how we could avoid them whenever possible. He explained how we should work when the "kapo" was watching: how to behave and how to answer when we were called before an infuriated SS-Mann; he warned us of the traps that the "Wächters" (guards) often set for the prisoners to have an excuse to torture or kill them. When we were going through the *Marsch und Gelenksübungen,* it was he who tried to lead us as far as he could from the prying eyes of the guards. He treated us with unusual kindness, which was bound to impress us as an unforgettable wonder in that savage place.

271

But this was not the strangest, most peculiar part of it. Right at the outset Dr. Zeische, the supposed Berliner, spoke to us in excellent Polish. It was not so pure that the foreign intonation could not be heard, but generally fluent and almost without mistakes. Why and how? He answered our questions, "Oh, I probably know Poland better than many a Pole."

For years he had spent his vacations in Poland as an enthusiastic tourist, wandering from the Tatras to the Holy Cross mountains, not to mention Cracow or Warsaw. And when you come right down to it, he was not so much of a Berliner. Of course, he had studied law in Germany, but he had also spent time in Prague, where he met Henryk Batowski, who soon kindled in him an unextinguishable liking for Poland. He began the study of the Polish language, followed by copious reading and roving tours.

It must be said that this Polonophile initiation was in a great measure facilitated by the fact that Zeische was not a German at all, but a Lusatian, and thus a close kinsman. Neither was he Zeische. It was the Germans who imposed on him this version of his good family name. He was called simply Cyż, tracing his descent from the old and worthy line of Lusatian Cyż's. Since he was an activist of Slavic nationalism, the German government did not permit him to open an attorney's office in his native land; thus he had to settle in Berlin. Even from there he did not cease to be an advocate of the national consciousness of Lusatia, and this was what opened the hospitable gates of Sachsenhausen camp to him.

I felt an immediate liking for this kinsman. The name of Cyż was not unfamiliar to me. I remembered it from somewhere, from something I had read long ago, and it came back to me in some honorable association. But what was it? I was able to check it right after my return home. But to grasp this association, we must go back nearly a hundred years.

In 1849, the young poet Teofil Lenartowicz, still warmed by the rays of the Spring of Nations (revolutions of 1848), set out from Dresden on an extended journey through Lusatia. Many things drew him there. First of all, the venerable and august history of the origins of these people. It is because of this that

Lusatians generally enjoy a great deal of respect in Poland and evoke a sincere attachment. We feel something in the nature of a wistful affection toward our old good neighbor. And what a neighbor they have been! Already in the ninth century a Bavarian geographer wrote about the Lusatians: *"Zeriuani, quod tantum est regnum, ut ex eo cunctae gentes Sclavorum exortae sunt et originem ducunt."* (The Sorbs, from whose abode all Slavic tribes arose and took origin.)

According to this, then, the Slavs sprang from them, and here was the origin of their national consciousness. Neither should we forget that for a long time Lusatia formed a part of the Polish state within the borders delimitated by the thunderbolt of Boleslaw's sword. Our kinsmanship was fixed centuries ago.

Lusatian colleagues had invited Lenartowicz to come for a visit, painting an alluring picture of their country and offering to share with him whatever they had. He was also enticed to go there by his friend, the young Roman Zmorski, who felt at home in Lusatia; wandering from village to village, he had been collecting songs and legends for some time, had formed literary friendships, had initiated and even led the budding publishing movement.

Reminiscing over this trip some forty years later, Lenartowicz could not hold back his emotion. How charming it had been! The landscape so beautiful, the people friendly, and the old national heritage blossoming forth from under the German deluge like spring flowers from under the snow. He was greeted nearly the same way as in his native Mazovia: "Blessed be Jesus Christ!"—"For ever and ever, Amen."

There was love for the fatherland there, *"nasz srbski kraj, ridny kraj"* (our Sorbian land, our native land), and a Pole was received with hospitality, with an open heart.

Lenartowicz accepted these invitations, staying in the region for a long time. He had his stops all planned with the more outstanding leaders of the awakening Lusatian national spirit: Jan A. Smoleri, Imisz, Koczko, Fr. Broszko. But he started with someone else, searching for him in the countryside. Directly from Budziszyn he went to the vicinity of Chociebuz, to the patrimony of his young friend and colleague by the name of

Cyż. He did not find his friend at home, but his father, "a rich peasant, a real Piast-apiarist," welcomed him with open arms. Our poet spent quite a few days there.

"At the house of the Old Cyż," he recalled years later, "I took up quarters in his son's room, where I found all editions of the Czech Matica, the Lusatian bible and an abundance of other books. I read them for days on end. . . . I observed the good management and exemplary life of these patriarchal people. . . . Work—and what work! From morning to night, but gaily, because it was on their own land and for the improvement of their lot. To this day I remember this old apiarist (owner of about three hundred bee hives), drawing himself up at the table and solemnly, with voice raised, invoking God's blessing for his family; throughout my stay in this peasant cottage I never heard a cross word."

Who could have foreseen that we would take up the thread of intimacy relinquished by Lenartowicz, and under what conditions we might begin weaving it anew? Who could have imagined that the grandsons would pick up the conversation interrupted by their grandfathers, in the same friendly comradeship, only ander ominously gathering clouds that threatened extermination? There could be some justification for considering this incident more momentous than it appeared. There was a broader meaning to it. The barbed wire of the camp had dealt us, as well as Cyż, our age-old common fate. For a thousand years we had both been assaulted by the insatiable German rapacity. Since the Lusatians were closer, they were assaulted more aggressively and voraciously. From the middle of the seventeenth century, the enemy invasion flooded Lusatia and did not let up. But it did not succeed in depriving the Lusatians of a feeling of national identity; under the crushing pressure it blossomed even more intensely in the nineteenth century. Now the hereditary enemy, raving with fury, dealt them a decisive blow. Dr. Cyż was a victim of this fury, as were we. What a joy it is to realize today that the blow finally struck the evildoer, and not the victim!

I cannot say when Cyż left the camp. Could it have been as late as the spring of 1945? I do not know how he returned to his native land and what he found there. I heard somewhere that the camp ordeal had ruined his health and caused his death shortly afterwards. But surely at the old homestead near Chociebuz there still lives the long-settled clan of Lusatian Cyż's, the peasant apiarists who for generations had had their hearts open to Poland. Perhaps the kinsmanship we developed at the camp strengthened this bond in some way. This would be a small sign confirming the historical curse on an evil deed.

2. A HUMAN VOICE IN THE RUFFIANS' CAVE

A quarter of a century has passed since a group of professors from the Jagellonian University was deported to the concentration camp in Sachsenhausen. As an unprecedented event in the history of learning, this fact still attracts a great deal of attention, giving rise to reminiscences, both written and oral, historical commentaries, and emotional reflections. Under these circumstances, it is natural that the event itself becomes enveloped in legend. And a legend, by its very nature, inevitably displaces events a little. Sometimes changing perspectives, it draws some incidents to the fore, while keeping others completely in the dark. This is unavoidable. Sometimes this benefits the truth (when, for instance, new details emerge), but often it acts to its detriment, to the prejudice of a valid appraisal of historical events, of historical justice. After all, the proper emphasis on one detail or another sometimes depends on a turn of chance. Sometimes this is fortunate, but at other times it is a pity. In this case it is too bad! It is a shame even when this slight concerns a trifle. Who is to decide and judge once and for all what is an unimportant detail? When considered from another angle one day, may it not take on a deeper meaning?

These are the considerations that induce me to reach into the (already dusky) stock of memory to draw out a few sketches from those times, slender to be sure, but somehow significantly interconnected and important, if only because they have remained engraved in my memory and are thus perhaps not wholly insignificant. In any case, they seemed important to me already at the time.

The final leg of our journey to the camp was as follows. Night had fallen when we arrived at a terminal station by train from Wrocław. We were herded out of the cars, lined up in rows and pushed on our way. It was quite a distance from the station to the camp, and the way was muddy. In a darkness incessantly shattered by the blinding rays of electric flashlights, surrounded by guards, we pushed on—as was the custom there—on the double, stumbling over chuckholes in the road, urged on by the shouts of our escort. The older men among us, those with heart conditions, grew weak and fell down, which caused momentary confusion, until the fallen man was kicked out of the file and dragged off separately.

Those who arrived within the area of the camp were lined up in a square before the administration building. After checking whether the transport was complete, they sorted us out: the priests separately, the Jews separately; those who remained were divided into four groups, so that they could be squeezed into the already greatly overcrowded barracks (blocks) 45 and 46. Naturally, no one displayed any hospitality or pity toward us on this occasion. We were led through the "reception hall," had our "effects" removed, went through a brutal check to see whether we were not bringing in any vermin, and finally we were ordered to change into striped suits. Even during this procedure we were not spared outbursts of savagery. Privatdozent Stefan Harassek was beaten because he leaned against the wall for a moment while he put on the tight clogs doled out to him. An enraged guard tore a cross from the neck of a young priest; seizing a breviary from his hands, he ripped it to pieces and stomped on it.

In our barrack, we found a crowd of inmates, mostly Germans but Poles as well. As we soon found out, the Poles were nationalist activists from Westphalia and Pomerania. They all crowded around us to get a look at these "Professoren." We all walked in together.

To make the events that I want to present here sufficiently clear, I must make a more general observation. The camp at Sachsenhausen had existed for several years. Shortly after Hitler's coup, it was set up on a clearing cut out of the woods, with barracks built by the prisoners; it was populated by political opponents of the party, mainly German communists. Later this changed. Already in the first weeks of the war throngs of disloyal citizens were herded from all parts of the country, along with those suspected of disloyalty, and also put behind the barbed wire of this camp. Thus, thousands of people of different kinds found themselves together in this crowd, since authentic criminals were mixed in with political prisoners, along with various sectarians, loafers, and vagabonds ("Arbeitsscheue," which included Gypsies); there was even a separate barrack for "fallen angels," or Gestapo men thrown out of the ranks for some offense or other.

From this we could see that conditions did not exist as was popularly assumed—that behind the barbed wire could be found only virtuous martyrs in striped suits and devils in uniform who tortured them. Among the prisoners there was no shortage of quarter, half, or at least potential devils. They did not have a bad time there. Birds of a feather soon flocked together. As the size of the camp was increased, the command found that it needed helpers, and the commanders chose them from among the prisoners. In a small way they formed something in the nature of a spider web of camp self-government. A hierarchy of sorts arose from among these—to a certain extent authorized—helpers. There was a prisoner principal leader ("der Lagerälteste"), a barrack manager ("Blockälteste"), a room keeper ("Stubenälteste"), and even a table steward ("Tischälteste"), as well as so-called kitchen helpers. Similarly, in the administrative section there were store managers, tailors, cooks, and hospital attendants, among others. Every one of the lucky chosen people gained certain rights along with certain duties, in particular the protection of the "authorities"; any attempt at resistance, not to speak of raising one's hand against one of these sub-sovereigns, was considered rebellion and resulted in serious consequences. And what opportunities there were for oppression and abuses! It was enough for the "authorized" fellow to be in charge of sweeping or washing the floor in the barrack for him to bark out orders whenever he had the chance and to use his fists on those who did not obey eagerly enough. It was a paradise for sadists of all sorts; a great opportunity for getting away with bestial behavior with impunity.

The more profitable the assilnment, the more scoundrels crowded around. For instance, the "hospital attendants" worked in a heated barrack ("district"); they were exempt from roll call; they enjoyed an ample food supply. It was something worth trying for, and, as a result, the chosen ones outdid each other in their zealousness toward the authorities, and thus also in cruelty. Supposedly, they were to be helpful to their suffering fellow prisoners. They simplified their job by treating the sick like annoying rubbish, as insufferable intruders who disturbed their peace. They did not make a fuss about anyone. In the camp, where half-rotten turnips were the basis of the diet, dysentery was rahpant. The hospital attendants cleaned off a patient who could no longer stand on his feet, and therefore was soiled, by dousing him with icy water from a hydrant. We heard a great deal about the torturing of the sick, and it all turned out to be true. After the widow of Professor Feliks Rogoziński had been notified of her husband's death and had managed to come to the camp in time to view the body, she noticed a deep wound on the temple of her dead husband, obviously made by a shoe. The guard she questioned about this interrupted his whistling of a lilting tune long enough to reply: "He must have fallen down. . . ."

Among the most brutal lackeys (at least in my barrack) were the cooks. Naturally, they did not suffer from hunger, so they had plenty of strength to take out their sadistic impulses on the weak. No one went into the kitchen eagerly. Once Professor Adam Heydl and another man from our room went there with buckets to fetch our dinner. A moment later they returned—cursed out, black and blue, and without the hogwash called "Eintopfgericht." It seems that they stood in some line not as they should have, or spoke when they shouldn't have. So it seems that the camp tormentors made use of subtormentors, a job for which they found as many willing recruits among the prisoners as they wanted. The degree to which the stay in the barrack was onerous depended a great deal on the character of the manager and his assistants, and thus on fellow prisoners. They did not always leave a good name behind them.

But even here there were exceptions sometimes.

Let us now return to the course of our camp initiation. Already properly dressed and terrorized, we were shoved into the hall of barrack 46. There we were received by its manager, "der Blockälteste." He had his bed and night table in the corner by the window, separated from the rest of the room by a linen screen. When he came out of there to greet us, he already knew what a bunch he was getting. As we stood lined up in a row, he spoke a few words to us, letting us in on the elementary principles of camp discipline, the prescribed penalties, and finally told us: "Mingle with your fellow prisoners, blend into the mass of them without any distinction. It does not matter what you were up to now. I will treat you like people, in accordance with the principle of equal justice."

"Like people." I will not forget these words. This was the first human voice in this shrieking pandemonium. Fortunately, it was not an empty promise.

I became interested in this unusual "block manager." During the days that followed, I was able to find out a little about him. He was middle aged, with an expressionless face that nevertheless inspired confidence. He hailed from East Prussia, was a railroad worker by profession, probably with a secondary or even only a primary education. His name was Dobschatt, and from something he happened to mention one day I found out that he came from a family of Germanized Prussians who retained some feeling of racial distinctness. As an active Communist, he had been put in the camp right after the Hitler coup, so that he was a well-settled resident by the time we arrived. In later talks with us he dropped a few hints about himself once in a while. Already after his deportation, he learned by chance that his wife had borne him a son. In 1939, the child must have already been quite a big boy. Since no one was allowed to send photographs into the camp, the father had no idea how the boy looked. From his wife's cards he knew only that his son was alive.

Dobschatt felt quite at home at the camp. He knew the local conditions well, and kept some sort of secret contact with his ideological companions. Like the masons, the Communists had a special distinguishing sign when they met.

Dobschatt had not just promised to treat us as human beings.

He tried to keep our group together, assigning us adjoining places in the barrack and at the tables. Although he shouted at us as well as at the others, since there could be no life there without shouting, he did not bully us, nor torture or harm anyone, as did many others in his position in other barracks. There could even be some basis for saying that he displayed a guarded friendliness. We felt it more than once. It may be worthwhile to mention a few examples.

Among the camp duties was peeling potatoes for the kitchen. This was done in a remote place, only at night, after the completion of compulsory daytime work; it lasted quite a long time, sometimes all night. Even so, in the morning one had to get up as usual with the others for roll call and work. Dobschatt quite obviously tried to prevent us from being assigned to nighttime burdens; only seldom, in case of unusual need, would he add us to the list of potato peelers.

Besides hard work and savage discipline, a source of our anguish through December 1939 and January 1940 was the dreadful cold and the fierce "wind from the sea"; every day the thermometer dipped well below 20° (we had no thermometers, but we estimated the temperature well). Dressed in torn recruits' shirts, often without sleeves, in thin fustian striped jackets, we froze unbearably. The cold took its toll. Professor Haborski froze his toes, and since he was not given first aid in time, he hobbled to the roll call on his heels for a few days. When he finally got into the first aid, they scraped his toes of the decaying flesh like sticks of wood. It was too late to prevent gangrene, and anyway no one took any special pains about it.

Every one of us gave a lot of thought to how he could save himself by some means. We were herded out for the roll call early, much ahead of time. Before we were marshaled into rows, we huddled together tightly, taking the weakest in the middle. This did not help much in the penetrating wind. I also tried to craftily gain some semblance of protection for myself by safeguarding my feet. Stealthily, I pilfered some straw from my mattress, and in the tried peasant manner lined my soles with it, covering the wisps with paper. I had the opportunity to confirm what a wonderfully effective method this was. There still remained the problem of the trunk of my body, especially the thorax, covered with the thin, draughty striped coat. Here I lay in wait for a newspaper. We did not receive papers either often or with regularity; sometimes we were thrown some issue of *Stürmer,* but only very seldom a daily. It was grabbed up immediately, although not necessarily for reading. I came upon a newspaper slyly one day. I knew (from experience) that paper was a poor conductor of heat and in a pinch could be used instead of a lining. Before the morning roll call, I imperceptibly—as I thought—slipped the paper under my blouse.

Some imperceptibility! One of my table companions, a grumpy ruffian, witnessed my crime and ran to tattle to Dobschatt. I do not know what motivated him. We had never exchanged one word before this time. I had had no occasion to antagonize him. Everyone knew that the crime was a serious one. To take steps on your own to save your skin—what impudence! Things could have been bad for me if news of my offense had reached the henchman of a noncom; but luck was with me. It was part of the basic camp discipline that none of the prisoners could begin a conversation with a noncom guard on his own initiative. The Blockälteste was the only level of official accessible to us. And that is what saved me. After he was notified of my misdeed, Dobschatt summoned me; he sharply reminded me of the seriousness of my crime and that there were no light penalties at the camp. Of course, he took away the newspaper. That was the end of the affair for me, but not for Dobschatt. He called the informer and spoke to him alone for a long time. He must not have been paying him compliments during this time, since the ruffian continued to favor me with dirty looks for a long time afterwards.

A later, somewhat similar incident I want to recount here was also connected with the cold but was of much larger dimensions. It did not involve me directly. On a Thursday, January 18, a day not to be forgotten by any of us, when the thermometer must have plummeted lower than ever before, it happened that they were one prisoner short during the morning roll call; the suspicion arose that someone had tried to escape. In such cases it was a standing rule that all prisoners were kept out on the parade ground until the escapee had been caught. This could last half a day, all day, or even the night as well. So, then, on that day we were kept on the square, standing in rows, until dusk in our flimsy garments, while the catchers searched through the barracks and every nook and cranny of the camp. The weather was unusually cold and windy. The older and weaker among the prisoners could not stand it. One after the other they fainted from exhaustion or the cold. All we could do for them was to carry them to the so-called "rewir" (infirmary) or hospital barrack.

Not everyone in our group of professors could weather this ordeal. Professor Leon Wachholz, standing next to me, fainted and fell over. Two of us picked him up and carried the unconscious man to the "rewir." But the doors of the barrack were locked and before them lay—one next to the other—a number of other unconscious men like Wachholz, slowly freezing to death. Through the windows we glimpsed the smug and laughing mugs of several hospital attendants (of course, our fellow prisoners), who were amusing themselves with banter about such a fantastic joke. What were we to do? We put our unfortunate colleague down alongside the others and left him there unconscious, but we quietly presented the matter to Dobschatt. And now it was he who committed a crime. He gave us a key to the barrack, telling us to take the fainted man there and try to revive him. After being rubbed with snow, Wachholz regained consciousness and sat up. Nothing was said about the crime of our block manager, because nothing could be said. Professor Wachholz returned with us to Cracow.

What I have written here might have created the impression that Dobschatt favored us professors in some way, granting us special privileges. It was not so. He was a strict military disciplinarian, demanded order, drove people to it, and could be strict. But he was equally strict with everyone—only without savagery. He did not even shout as brutally and foul-mouthedly as was the custom in the camp. He treated us all fairly. He always divided justly the meager food portions received for us, although as close as the other side of the barrack we could see how the room manager, a ferocious brute, a former German sailor, shamelessly, before everyone's eyes, cut a thick slab from each loaf of bread and lay it aside on his table. It was rank theft, but the thief shrieked with cynical laughter as he perpetrated it.

Dobschatt never said a word of criticism about what was going on around us, but there was no doubt what he thought about it. If he did hint at something, he did it with a great deal of caution.

An occasion for this arose when a resident of our barrack was beaten publicly.

People were beaten at the camp for the slightest infraction: for lining up badly, for not saluting a noncom quickly enough or not saluting the displayed flag, or often just for simple sadistic pleasure. But there were also executions with special ceremony, carried out publicly on the parade ground for infractions of discipline, among other things. A distinct category were multiple executions designed to systematically finish off a number of "culprits" to a crime. These were deliberate acts of terror; the death of the prisoners was meant to frighten the other prisoners thoroughly. We had a chance to observe such an incident at close range.

Among the prisoners there was a farmer, a bulky fellow, no longer young and rather stout, some kind of Bavarian "Grossbauer." It was said of him that he had raised his hand against a Hitlerite soldier. A military unit had invaded his farm with a requisition. The farmer tried to fight back against its ruthlessness and, pushed or slapped by a noncom, impetuously returned the blow.

He was sent to the camp for a slow "exemplary" death. After the roll call, two or three tormentors approached him and the torture began, with fists, with bludgeons. When he fell down, they kicked him with their boots in the head, the ribs, in the groin. When he passed out he was left lying in the square. On the next day and the days that followed, the torture began with the question: "What? You haven't hung yourself yet?"

And then the whole procedure began as the day before. And in fact we soon stopped seeing him in the square.

The most frequent occasions for beatings were incidents of theft among the prisoners. Theft was prevented by means of terror—as showy as possible—precisely for educational purposes. It happened that one time a prisoner from our block was sentenced to a flogging. I cannot say whether the accusation was just or not, but the opinion of the block had it that the suspicion was unfounded. The flogging was meted out publicly, on the parade ground, in front of everyone. The victim was tied to a slanted pillory of sorts, with the necessary piece of his clothing pulled down. Two strong men designated for the task beat him with thick rubber hoses.

When our martyred block-mate dragged himself back to the barrack late that evening, at a time when there was less likelihood of an unexpected visit by one of the noncoms, Dobschatt ordered him to undress and stand with his face to the wall. He gave us something in the nature of an object lesson. He said a few words about camp discipline and showed the culprit as an illustration. The sight turned out to be macabre. The entire middle of his trunk, from the loins down, was thickly covered with bloody black stripes; the stripes blended into each other— so that it was difficult to count the number of blows. Dobschatt kept the victim on display for some time so that—as he said—we would see and remember. "Damit sie merken." And in fact none of us forgot. . . .

After we learned that some of us would be released from the camp, we spoke more freely with our "host." He wished us liberation and mentioned that when this terrible cataclysm blew over, he would be happy to visit us in Cracow. To a man, we invited him to come, but nothing came of it. I do not know what happened to him. I understand that he survived the war and held some important position in the German Democratic Republic (East Germany), but I am certain that he is no longer alive.

Of course, then, these words will not reach him. Nevertheless, I feel that they had to be said. A small matter, a trivial incident; I cannot even say how unique it was within Sachsenhausen itself, of whether a similar one occurred somewhere else. But it is worth recalling, worth bringing to mind this human voice in a cave of raging ruffians. It did not pass without leaving a mark. In the din of triumphant villainy it sustained our faith in the inner integrity of man.

3. UNDER THE THREAT OF EXTERMINATION

It is most difficult to find the end of the thread in a tangled skein; if you grab it, the skein falls out of your hand, as if some sort of desire to elude and stretch itself out were released in the thread. This is how it is with the thread of memory generally, and in this case of prison memories of a quarter-century ago. I presented the reader with a short fragment from them a little while ago, and already further memories come crowding in. Faces and incidents from that time come before my memory and say accusingly: "Have you forgotten us?"

I have not forgotten, but it is difficult to cope with scruples about whether we—jailbirds—will not bother outsiders with these memories, people for whom these incidents and experiences are after all only someone else's distant adventures, perhaps not always believable.

In the course of those terrible months, there is one thing that particularly fascinates me: the process of psychic adaptation by my professor-colleagues to such unexpected and frightening circumstances, a distinct process because of the very fact that it was so condensed. Nearly two hundred people with fully formed personalities, people who knew each other, but not very intimately, suddenly found themselves isolated: Around them was a void; they were alone in indifferent, strange and often hostile surroundings. Like a bunch of castaways who found themselves in a cockboat without oars or rudder, tossed by a storm in the depths. How will they act? How will each one act individually? Who will stand it, and who will break down? On which of them can you count at least a little? You look around at the others with dismay. . . . It was something like that with us.

Helpless, completely lost, indeed tossed overboard, thrust together by fate into a close-knit body of desperadoes, we crowded together, became more familiar with each other— eyeing each other guardedly and not without fear. Everyone seemed to be asking: Who are my neighbors, how will each of them turn out to be, in whom does a spark of hope smoulder, and in whom does the emptiness of despair lurk? On whom can I count, and who is not worth counting on? Whom would it be better to avoid carefully? In this panic, we formed ties that have

lasted through the years. How did it happen? Under what circumstances?

In this comparatively short time of imprisonment (I speak of
the older colleagues, who were released in February 1940), we
went through three stages of feelings, as if through three levels
leading to the depths of a mine shaft. The first stage, still almost
idyllic, took place in a Wrocław prison. We all felt that the
madness of this outburst of the occupant's police could not,
after all, last long. They struck at the University, terrorized the
Polish population right at the outset of the occupation, but that
was enough. They achieved their goal, so they were bound to
free us from here very soon.

They did not let us go. I will never forget the day before we
were deported from Wrocław. I associate it with a curious
character we met—a professional prison provost who helped us
to clean out our cells. Our adventure with him could be used by
Tadeusz Mikulski for his series "Wrocław Meetings." He was
also a specimen of the fading past of that region. A peasant by
birth, he seemed a German through and through, who spoke to
us only in German, but one day, when we were alone, he
blurted out: "My mother," he said, "called 'Handmühle'
[handmill], 'zorna.' " It was obvious that he heard Polish spoken
at home. He came from the vicinity of Wrocław; he was the first
to be forced outside his tribal area by the pressure of Germani-
zation. But not completely; still his memory served him and an
affinity with the Poles stirred within him. The day before our
departure he somehow dug into his fund of knowledge of his
mother tongue and whispered to us fearfully, in dialect: "You
will go to a camp."

And indeed on the following day our second stage began,
already behind the barbed wire of Sachsenhausen. But even
this stage did not break our spirit. Here again, with the desperate hope of the condemned, we clutched at the thought that
there would be only weeks of this ordeal. They want to terrorize
us, "teach us a lesson"; they will reveal to us the horror of the
camp and soon—surely before Christmas—they will let us go.
In this expectation, my colleagues still kept their heads high;
they did not abandon their intellectual interests, and weathered
the cruelty of the cold and the brutality of the guards.

Again we were deluding ourselves. Christmas passed—and we were not released. This was our descent to the third stage, which for many was the moment of collapse. There was not enough strength left. A series of deaths among our older colleagues proceeded in rapid succession. Dread hovered over our group. The day after Christmas I had a chance to talk with Professor Chrzanowski for a little while. He did not bear up well under the camp conditions; he had been among those who had desperately clung to the forlorn hope that we would be home for Christmas. When this hope was extinguished, he was deeply shaken; his usual serenity let him down. "Well, Mr. Stach," he began, "you seem to have lost heart. . . ." "Not at all," I answered. "Even if it drives them crazy, I will get through it somehow." "Oh, well, you see," he said quietly, "and I won't. I will stay here." He looked at me deeply with his sad eyes. This plaintive look went right through me, and I will never forget it.

These harbinger eyes in the camp are another subject in itself. I have looked into them to excess. We grew to understand their meaning through experience. As a farmer can predict tomorrow's rain by the clouds around the setting sun, so we, from the quality of someone's gaze, determined the distance of stealthily approaching death. One could tell the end of a man three days before it happened. I will not forget one of my meetings with Professor Michał Siedlecki. I liked and respected him; I had come to Wilno during his term as president. It was he who had brought me to the department and introduced me to everyone there. Now we stood on the parade ground and exchanged a few words. One moment and one look in his eyes were enough. He had the gaze of a mortally wounded fawn, somehow surprised, extinguished, mournful, deeply sad—even though the course of our casual conversation gave no cause for it. Well, I thought, you haven't long, my poor soul. . . . And that is how it was. I went through this more than once.

Here I might venture to discuss a difficult matter. How did it happen that among our colleagues death so unpredictably struck some and spared others? We all lived under the same external conditions: meteorological, gastronomic, and all others. One might think that age would be of primary importance: the old would die and the young survive. But no. Bossowski, Smoleński, Metallmann were not the oldest among us, but they perished. And on the other hand, Adam Krzyżanowski, the oldest of us, lived through it; Lewkowicz, Maziarski, Kutrzeba—men well along in years—escaped death.

One could also take another factor into consideration—that extermination pushed its way among us from another source as well.

We were all doomed to hunger at the camp; we were all underfed. No one had calculated our meals in calories, but it was safe to say that they were down in the lowest category possible. Nevertheless, it would be correct to say that although we were all equalized, subjected to the same torment, we did not all react to it in the same way. Hunger bothered some beyond belief, while others bore it somehow.

In point of fact, I am among the more enduring in this respect, as I had a chance to prove to myself more than once. It takes quite a lot for hunger to really bother me. During my student years, a few friends and I purposely underwent experiments of this kind. And it was not on a whim. I belonged to a generation which sporadically, but not without incentive and a system, tested itself in a disciplined training of the will. This was popular then. We read the books of Jules Payot and Wincenty Lutosławski, and went through the exercises described there.

There were some among them that led to the control of emotional impulses or body functions, including the suppression of sensibility to hunger. I had a friend who beat all of our records: he survived forty days without taking a bite to eat, living only on water and lemon juice. I myself did not manage such a feat, but I did get through a week of such experiment without any particular effort or suffering. To this day total fast is no great trouble for me. The whole trick is to curb the voracity of the stomach and steer your imagination away from these matters.

But I know that everyone is not capable of the same control, and in the camp I saw a lot of people whom the torments of hunger shattered physically and mentally. An example immediately comes to mind. One such martyr of hunger was assigned to our table. He was a comparatively young Russian farmhand, whom already before the war fate had thrown in the

service of a farmer in East Prussia. The Gestapo fished him out
of there in no time. This unfortunate fellow constantly writhed
with hunger on our camp diet. Whenever I looked at him, I was
reminded of the hero of Dygasiński's novel *Żerty chłop* (The
Greedy Peasant). In his anguish he would have chewed shoe
leather, could he have managed it. He ate everything that was
even remotely edible.

Sometimes we were given potatoes boiled in the skin for supper: five poor little potatoes per head (or rather per stomach).
Since there were plenty among them that were half-rotten or
covered with black growths, we peeled them and removed the
inedible portions. Our companion swept these scraps up with
assiduous care and ate them all. He laughed gaily at our ad-
monitions that he might get mortally ill from them:

"I never saw anyone die from eating! From hunger—yes. But
from eating? . . ."

There was no shortage among us of people whom hunger
crushed and knocked off their feet. But this did not necessarily
lead to the final catastrophe. Already during the course of my
youthful reading and training I discovered a secret that became
important at the camp. The feeling of hunger does not have
absolute power over man. It rises to some high limit, to an
intensity such that it seems to tear at our insides. But after a
while it quiets down and slowly subsides. The body switches
over to its own resources. The first three days are the hardest to
stand, and then one can live with it. It is another matter that
after some time the starveling faints at the slightest strain.
Thus, one can stand hunger for quite a long time, longer than
is generally supposed. Even in our most bothersome trouble—
undernourishment—we were not entirely helpless.

As I believe, the secret lay in one's psychic armor. Every one
of us was besieged like a bastion by the unyielding furies of
destruction and for each of us it was most important not to
suffer weakness within the fortress, not to admit the most terrible enemy—despair and defeatism—to our side.

In olden times, fortresses were sometimes built on two levels.
Above the "lower castle," a "high castle" was always perched on
a crag. Even though the first fell, the second could still be defended for a long time. We also had to find in ourselves such a

"high castle" in the face of this ominous violence, to find a mainstay, strong and imperturbable as possible, to defend it with all our might and not let go even for a moment. Not to give way to doubt, prostration, dig in deep within ourselves and—stand fast like a rock. Let them try to dislodge me! That was the only way to salvation. These are not idle words. I myself reached such a point of resistance, and this is probably why I survived. This protected me from the deluge of aggressive hatred. And such armor did not depend on age or exclusively on the fund of vital forces.

I have described one of the prisoners' tactics to save themselves from the overwhelming avalanche of evil and destruction. But some of the prisoners relied on another to try to save themselves as well. (It is true that one did not often meet anyone who had the temerity to try it.) They would resort to a peculiar kind of ataraxia and an internal woodenness that was hard to understand. The individual, called half-contemptuously and half-compassionately "Moslem," assumed this to withstand the brutal treatment. He would show a complete indifference toward the threat of death: he had conquered pain and could choke back suffering, not to flinch before the horror of pain.

There was such a man in our barrack, and I watched him with growing horror. Haggard, barely able to stand on his feet, he went unhesitatingly to the center of torment with a stubborn defiance: "Well, then, finish me off!" And it sometimes happened—wonder of wonders—that the devil of cruelty turned his enraged eyes away from him and crept away defeated. I have seen it myself.

Quite often the so-called "*stójka*" (punishment by standing, or *Stehkommando*) was employed against us older men. A large number of men were crowded together in a barracks. The guards surrounded the prisoners around the walls, armed with bludgeons. We had to stand in this crush for hours, until our feet swelled. There was no question of sitting or even kneeling on the floor. In another form of torment, the prisoners were locked in a room, and allowed to leave for the latrine only at certain times. For the many among us who suffered from dysentery, this was the source of a new torture. However, our

"Moslem" was sick, and he asked to go through the barrier; when he came back, after about fifteen minutes, he again put in his request. When he was refused, he stubbornly returned to the guard. Beaten, kicked around, he again struggled to his feet and refused to give up. He again invited the bludgeon. He suffered the blows in silence, stifling his cries. And so he did for the third and fourth time, until finally the infuriated tormentor either weakened or became frightened. He opened the door and with a swift kick threw out the bothersome fellow. The "Moslem" achieved his aim, but a clammy fear gripped those who looked on this fury of brutishness; nevertheless some superhuman doggedness clearly won out over the bestiality of the tormentor.

My colleagues who have written about their camp experiences have discussed at length the deluge of evil which inundated us from outside our midst and finished off so many of us. Of course, there were as many reactions to the evil as there were personalities among us. But the one reaction to this that almost all of us made was to develop a deep-seated desire to survive. Each one of us was thrown upon his own resources and tried to save himself the best he could. Naturally, there were those who let panic overtake them and plunge them into black despair. But they were not many. The great majority fought back in a variety of ways, gathering in themselves the forces of resistance like glowing embers in a fire that gives the outward appearance of dying out. Some surrounded themselves with a layer of unconcern. Thus, Karol Dziewoński filled each free moment quietly and serenely doing calisthenics. Roman Prawocheński displayed an inexhaustible reserve of serene vitality. At one time, his daughter had sent him a small package: a little sugar, some biscuits grilled in butter, a chocolate bar. The package arrived. The addressee was called to the office, paid the cost of delivery, and when the package was finally opened, it was announced that it would be divided among the noncoms. They work so hard. . . . They deserved something for it. The recipient did not even get a chance to smell the contents of the package. The professor recounted this scene to us later with unruffled good humor. He did not take it to heart. Even illness did not knock him off his feet. It must have been serious, since he was taken to the infirmary, where usually people were taken only to die. But by some miracle he came back healthy. Although well along in years, he did not give in to death. He came back to Cracow with us, too—always in good spirits. And there he lived for another twenty years.

The enemy also wanted to blunt and annihilate us intellectually. There was no question of a library; periodicals, aside from cheap propaganda, were not allowed in the camp. A project that lasted the longest and turned out to be most useful was a General Camp University launched, if I am not mistaken, by Professor Władysław Konopczyński, with the active and zealous participation of many colleagues from our barrack, especially Adam Heydl and others. During the evening, when the guards had settled down in the canteen and there was no danger of unexpected checks, we held "lectures." Some of these lectures have remained engraved in my memory more distinctly than others, sometimes because of their merit, and sometimes their peculiarity. I remember a discourse by one of my colleagues about the human personality. It propounded the idea that man is something in the nature of Peer Gynt's onion: He seems to exist. He changes. Life peels one husk after another from him but can never reach the "core" of his being, which, in its final manifestation, will turn out to be only a tiny leaf. No one will ever guess what the essence of his being had been. I recall the natural history lectures of Skowron and Starmach, the brisk controversy between Stanisław Szczotka and Władysław Semkowicz over the history of the peasants as a distinct branch of study, and a few others. I gave a few talks myself: I spoke about the vicissitudes of the so-called "Sejm edition" of Mickiewicz, and about the limits of Norwid's "incomprehensibility," among others. We also organized a memory contest. Tadeusz Estreicher outdistanced us all, by reciting *ex abrupto* some eighty of Asnyk's lyric poems.

The point was not to amuse ourselves but to save ourselves by returning in thought to our old pursuits: at least for a moment to escape from the baleful, unbearable present! We would evoke the distant past or intellectual interests, to the day before yesterday rather than yesterday—anything but recent times, still fresh and alluring in their blissfulness. But this proved most difficult and seldom successful. I will tell one story to illustrate. We had almost two months of prison behind us; Christmas Eve was approaching. The camp command marked this date ostentatiously: a tall, spruce Christmas tree was put up in the parade ground and hung with colored bulbs. Our group debated whether we should observe this evening in some way or not. Among those opposing this idea most vehemently was Professor Jan Nowak. It makes no sense, he said, what is the use of this sentimentalism, why pour salt on the wound, aggravate it with these gushy scenes! More anguish, that's all. But his advice was not followed. We arranged our poor prison Christmas Eve supper the best we could. The head of our table, the Pomeranian Mozalewski, cut the meager bread portion into paper-thin slices. As we broke a wafer, we wished each other only one thing: freedom. And later, when we sang the carol *Wśród nocnej ciszy* (In the Silence of the Night), we all broke down. But at neighboring tables our German comrades were going through the same thing as they sang "Stille Nacht, Heilige Nacht." Whatever the convictions, beliefs, or world outlooks, we all sang. It was a strange occasion. It took us some time to collect ourselves and spin cocoons of stubborn resistance once again, but none of us will ever forget that night.

I especially want to say something about my fellow professors, who had been the closest to me. I was separated from Professor Chrzanowski right on the first day; we were in different barracks, so that I could see him only during evening visits lasting only a few minutes. These were painful encounters, since the Professor was sinking fast. He, who had been so jaunty in Wrocław, so eager for reminiscences and even anecdotes, and still quite alert at the camp in December, after Christmas quite obviously broke down. He practically stopped speaking, except to complain of constant headaches and fears that he would catch a cold. He could not avoid it; the cold came—the last. At the very end he was taken to the infirmary, usually the antechamber of death. On the morning of January 20 we got the news that he had died during the night: "wegen Lungenentzündung verstorben," as his widow was notified by telegram. . . .

I spent a great deal of time together with my colleagues Kamykowski and Kołaczkowski, sitting at neighboring tables and sleeping on neighboring bunks. Kamykowski, who at one time had pulled through tuberculosis, now suffered from the difficult conditions of the camp. Seemingly burly, broad-shouldered, he was assigned the most arduous work, and never shied away from it. After a few hours he would come back worn out to the point of exhaustion. But he never complained. This could be termed a heroic endurance of grim hopelessness; he persisted in it doggedly. And eventually he returned to Cracow and soon even began teaching again. But death did not grant him much time for this. It was different with Stefan Kołaczkowski. Through all our time in prison he simply bubbled with energy. . . .

When we arrived at Sachsenhausen, we found quite a sizeable group of Poles already there. The Hitlerites had prudently thrown out on this rubbish heap of death all that was most valuable among their national minorities, and first the Poles who were German citizens. We soon met them. The former Reichstag deputy from Western Pomerania, Jan Baczewski, would have to be considered their obvious leader. This was unavoidable if only for physical reasons. A grenadier-sized man, rangy, corpulent but well formed, he was a head taller than the other residents of the barrack; during roll call he was visible from afar, at the right wing of the detachment. He enjoyed a profound respect and authority among the prisoners. I have not been able to learn what became of him later.

The Gestapo had not managed to catch up with the spiritual leader of the Polish minority, the president of the Union of Poles in Germany, Father Bolesław Domański of Złotów. He "eluded them" by dying shortly before the outbreak of the war. But they did imprison the circle of his closest collaborators. His church subordinate—a sacristan or organist whose name I can no longer recall—was in our barrack. He was taken prisoner together with his teen-aged son. The boy was assigned to the team that worked hard at the clinker-brick factory. Every day he left the camp early with the rest of the team, to return only toward evening. One day he did not return; his fellow prisoners pulled him in, loaded on a carriage filled with dead bodies. The boy's body was thrown on a pile in front of the mortuary. One of his fellow workers notified his father. Crushed by the blow, the father begged for permission to see the boy, to take him in his arms for the last time. In vain. They would not hear of it. The bereaved father, rent with wild sobs, spent that evening with us; in the evenings that followed, he presented a living image of grief. The ancient myth about Niobe does not even mention the name of the father of the innocent children slain by the terrible god in his vindictiveness; it only immortalizes the mother's grief. We had before us the image of a father changed to stone from such sorrow. It was unforgettable.

This was an example of an individual who was bestially annihilated as an "internal enemy." But large groups of these "internal enemies" also were imprisoned. I well remember such a group of Polish miners from Westphalia. Just before the outbreak of the war, the strongest and most energetic activists amongst the miners were "preventively" pushed behind the barbed wire of the camp. They took it good-naturedly, treating it rather as a distinction, and did not seem to be intimidated. One of them, a young boy, practically a lad, once told me proudly: "Not everyone can get into a concentration camp right away. You have to be somebody!" This pugnacious pride of theirs was often sorely tried, e.g., in the outbreak of a violent argument between a Berlin German and a Pole from Westphalia. They were arguing over the recent wartime events. The German did not hide his exasperation over the results of the September campaign. He was disillusioned with the Poles. "We were waiting," he shouted, "for you to free us from oppression, and you ran away like rabbits!" Before the neighbors stopped them, the Westphalian threw in: "I am proud to be a Pole." That was not the end of the incident. The next day a brutal guard summoned the impetuous Pole by name and tormented him mercilessly in front of the others. We all knew why. His antagonist of the previous day must have run to inform on him. Feelings of national pride had to be paid for on more than one occasion. But the boy's tough stand could not be crushed.

The Westphalian miners and I were old friends. When I was still a student I belonged to a group who devoted a good bit of time to the patriotic education of Polish miners in Silesia and Westphalia. I edited a paper for them; we met sometimes in Bochum, but more often in Cracow. There were many outstanding individuals among these miners: Stanisław Janicki, Jan Kaczor, and others. I searched for these old friends among my fellow prisoners, but they were not there; the Gestapo chose younger men. However, these younger men knew them and spoke of them with respect. So our friendship also grew and soon became intimate.

I introduced Kołaczkowski to these miners. He set about getting to know the men, questioning them about conditions where they came from. "What wonderful asset for Poland," he exclaimed. "As soon as we return to work, we must make up for this neglect; we must try to understand them." We were not destined to carry out this plan. Kołaczkowski did return from the camp, but so exhausted by dysentery that from the railway station he was carried straight to St. Lazarus Hospital. Neither a blood transfusion nor other medical treatment helped. He died a week later on February 16, 1940.

4. THE SAMARITANS

Writing about my fellow prisoners, I cannot leave out the physicians, who constituted a sizable proportion of the prisoners. We, ordinary patients, consider doctors as superior people—beings apart—calm, controlled, regarding man as a subordinate object of their knowledge and art, and thus we see them as creatures who view life from a position of strength. What others do not know, they know, what others cannot do, they can do, about such awesome matters as suffering and the aggression of death. Therefore, it was something quite extraordinary to discover that they suffered as much as other people and were just as helpless as we. Through this realization, we came closer to them and became their friends.

I made this discovery at the very outset of this bleak adventure. We were removed from barrack 20 in Cracow one afternoon and deported to Wrocław by passenger train. I shared a compartment with seven colleagues, mostly young physicians. We talked about what we were bound to talk about: the fate that awaited us. During this conversation, one of the doctors, Miodoński, seated opposite me, suddenly broke out into spasmodic sobbing—his control snapped. His friends tried to calm

him down: "Janek, stop it! We'll get through it and come back."
"It's easy for you to talk," he answered, "I left my wife at home
with a child a few days old, and no money. How will she manage?" Actually, she did manage somehow. Other doctors who
had not been arrested watched over the fate of his wife, and
regularly contributed money for her needs. After a while
Miodoński found out about it too. But that moment in the train
was enough to reveal his human, vulnerable tenderness.

The camp command did not put to use the knowledge and
experience of any of our doctors, did not assign them to the
infirmary as auxiliary physicians or even as hospital attendants.
Did they seem superfluous? Was the medical care there on such
a high and adequate level? Not in the least! The last doctor we
saw face-to-face was in the Wrocław prison. The kindly old
milksop made official visits to our cells and cheerfully prescribed various preparations, an extra-fortifying diet for the
old, drops of some sort. We did not get much out of it, since the
prescriptions were never filled, but we were always glad to see
him. After all, he represented the semblance of some kind of
care. Nothing like that ever happened to us in Sachsenhausen.
Perhaps some sort of doctor did stop in at the infirmary once in
a while, but certainly not with the idea of saving the poor
wretches there. Throughout the camp, in the barracks, there
was not a doctor to be found. We could have used one, if only to
check on the hygienic condition of the accommodations.

Our physicians were not left idle because they were not
needed. Rather, they were not wanted, for we had not been
herded to the camp for a health cure. We were all to share the
same fate. Sanitary standards were maintained only to the degree that was absolutely necessary. In such crowded conditions,
epidemics spread very easily. Therefore, we were all carefully
shaved, but we were taken to the showers only once during that
whole period of three months. Daily washing in ice-cold water
was carried on under the gush of a waterspout and in such a
crowd that one had to complete the job in a great hurry. The
actual plan that was applied to combat any epidemic was simple.
When a disease, such as typhoid, spread in a block, it would be
surrounded with barbed wire. And the fence would be taken
down only when the contagion in the barrack was quelled—
speaking plainly—when everyone had died.

How did we manage to overcome our illnesses? We managed in various ways, and usually resorting to very primitive methods. For instance, a prison witch doctor was relied upon—an old, burly German peasant with a rough-hewn face. He cured through magnetism, the pulling of hands. And in fact, when our block manager's cold turned to flu, he cured him in one evening. When I induced him to apply similar measures to Professor Chrzanowski, who suffered from acute, prolonged headaches, he treated him with his pullings and massage, but to no avail.

We coped with familiar illnesses ourselves. The most common of these was diarrhea, and there was one common remedy. It was necessary to pilfer a piece of charcoal from one of the furnaces, crush it into powder (a bottle was most useful for this purpose) and take this preparation in small doses. This helped a little.

In my own affliction, however, I decided to fast for three days—and was cured.

Illnesses raged among us even though our own physicians were imprisoned with us. Many among us walked around with chills, frostbite, wounds, and one man had boiling water spilled on his hand in the kitchen; for weeks he went around with a huge, blackening blister on his hand and forearm, until his tough system fought off the infection. And another had long suffered from a bladder infection. The catheter he needed had been left behind at his apartment in Cracow. Exhausted by excruciating pain, he was one of the first victims of the senseless ill will of these henchmen.

The small infirmary was always crowded. The sick who swayed on their feet from exhaustion but had no fever were not admitted; they had to remain in the barrack and stand for roll call. Friends dragged them out on the square by supporting them under the arms. For inspection, they were lined up on the ground on the left flank. Then, during the day, the bedroom part of the barrack was closed; it was impossible to put the sick man in the crowded day room. We ended up by wrapping some unfortunate fellow in a blanket and putting him down in the freezing little alcove that served as our washroom, on the concrete floor, in the corner, so that he would not be trampled.

Occasionally, one would slowly die there over a period of a few days.

In the face of all this horror, our doctors, just as the rest of us, were quite helpless, mixed into the gray crowd decked out in prison stripes—all equally driven, equally terrorized.

But there was among the doctors one who managed to cut himself off somehow from this pattern, to make his mark: he was Eugeniusz Brzezicki. He did this in a curious way. Naturally, not as a physician, or even as a hospital attendant, but as a stubborn, uninvited sanitary helper who was pushed and even kicked aside. Somehow, he succeeded in getting through to the infirmary and went there quite often. He took our seriously ill to the infirmary, placed them there as best as he could and—to the meager degree he had eked out for himself—brought them relief, of course, spiritual rather than physical. He brought them a little news of their colleagues, cheered them up, talked with them. He was often the recipient of the last words of the dying and, perforce, he became a messenger of death. Every morning we learned from him which of our colleagues in the infirmary had left us forever. We valued and respected these truly samaritan services.

The doctor I myself became most friendly with was Professor Aleksander Oszacki. He had had an unusual career, for at a tender age he had taken part in the physicians' consultations about the health of Emperor Franz Josef, and in Cracow, he soon achieved a leading position as a scientist and professor. His grandmother, Sabina Grzegorzewska, brought up in Puławy, had made a name for herself in literature. Aleksander himself, possessed of great esthetic sensitivity, also had close connections with literary circles, and was especially fascinated by the religions and philosophies of the Far East.

But this brilliant doctor of internal medicine—even he was helpless in face of the adversities of the camp. I had an opportunity to painfully confirm this myself. At the camp I experienced the first symptoms of arteriosclerosis. Very unpleasant. The pain began somewhere in the vicinity of the stomach, rose to the breastbone and there tugged at me like a wrench. This went on night after night. I first thought it to be some sort of stomach trouble. A tumor or something. I could not do anything to help myself. In my need, I described my symptoms to Oszacki. He spread his hands helplessly: "I can only know as much about this as you, even less. In order to know more, I would have to examine you, sound you out, feel you, listen to your heart, and I can do none of these things. I am helpless." And indeed it was only in Cracow, when he got back to his clinic, that he admitted me there for three weeks, examined me thoroughly and undertook a series of treatments. To a certain degree, he put me back on my feet.

How different it was on the other side! A different professional ethic was in force there.

During the war, my friend Dr. Henryk Biernacki told me the following story: "My German director cursed me out when I mentioned to him that I had a serious case for which there was no medicine in the clinic pharmacy. He snorted angrily: 'What's all the fuss about? An injection, a bit of phenol—and everything's quiet.' "

Was this a Samaritan too?

When I remember these terrible times, I shudder at the thought that I might have to go through such things again, that anyone might have to go through them. But I did derive certain advantages from these months of oppression. Among the most precious are the bonds of friendship that tightened there. At the nadir of humiliation, in face of the threat of annihilation lurking everywhere, it is easy to see through a man and realize his worth. It is easy to see where in this gray dust there is gold, where there is iron, and where there is dross and common slag. It taught me a great deal—this ordeal by fire.

Notes on the Authors

Henryk Barycz, Professor of the History of Education and Culture, at the University of Cracow, archivist and editor. His bibliography includes more than a hundred items. The essay appearing here has been excerpted from his book *Spojrzenie w przeszłość polsko-włoską* (A Glance at the Polish-Italian Past).

Cezaria Baudouin de Courtenay Jędrzejewicz (1885–1967), Professor of Ethnography at the Universities of Wilno and Warsaw and subsequently of the Polish University in Exile (England) of which she became the Rector. The essay published here has been excerpted from the collective work *Polska i jej dorobek dziejowy* (Poland and Her Historical Attainments).

Wacław Berent (1873–1940), a prominent novelist who particularly distinguished himself in historical and biographical essays resembling "vies romancées" which were based on thorough study of the respective period. The essay included here has been excerpted from the volume, *Zmierzch wodzów* (Twilight of the Leaders).

Aleksander Brückner (1856–1939), a prominent linguist, Slavist and historian of literature and culture of international repute. In 1881–1924, Professor of Slavic Languages and Literatures at the University of Berlin. His vast bibliography includes significant works in several languages. His versatile and prolific research embraces Slavic and comparative literatures, linguistics, and folklore. The essay published here has been excerpted from his major work *Dzieje kultury polskiej* (History of Polish Culture).

Feliks Gross, Professor of Sociology at Brooklyn College and the Graduate School, City University of New York; from 1945–1968 Visiting Professor in the Department of Politics, New York University. Fulbright lecturer at the University of

Rome. Active in Polish Labor Movement. During World War II, Secretary General of Central European Planning Board of Czechoslovakia, Greece, Yugoslavia and Poland. Author of numerous articles and studies in the fields of Sociology, Anthropology and International Relations in Polish, English, Italian, French and Spanish. The essay published here has been excerpted from his work, *The Polish Worker* (New York: Roy Publishers, 1945).

Stanisław Kot (1885–1975), internationally known scholar, Professor of the History of Polish Culture at the Jagellonian University. His research concentrated mainly on the political and religious doctrines of the XVI and XVII centuries. Of particular significance was his long time editorship of the quarterly, *The Reformation in Poland*. Also active in politics, he was a member of the Polish Government in Exile (England) and served as Ambassador to the U.S.S.R. After a brief stay in Poland after 1945, he again went into exile continuing his scholarly activity in London. The essay published here is a chapter from *Socinianism in Poland: the Social and Political Ideas of the Polish Antitrinitarians in the Sixteenth and Seventeenth Centuries.*

Alexandre André Koyré (1892–1964), historian of science, taught at the Sorbonne and at the University of Montpellier, was also Visiting Professor in Cairo. During World War II, he became associated with the New School for Social Research and the Ecole Libre des Hautes Etudes in New York, as well as later with the Universities of Chicago, Johns Hopkins and Wisconsin. He was also elected to membership in the Institute for Advanced Studies in Princeton. Some of his many works were translated into English. The essay published here is a paper read at the Copernicus celebration in the Polish Institute of Arts and Sciences in America, May 3, 1943.

Wacław Lednicki (1891–1967), scholar in Slavic and Comparative Literature, successively Professor at the Universities of Cracow, Brussels, Harvard and California in Berkeley where he became chairman of the Slavic Department. His imposing bibliography includes works in Polish, Russian, English, and French. The essay reprinted here is excerpted from *Bits of Table Talks*.

Isaac Lewin, Professor of History at Yeshiva University in New

York. Until 1939, he lived in Łódź, Poland, where he was a member of the City Council. Since 1948, he has been the representative of the Agudas Israel World Organization to the United Nations Economic and Social Council. His many publications include books in Polish, English, Hebrew and Yiddish. The essay published here is an updated version of his lecture delivered by him on January 20, 1943, at the Polish Institute of Arts and Sciences in America.

Jan Chryzostom Pasek (1636–1701), a gifted narrator and diarist, famous for his uninhibited memoirs, typical of the gentry class of the second half of the XVII century. The essay published here is the translation of two chapters from his *Memoirs*.

Stanisław Pigoń (1885–1968), literary scholar, successively Professor at the Universities of Poznań, Wilno, and Cracow. In 1939, imprisoned with many Cracow University faculty members in the Oranienburg-Sachsenhausen concentration camp. A leading expert on Mickiewicz, his scholarship included a wide range of Polish literary history. The essay printed here is excerpted from Pigoń's reminiscences *Z przędziwa pamięci* (From the Yarn of Memory).

Józef Piłsudski (1867–1935), soldier, statesman, fighter for Poland's independence, co-founder and editor of the newspaper "Robotnik" (The Worker), member of the Polish Socialist Party. Organizer of para-military units later known as "Legions" which fought in World War I against Russia. Imprisoned by the Germans in the fortress of Magdeburg, he returned to Warsaw after the victory of the Allied Powers and became Chief of State of the reborn Poland. As Commander-in-Chief of the Polish Armed Forces, he fought against the invading Bolsheviks and won a victory in the crucial Battle of Warsaw. Withdrawing from politics, he returned to power in the coup d'etat of May 1926. He remained the dominant personality in Poland until his death. His writings include books on military events, reminiscences of his underground fighting and political essays. The essay published here is a translation of an article published in the Socialist Cracow daily *Naprzód* in November, 1903.

Jan Ptaśnik (1876–1930), historian and scholar in Polish culture specializing in the past of Polish cities. Professor at the

Jagellonian University and editor of *Kwartalnik Historyczny* (Historical Quarterly). The essay included here is excerpted from his work, *Miasta i Mieszczanstwo w dawnej Polsce* (Towns and Townsmen in Ancient Poland).

Adam Żółtowski (1881–1958), philosopher and historian, successively Professor at the Universities of Cracow and Poznań, director of the Polish Research Center in London. His many books include *The Border of Europe, East and West in European History,* and studies of Descartes and particularly of the great philosopher of the Romantic era, August Cieszkowski. The essay included here is a chapter from *Church and Society*, Rev. Joseph N. Moody, Ed., entitled "Catholicism and Christian Democracy in Poland."

INDEX